To John

Thank you for
do for me

I hope you enjoy this book.

Love,
Grandee Raven

U
TURN

George Barna and **David Barton**

The word *church* is capitalized when referring to the larger body of believers, the Church universal, as opposed to local congregations.

Many early American historical quotes have been used in this book—quotes made at a time when grammatical usage and spelling were quite different from what is practiced today. In an effort to improve readability, we have modernized some spellings, capitalizations, and punctuations, leaving the historical content unimpaired.

Copyright © 2014 by George Barna and David Barton
All rights reserved

Cover design by Justin Evans

Visit the authors' websites at www.georgebarna.org, www.wallbuilders.com.

Library of Congress Control Number: 2014947918
International Standard Book Number: 978-1-62998-024-9
E-book ISBN: 978-1-62998-025-6

First edition

14 15 16 17 18 — 9 8 7 6 5 4 3 2 1
Printed in the United States of America

CONTENTS

MAKE A U-TURN. NOW!

T HE WISEST MAN who ever lived earned that reputation. He wrote some blunt and wonderfully insightful observations that we ought to heed. For instance:

> History merely repeats itself. It has all been done before. Nothing under the sun is truly new. Sometimes people say, "Here is something new!" But actually it is old; nothing is ever truly new.
> —ECCLESIASTES 1:9–10

Technology changes across the ages, but human issues and human behavior do not. There is nothing new in the problems we face right now as individuals or as a nation. The problems are new only to this generation. And the solutions do not really change either. The answers to human problems and behavioral challenges are the same today as they were in the past.

The United States is now entering its own version of the Dark Ages. Other once-great nations walked the same path we are traversing today, only to discover it led to their demise. Of course, we have convinced ourselves that we are different—that we are enlightened and sophisticated and will blaze a trail to new heights of human experience.

Alas, such self-deception is also nothing new. History reveals that it is what the people in every declining society do before they crash.

Maybe the saddest realization is that we knew this day of reckoning was coming. We have been receiving vivid warnings of its imminence for several decades. A popular expression reminds us that "data don't lie"—and for more than a quarter century it hasn't been lying. But we have ignored or denied the unpleasant realities and have delayed making the tough choices. We persuaded one another that if we "stayed the course" and maintained a positive attitude, things would turn around.

Except they didn't. And on our present path they won't.

So today America is mired in an undesirable position, and it is getting worse. And we know it.

We understand that our lifestyles and our standards of living are on the downslide:

- Seventy-four percent are dissatisfied with the way things are going in America.[1]

- Seventy-five percent are trying to find ways to lead a more meaningful life.[2]

- Sixty-three percent believe America is in a state of decline.[3]

- Sixty-three percent argue that things in the nation are generally headed in the wrong direction.[4]

- Fifty-four percent no longer believe the United States is a country where anyone can get ahead and have a better standard of living.[5]

We likewise realize that the moral and spiritual conditions of America are in decline:

- Seventy-seven percent say religion is losing its influence on American life.[6]

- Seventy-four percent argue that the state of moral values in the nation is getting worse.[7]

- Fifty-seven percent recognize that religious freedoms are being more restricted because activist groups are trying to move society away from traditional Christian values.[8]

♦ Fifty-six percent believe that the Bible does not have enough influence on American society these days.[9]

We are keenly aware that government and politics are deteriorating before our very eyes:

♦ Eighty-five percent say Congress is more interested in serving special interest groups than the people they were elected to represent.[10]

♦ Eighty-one percent acknowledge that most voters are not sufficiently informed about the issues to vote wisely.[11]

♦ Seventy-four percent are dissatisfied with the way the nation is being governed.[12]

♦ Seventy-two percent perceive that America is more divided now than at any other time during their lifetime.[13]

♦ Seventy-one percent say the signers of the Declaration of Independence would be disappointed in how the United States turned out.[14]

♦ Sixty-seven percent say that our government will never change for the better.[15]

♦ Sixty-three percent indicate that they usually wind up being disappointed by the people they vote for.[16]

♦ Sixty-one percent agree that Hollywood has too much influence on American politics and social values.[17]

♦ Sixty percent admit that the media coverage of our presidential elections in unbalanced and biased.[18]

♦ Fourteen percent strongly believe that they can make a difference if they get politically active.[19]

- Six percent are very certain that the government has their best interests at heart.[20]

All of this has led most Americans to worry about the future— theirs and their children's:

- Seventy-seven percent of Americans are concerned about the future.[21]

- Only 17 percent say it is very likely that today's youth will have a better life than their parents did.[22]

It's not a pretty picture, but it's one we can take full credit for producing. As a nation, our choices over the past fifty years have been steadily redefining who we are. These choices of societal disengagement have put us on a path of self-destruction. A simple list of major policy and procedural changes embraced during that time paints a clear portrait of who we have chosen to be and the values we have chosen to embrace:

- Removing the Bible and prayer from public schools

- Legalizing abortion

- Legalizing same-sex marriage

- Government spending beyond its means

- Working on the Sabbath

- Protecting pornography as free speech

- Facilitating divorce

- Penalizing families, including for homeschooling

- Reducing religious liberties

- Instituting unprecedented expansion of entitlement programs

- Enabling government eavesdropping and data collection of all citizens and businesses

♦ Pursuing foreign policies that have severely weakened our economy and global relationships

♦ Creating countless laws through judicial rulings and executive orders

When the pilgrims put their lives on the line to sail across the ocean in search of religious and political freedom, their intent was to create a place where the God of Israel would be worshipped and served with as much passion and purity as they could muster. Over the course of the past three hundred years, we have recklessly diluted that founding purpose and turned our collective back on the beliefs and practices that made America unique and special. We have mentally (and, in a growing number of cases, on paper) rewritten our history to be one of a nation dedicated to diversity, tolerance, happiness, and comfort rather than a nation devoted to the pursuit of holiness, humility, submission to God, and gratitude for His blessings.

One of the running gags in our culture concerns the myth that men who get lost while driving refuse to ask for directions. That prideful persona is analogous to what has happened to America across recent decades. Every once in a while, uncertain of who we are, who we want to be, where we are heading, or what our ultimate national and personal goals are, we take a wrong turn. Add up decades of wrong turns and we are now hopelessly off track and utterly lost. We have no recollection of the original destination. But rather than stop and get directions that would enable us to return to the proper path, we keep moving forward, convinced that we are just one turn from getting back on track. As we get deeper and deeper into uncharted territory and all the signs convey our lostness, we secretly realize we're in deep weeds.

Millions of Americans who are frustrated, or even scared, simply throw up their hands in despair and ask, "What can we possibly do now?" The answer is the same now as it always has been: ask God to forgive us and to lead us out of the wilderness where we have now spent so many years. And if we do so, we will undoubtedly be given a simple command: "Make a U-Turn. Now!"

If you have read the Bible much, then you know that God never immediately and painlessly removes people from their own mess. If we truly repent—which means to make a U-turn—then He will provide the guidance and resources we so desperately need. But because one of the inviolable principles of the universe is that choices do have consequences (as we so often teach our own children), we must experience the natural results of the bad choices we have made over and over again for decades. If we earnestly seek to follow God and follow His ways and commands, there can be restoration. It will not be simple, quick, or painless, and it may not even be immediately obvious, but that restoration can be ours—if we are willing to make that U-turn. Now.

Making a U-turn implies that you realize you were headed in the wrong direction. It means you need to follow a different path and that you are willing to do so. It represents a course correction in order to arrive at the original destination. U-turns require backtracking along some of the same ground that was just covered, admitting that such ground should never have been traversed.

But making a U-turn without accurate knowledge of how to arrive at the desired destination leaves you no better off than if you had simply continued down the original misguided path. In fact, it might be more painful because now you realize you're on yet another wrong path and must agonize over making continued progress (again) toward an overtly wrong destination.

So let's consider the new and improved plan. The first step is to know where you want to go. The second step is to acknowledge that the path you're on will not get you there. The third step is to consider the possibilities and choose the best approach for arriving at your desired destination. The fourth step is to pull a U and begin to move toward the desired destination. The fifth step is to carefully monitor your progress to ensure that you do not wander off track again.

This book is designed to provide the information required to follow that plan.

Just a few words of caution before you dive in.

If you are seeking a new plan that moves America forward without full dependence on God and a determination to do things His way, this is not the book for you. We believe that without God at the center of the equation, we cannot possibly arrive at the right answer. Our success over the last couple of centuries is fully attributable to God's blessings, and the current state of decline is fully attributable to our own arrogance and ignorance apart from Him. Unless we invite God to be at the center of our process and operate in strict accordance with His principles, we are doomed to continue our downward slide. Because He has proven Himself to be a merciful ruler, though, if we will humble ourselves before Him, there is hope. This book will describe the radical action we must take in partnership with God to restore the nation's heartbeat.

If you are searching for a guideline that tells elected leaders how to get it right, this is not the book for you—it is not about them; it is about us. The only way America gets turned around is if each of us individually takes responsibility for the abysmal choices we have made and commits to doing what is right in God's eyes. The required turnaround is not a top-down effort; it is a bottom-up requirement that puts the burden on your shoulders and ours.

If you are trying to find a simple, quick turnaround strategy, believing that the best solutions are always the simplest solutions, this is not the book for you. The accumulation of decades and decades of atrocious choices has annihilated the possibility of an easy restoration process. We are at the stage of the disease where all of the necessary medicines are harsh. But at least we still have the hope of becoming well again if we immediately begin taking that medicine and strictly adhere to the prescribed protocol.

America has been one of the greatest nations in human history. It can perhaps regain that status if we unite in following the precepts and principles that enabled the United States to be uniquely blessed. But one thing is necessary if we want to attain such greatness again: We must make a U-turn. Now!

Chapter 1

A NEW AMERICAN DREAM

O<small>NE OF THE</small> hottest political and business stories of the day relates to what has become known as Big Data. This is a new and rapidly growing industry based upon the flood of consumer data derived from tracking online behavior and other information available through new technologies. Every time you use the Internet, mobile devices, social media, and most other forms of communications technology, you leave behind clues about who you are, what you like, and how you respond to specific stimuli.

Billions of pieces of consumption behavior data are captured, and the Big Data professionals slice and dice it to make behavioral inferences that can result in smarter marketing decisions. Using sophisticated software, these data analysts search for and identify correlations and patterns that improve the ability to predict what choices people will make. With each passing month, data analytics are becoming more accurate and useful—and more mainstream.

Sometimes Big Data provides us with new and amazing insights into how people think and behave. Other times the results of the sophisticated algorithms and statistical models simply confirm what we already knew or suspected. Such confirmations may not possess the same wow factor as bold, original discoveries, but they are no less valuable. In a world where reality is often staged and contrived, truth is valuable whether it is a unique revelation or the confirmation of a time-worn truism.

One of the confirmations provided by data mining and analysis is simple but profound: *you do what you believe.* You probably put this truth into practice a thousand times in a thousand different ways every day.

- ◆ If you're like most people, you don't like wearing a seat belt, but you strap yourself in every time you get behind the wheel of your car. Why? Because you believe that it could save your life—and you believe that snapping the belt into place will protect you from a costly fine that would be assessed if you were caught not wearing it.

- ◆ You pray to a God you have never seen or touched and whom you cannot control because you believe that He exists, that He listens to your prayers, that He has the power to do what you ask, and that He is pleased by your prayers to Him. Even if your prayers do not get the desired response, you believe that you are better off praying than not praying.

- ◆ Occasionally you get angry with certain people or organizations. You do not stalk the people who made you angry and kill them. Why not? After all, you have the right to buy a gun or a knife. You've seen how murder is done hundreds, if not thousands, of times in movies and TV shows. With a bit of planning and by carefully implementing that plan, you would probably be able to accomplish the murder, and you might even get away undetected or exonerated by a court of law. But you don't kill those who make you angry because you believe that there are more appropriate responses. You may even believe that you do not have the right to terminate the life of another person in response to your anger. Perhaps you are restrained from murdering others simply because you believe you would be caught and the consequences do not justify the behavior.

- ◆ Your child may protest having to get up early, get dressed, go to school, become bored in the classroom, and do homework instead of laying around the house in pajamas playing video games. Frankly, it might be a lot easier to let the rascal sleep in and enable various media tools to babysit the child while you focus on your challenges. Instead, you battle the child, deliver him to school, and prod him to do his homework after school because you believe that getting an education is a critical factor in becoming a self-supporting, fulfilled, and productive member of society.

In each of these situations and numerous others you can undoubtedly identify in your daily routine, your actions reflect your deepseated values and beliefs—the things you are confident are true. Your values and beliefs fuel your choices, large and small.

Focus on Values

Values are the guiding principles that combine with our core beliefs to affect our attitudes, opinions, choices, and behavior. Values identify what we maintain to be right and desirable in life, and they therefore influence our goals as well.

Before you arrive at a conclusion, you usually consider the alternative courses of action in light of what you believe about the moral, spiritual, relational, perceptual, cultural, intellectual, and emotional implications of those choices. Realistically, though, we rarely, if ever, take the time to painstakingly dissect every option according to all those dimensions. In most situations you instantaneously arrive at a decision based on the core values and beliefs you have carefully tested and embraced over time.

You reflect your values every minute of every day. Those values were primarily developed and adopted before you reached your teenage years. They were influenced mostly by your parents, the media to which you were exposed, and your understanding of the law and the dominant values of the culture you were growing into. Those values were either reinforced or refined largely by the key people in your life: your family, friends, and elementary and middle-school teachers. While our values occasionally change as we age, such shifts are the exception.

AMERICA IS THE PRODUCT OF ITS VALUES

Just as the behavior of every individual is an outgrowth of the person's values, the same is true for nations. America is the product of the cumulative values of its people. It always has been and always will be. There is no way around it. As a person, you do what you believe; as a nation, our behavioral patterns represent what we, as a nation, value and believe. Our moment-to-moment choices are based on the points of view that emerge from our values and religious beliefs. Truly grasping this insight explains more than you realize about the past, present, and future condition of America.

More than three hundred years ago many groups of disenchanted European citizens risked their lives to journey to the New World and initiate a new life in a land that came to be known as America. The driving force behind people's decision to abandon their homeland, leave behind friends and perhaps family, brave the treacherous ocean swells and despicable living conditions on overcrowded ships, and start from scratch in unsettled lands to the east—ignoring those dangers in favor of a new start—was prompted by the force of values. Once they landed and began making the best of their new situation, the lifestyle of the residents of the New World consistently reflected those values. Fed up with the values in their native country, these brave souls put their lives on the line to be true to what they held to be right, important, defensible, and true.

Some had made the journey to seek religious freedom. Others were compelled by oppressive politics and government. Others sought the thrill and adventure of the gambit. A share of the new arrivals needed a fresh start after ruining their reputations or experiencing run-ins with the law in England. No matter what the motivation was, their values compelled them to board the ship and settle the new land.

The more you study our nation's beginnings, the more difficult it is to overlook the role of values in the shaping of the emergent country. The central documents that defined our nation—the Declaration of Independence, the Constitution, the Bill of Rights—are the product of the values of the people, the Founding Fathers, and the nation's leaders. The compelling motivation to leave their homeland for a new country, as noted above, was driven by core values.

We can identify many of the dominant values of the American people at the time the United States was founded. But even under the best of circumstances, grasping and describing the values that people throughout a country possess is no simple task. Each of us embraces dozens of values. Multiply that by the number of people inhabiting a country, and the challenge becomes monumental.

To identify the values of the early days, we can turn to a wide array of their historical documents from the arenas of law, politics, education, entertainment, religion, journalism, and other fields that enable us to re-create what such a list might have looked like in the last couple decades of the eighteenth century. There were a number of individuals who helped to document the prevailing worldviews and ways of processing daily life. For instance, the renowned Benjamin Franklin, the industrious creative who published countless articles, pamphlets, journals, and other thought-provoking resources, wrote about the thirteen "virtues of life" as examples of what made someone a good person.[1] Insight into the values of the day can also be gleaned from documents that detail the era's most common preaching topics, public speaking emphases, leadership themes, public laws, and newspaper reports.

Making the task a bit murkier is the realization that not all values are created equal. Each of us embraces a set of core values as well as a series of support values. Core values represent the ideals and principles that are the non-negotiable values possessing the greatest influence on our thoughts and deeds. Support values are those that are consistent with and provide breadth and depth to our ideals. Core values are our primary values; support values are our secondary values.

To simplify this exercise (for the moment), let's identify the core values that seem to have been most prevalent at the end of the eighteenth century. The list probably looked something like this:

- Freedom
- Truth and honesty
- Hard work
- Civic duty
- Family
- Humility
- Faith and piety
- Rule of law
- Self-control
- Happiness
- Contentment
- Moderation
- Frugality
- Justice
- Chastity
- Simplicity

If you analyze these values, you will see that they represent a well-balanced set of ideals. They indicate a focus on protecting the common good, serving humanity, protecting revered social customs, upholding central spiritual truths, exhibiting restraint and self-control, facilitating stability and security, contributing one's just share, committing to productivity and growth, and investing in people. That became a recipe for a strong and emerging nation that experienced unprecedented success. Without those values in place, such strength and vitality could not have occurred. This values profile was truly unique. Other nations of the world had values that reflected a greater emphasis upon hedonism, selfishness, power, and ambivalence toward righteousness.

America became a land where a new mind-set triumphed over the Old World's failed body of values. It was not perfect, of course, but the outcome was a different daily experience for those who settled in the new land to the east.

TODAY'S CORE VALUES

Jump forward a quarter of a millennium to the United States that we experience today. The nation is barely recognizable when compared to its humble beginnings. While the government, institutions, economy, and land have developed in ways that would have been unimaginable two hundred fifty years ago, the biggest transformation of all has been in the people. Perhaps the most efficient way of judging those differences is by comparing the values of early Americans with those of contemporary citizens.

Here are the values that are at the heart of the nation today:[2]

- Belonging/acceptance
- Comfort
- Entertainment
- Experiences
- Expressiveness
- Financial security
- Flexibility
- Freedom
- Happiness
- Individuality
- Love
- Meaning and purpose of life

- Personal control

- Physical security

- Self-reliance/independence

- Speed

- Stability

We should point out that had we written this book just twenty-five years ago, that list would have looked substantially different. One of the most startling outgrowths of the past quarter century has been the rapid and broad transition in our core values. Dominant values typically do not change quickly or in great number, but the recent past has seen a break with that pattern and an influx of nearly a dozen new core values—and a concurrent abandonment of some longtime values.

BEYOND THE CORE

During the past twenty-five years, the United States has been redefining itself through a dramatic shift in its values. Understanding that shift is important, whether you choose to embrace the shift or to redirect it.

These shifts do not happen overnight. Consequently, a nation's slate of core values and primary beliefs are predictable. However, during the infrequent periods of substantial values shifting, there is a very visible and audible level of conflict between those who prefer the old values and others who embrace the new values. That kind of social conflict has been evident in the United States for the past two or three decades and has been chronicled under the rubric of the "culture war." Now, with many of these long-term shifts well established, we must acknowledge where we stand and decide how to handle the transition.

Our extensive examination of the nation's current values indicates that there are roughly one hundred values (106, to be exact) that are germane to the current American experience. We suggest that this long list of values can be best understood in six distinct but fluid categories. Here is one way of understanding the flow of American values:

- About 30 percent of the nation's current values have been around for quite some time and are still held by most Americans.

- One out of every ten of our presently held values has risen to prominence and acceptance within the past twenty years.

- Nearly two-fifths of our values are in transition. These include a large group of values (one-sixth of the total) that have been around for a long time but are now the subject of furious debate and challenge; one out of every ten is a new value being vetted carefully by society in anticipation of widespread adoption; and the remaining batch of values (slightly more than one-tenth of the total) are existing values being redefined and recontextualized.

- The remaining one-fifth of the lot constitutes values that served us in the past but have generally been abandoned by most Americans over the past decade or so.

Viewing values in these silos, if you will, enables us to get a glimpse of how the nation is changing. We are essentially experiencing a steady and serious values makeover. If the current patterns continue uninterrupted and we assume that half of the values (new or old) currently in dispute get adopted and half get jettisoned, then within the coming decade we will have a refashioned slate of values in which more than one-third (36 percent) of the combined primary and secondary values are new.

To place that in context, imagine working in a company for twenty years with a workforce that has remained consistently at about 106 full-time employees. However, due to attrition, firings, and departures, thirty-eight of your current fellow employees were not on staff when you started your tenure. That may not seem too radical—in fact, it might sound pretty normal—until you realize that since your first day of work for the company, that infusion of new talent, skills, experience, and personalities has really reshaped the nature of the company. It happened so discreetly that you may not have noticed it, apart from an especially outstanding or incompetent newcomer every once in a while. But now, as you look back and concentrate on the changes wrought by the influx of new blood, you can see that today's team is discernibly different compared to two decades ago. The company still produces the same category of products or services, but the firm itself is substantially different under the hood.

That's what has happened to America. Same basic land mass; considerably different tenants.

Specifically how have we changed? A deeper examination of the values that we have recently adopted or abandoned tells an interesting story about the heartbeat of contemporary America. The research reveals that there is no single type of value that dominates the field and no single shift that explains most of our transition.

However, there are four types of values that we seem increasingly likely to adopt. Those include values that reflect hedonism (i.e., a desire for personal pleasure and sensuous gratification), stimulation (i.e., exposure to heightened excitement and challenge), self-direction (i.e., independence in ideas and behavior), and belonging (i.e., creating more fulfilling relationships and connections).

At the same time, the trending indicates that there are three classes of values we are becoming less supportive of in our values mix. Those include values related to benevolence (i.e., consciously facilitating the well-being of others), tradition (i.e., preserving habits, customs, and views that have a historical role in mainstream culture), and conformity (i.e., maintaining activity and choices that fit with prevailing norms and expectations).

If we compare not only the direction in which change is moving but also which types of values are most prevalent within our mix, we might also add that values facilitating personal achievement and universalism (i.e., a global and holistic concern for people, animals, and the environment) have remained a consistent part of the mix.

IMPLICATIONS OF OUR SHIFTING VALUES

Let's return for a moment to the earlier discussion about the core values of early America and consider them in light of the core values of our nation today.

It does not take a lot of scrutiny to notice the dramatic difference between the values that undergirded the founding of the world's longest-lasting superpower in modern history and the values that drive that same nation today. This comparison leads to several conclusions.

First, the primary values of the early Americans were diverse in their coverage. In comparison, America's values these days are more narrowly focused; we embrace a larger number of values clustered within a smaller number of values categories. (For example, early American values included one that fell within the hedonistic set, compared to five such values today. The early Americans adopted core values that were drawn from nine different values categories, while contemporary Americans possess values that cover just seven categories.) The implication is that we have become more limited in what we value, creating people who are less conscious of their external responsibilities.

Second, today's core values are more self-centered and less others-centered. For instance, 60 percent of the current core values are connected to the hedonistic and self-directed categories. That's twice the proportion of values drawn from those categories that are reflected in the core values of early Americans.

TODAY'S CORE VALUES	EARLY AMERICAN CORE VALUES
Belonging/acceptance	Justice
Comfort	Contentment
Entertainment	Hard work

TODAY'S CORE VALUES	EARLY AMERICAN CORE VALUES
Experiences	Civic duty
Expressiveness	Truth and honesty
Financial security	Humility
Flexibility	Moderation
Freedom	Freedom
Happiness	Happiness
Individuality	Family
Love	Faith
Meaning and purpose of life	Rule of law
Personal control	Frugality
Physical security	Self-control
Self-reliance/independence	Chastity
Speed	Simplicity
Stability	Cleanliness

While few adults are likely to articulate the content of this transition, we intuitively know something is off track. Two-thirds of adults (68 percent) admit that they are concerned about the moral condition of the country[3]—and with good reason. More than three-quarters of adults concur that the morals and values of America are in decline.[4] Things have gotten so scary on this front that even 71 percent of adults in the eighteen-to-twenty-nine age group—the segment whose lifestyles and attitudes have contributed most profoundly and energetically to the degradation of our values and behaviors—agree that our morals and values are in decline.[5] The bottom line for that group is that they don't care enough about it to change the trajectory.

ANTICIPATING THE FUTURE

It seems unlikely that we will ever return to the nation whose values are in the list on the right in the previous table. However, we know that if you want to foresee the future, one of the keys to doing so successfully is to project the nature of a country based on the trajectory of its values and beliefs. Doing so enables us to also forecast future behavior because we do what we believe.

One way we can see the implications of our shifting values is to recognize that the American dream has been redefined as a result of the shift. The traditional American dream, which emerged after the end of World War II, was based upon working hard; exploiting opportunities to get ahead; pursuing happiness through the acquisition of a house, a car, an education, and a marriage bearing children; and becoming part of a community of like-minded people. The dream also featured religious freedom, the expectation of a better future, and pride in being an American.

That dream propelled the United States forward during an amazing growth spurt in the 1950s through the 1980s. But the 1990s ushered in the era of values transformation that we are reeling from today. Along with the shift to the values previously identified, we have replaced the American dream with a kind of new millennium dream. It consists of the following vision:

- Working only as hard as necessary to get by

- Demanding the freedom, rights, and services we are entitled to

- Seeking a customized family experience in which *family* is defined as "significant relationships, emotional commitments, and satisfying physical liaisons"

- Living according to a personalized moral code based on situational truth and a tailor-made faith system

- Extolling modern-day virtues: tolerance, diversity, sensitivity to feelings, blunt candor, authenticity, personal strength, and social justice

- Experiencing happiness through comfort, convenience, choices, connections, and experiences

How could such a radically different dream gain traction? Because of the shift in our values. The original dream was reliant upon interdependence, trust, loyalty, respect, hard work, consistency, stability, acceptance of personal responsibility, humility, service, and support for the common good. Almost every one of those ideals, and the associated values, has been replaced. You can see the result in the marketplace every day. You are *experiencing* the result.

This revised dream will serve as the anchor for our efforts as a people over the coming years. Will the dream change again? Undoubtedly. Change is now one of the consistent expectations of our population—particularly among our younger people, who have only known a society whose characteristics include constant change. When will it change? That depends upon how quickly people tire of our new values system and which of the prevailing values they choose to alter—or when those who reject the new dream offer a viable alternative.

Long-Held Values, Still Embraced

- Acquisition of knowledge
- Belonging/acceptance
- Comfort
- Control
- Creativity
- Cultural diversity Education
- Entertainment
- Equal opportunity
- Financial security
- Forgiveness
- Freedom
- Free will
- Generosity
- Happiness
- Innovation
- Intelligence

- Kindness
- Love
- Meaning and purpose in life
- Mobility
- Peace
- Perseverance
- Personal accomplishment
- Personal growth
- Physical security
- Power
- Service to others
- Stability
- Success
- Wealth
- Wisdom

Long-Held Values, Generally Rejected

- Accepting personal responsibility
- Chastity
- Civic duty
- Commitment
- Common good
- Conformity
- Consensus
- Continuity from the past
- Discipline
- Efficiency
- Family values
- Hard work
- Hierarchy
- Honesty
- Loyalty
- Majority rule

- Neighborliness
- Physical fitness
- Privacy
- Ritual
- Simplicity
- Tradition

Long-Held Values, Currently in Conflict

- Accountability
- Civic/national pride
- Courtesy
- Democracy
- Excellence
- Interpersonal respect
- National status
- Patience
- Personal sacrifice
- Quality of performance
- Respecting authority
- Right to bear arms
- Right to life
- Rule of law
- Self-help
- Service to others
- Trust

Long-Held Values, Currently Being Redefined

- Community
- Compassion
- Diversity
- Fairness
- Faith and spirituality
- Family

- Goodness
- Human rights
- Justice
- Leadership
- Patriotism
- Unity

New Values, Currently in Conflict

- Animal rights
- Blunt/direct communication
- Emotionalism/feelings
- Entitlement
- Environmental protection
- Fame/recognition
- Government power
- Life balance
- Nutrition
- Tolerance

New Values, Widely Accepted

- Celebrity worship
- Change
- Collaboration
- Experiences
- Experimentation
- Expressiveness
- Flexibility
- Global view
- Individuality
- Informality
- Self-reliance/independence
- Speed

Chapter 2

NEW BELIEFS FOR A NEW ERA

VALUES LARGELY REFLECT our emotional and experiential perspectives. Our beliefs typically stem more from our spirituality. Like values, beliefs play a powerful role in shaping our behavior. Our ideas about the existence, nature, and engagement of God; about the existence of absolute guidelines for right and wrong; about our ability to influence God's responses to humanity through prayer; and about our sense of eternal destiny—all of these perspectives play a discernible role in how we view ourselves and our world and in the decisions and actions that come to define our lives.

As you will see, we are in the midst of a major era of change on the beliefs front, occurring in tandem with the changes related to our shifting values. As you consider the transitions in our beliefs, notice the inescapable interplay between values and beliefs. Their mutual influence means that a change in one necessitates a related change in the other in order for us to minimize our personal cognitive dissonance.

Here is an overview of some of the central religious beliefs that characterize the American public today.

BELIEFS ABOUT THE ROLE OF FAITH

Americans are often referred to around the world—inaccurately— as the most religious people on earth. (Global studies persuasively show that nationals in many of the Arab nations are more religious than Americans, both in the consistency of their beliefs and the frequency of their religious practices.)[1] While the Founding

Fathers of the United States considered the appropriate priorities of Americans to be faith, nation, and family, in that order, current research indicates that faith is typically embraced as people's fifth- or sixth-highest priority these days, even trailing elements such as intelligent consumption and career optimization.

Sociologists have been busy proclaiming that Americans are now "less religious than ever before."[2] While there is more than a bit of hyperbole behind that claim, many indicators suggest that we are certainly moving further from the expansive religiosity that has long characterized the nation. A case in point is that only half of American adults (53 percent) contend that their religious faith is very important in their life these days.[3] That proportion has declined slowly but steadily over the last twenty years. A more convincing piece of evidence concerns the well-documented dismissal of faith by the under-thirty crowd. Most studies now show that roughly one-third of them have no connection to organized religion—and that their distaste for organized religion is growing steadily.[4]

But the issue at hand is even larger than simply embracing religiosity. The concepts of religion and being religious are even falling on hard times in our culture. A growing number of adults now describe themselves as "spiritual but not religious," by which they mean they are open to and accepting of things related to faith and the supernatural but not inclined toward routines, traditions, doctrines, and faith systems. This newer view is especially en vogue among people born after 1980.[5] Despite the expectations of a society that demands tolerance of all points of view, it is difficult to mask the fact that the shift toward being spiritual but not religious is taking a toll on America's devotion to God and its long-standing connection to Christianity.

Currently, barely one-third of adults describe themselves as deeply spiritual. Being spiritual but not religious means that a person can integrate faith into their life at their pace and in their own way without the accountability and expectations that accompany being religious, much less Christian. It allows the "spiritual but not religious" individual to be free from the restrictions that accompany the historical practices, beliefs, and purposes that form the heartbeat of a world religion, be it Christianity, Buddhism, Islam, or Judaism.[6]

Some of the desire to distance oneself from religion may be explained by the widespread perception that religion is losing influence in American society. Americans love an underdog, but they refuse to be associated with a loser. The advance of technology and information systems has conveyed the impression that we are a knowledgeable, intelligent society and that religion is old-fashioned, outdated, and irrelevant to the sophisticated life. Americans were certainly nervous about the role of religion at the turn of the millennium, when half of them admitted that it seemed as if religion was losing influence in our society. But today three-quarters of Americans contend that religion is losing influence;[7] the "religious" bandwagon is one that people are jumping from as if it were on fire. That sense of religious descent helps to explain why just four out of ten adults believe it is very important to lead a religious life.[8]

Just as damaging is the fact that fewer and fewer adults believe that religion holds the answers to most of life's important problems.[9] Further, when adults were asked to identify what it takes to have a happy life, only one out of every six adults (17 percent) said leading a religious life is the most important component. In fact, twice as many (34 percent) believe that a religious life may be the least important factor when compared to having good health, being married, having children, being wealthy, and having a successful career. Being wealthy and leading a religious life held the lowest positions on the list, deemed to be least important by similar numbers of adults.[10] It's one thing to be characterized as outdated. But to be perceived as both outdated and irrelevant is a sure ticket to cultural oblivion.

One tangential observation will add a bit of color to this discussion of the shifting beliefs of Americans. There has never been a time in the history of humankind when so much information has been collected and analyzed about what a single society thinks, does, says, feels, expects, and believes. There are more than three thousand marketing research firms in the nation that cumulatively interview millions of Americans in the hundreds of national surveys that are conducted every year. Yet it is telling that as we explore the questions being asked in those interviews, far fewer questions about faith and religion are being posed to survey respondents today than was true even twenty-five years ago. Why? Because the purpose of those questions is to elicit insight that will improve product development, marketing, sales, or other forms of institutional or cultural progress. There is now a smaller market for religious information than when people's faith was recognized as being central to their self-identity and self-image and the establishment of cultural boundaries. In other words, there is much more information about a wider range of topics than ever before—and yet the market for diverse religious information has shrunk. That reflects the contracting role of religion and faith in postmodern America.

BELIEFS ABOUT GOD AND JESUS

Most Americans believe in God—or at least some type of "higher power," "universal spirit," "supreme being," or God-like power. These days, 86 percent of adults believe in some such concept of God no matter how the individual defines that entity. That is a substantial decline from the 96 percent to 98 percent that registered such belief every year from the 1940s through mid-1990s.[11] The vast majority of those people (80 percent, although that too has dropped significantly in the past twenty years) indicate that they "never doubt the existence of God."[12]

However, perhaps the more useful insight relates to the nature of the divine reality that people believe in. It turns out that for millions of Americans, indicating that they believe in God does not mean they embrace the notion of a personal, omnipotent Creator being. Only about six out of ten adults (62 percent) describe their idea of the God they believe in as "the all-knowing, all-powerful creator of the universe who still rules the world today."[13] That view has declined from 73 percent in 1992.[14] Growing numbers of adults are defining God as their own capacity for divinity (24 percent).[15]

Relatively few Americans buy into the pantheistic notion of there being many external gods (3 percent).[16] And, of course, one of the fastest-growing and most-frequently-chronicled faith groups in the United States is the segment that holds a skeptical view of any and all forms of divinity (i.e., believing there is no God or that we cannot know if there is a divine being, now held by 12 percent).[17]

Undoubtedly, one of the motivations for belief in some type of God is borne from our own astonishment at how challenging and intricate world survival has become, leading to the conclusion that a power greater than the human mind and all of the resources it controls must be keeping the entire universe going. In fact, a slight majority (54 percent) agrees that the complexity of the universe is a convincing argument for the existence of God—that the enormity and sophistication of the universe is beyond the control of humanity, cannot be explained by chance, and thus requires the existence of a supreme being that is continually and expertly guiding all of creation.[18]

A deeper dive into our perceptions of a personal God reveals the widespread confusion that abounds. For instance, when asked about God's gender, 39 percent describe God as male, 1 percent as female, 10 percent as both, and 31 percent as neither.[19] We are clearly dubious about God's omnipotence too, with just 29 percent believing that God controls what happens on the earth, a larger share (37 percent) claiming that God does not control what happens here, just 8 percent asserting that God neither observes nor controls what happens, and the sizable remaining portion (25 percent) either not sure or dismissively maintaining there is no God.[20]

One of the more popular teachings over the past quarter century has been the idea that God cares enough about us individually to actually have a unique plan for each person's life. That view is currently held by a minority of Americans (41 percent).[21] The more popular view seems to be that God, if He exists, may guide us but that what we do is up to our own determination.

While most Americans believe in a personal God of some sort and ascribe various powers and qualities to Him, we are not blown away by His day-to-day job performance. One survey found that just 52 percent of adults "approve" of God's job performance.[22] His rating is clearly affected by peoples' lack of appreciation for how He handles natural disasters: just 50 percent approve.[23] We seem much more affirming of how we believe God handled the creation of the universe: 71 percent approve of His work in making everything out of nothing.[24]

With all the confusion about who God is among those who believe He exists, you might expect additional confusion regarding the person Christians consider to be the Son of God—Jesus Christ. You would not be disappointed. A large majority (82 percent) believes that Jesus Christ was a historical person—that is, He was a human being who walked the face of the earth some two thousand years ago.[25] Noticeably fewer people (two out of every three adults) believe that Jesus Christ is the Son of God.[26] Almost the same number believes that He died and was resurrected, as described in the Bible.[27] That statistic, however, has been steadily dropping for two decades, down from 87 percent in 1994[28] to 65 percent today.[29]

The notion of the Virgin Birth has also experienced a huge drop in popularity over the past twenty years. In 1994, 78 percent accepted it as a true, historical event.[30] The Virgin Birth of Jesus by Mary is now accepted by just 57 percent of the adult public.[31]

Despite the obvious concerns a growing number of Americans have about Jesus Christ, the proportion who claim they have made a personal commitment to Him that is still important in their life today has remained steady over the past two decades. In 1994, 64 percent claimed such a commitment to Christ,[32] which remained consistent in 2004[33] and was an equivalent 62 percent in 2014.[34]

BELIEFS ABOUT THE BIBLE

So much of the American belief system comes down to what people make of the Bible. It remains a best-selling book year after year— recording such consistently high sales figures that those who track book sales simply dropped it off the best-seller lists in order to make the lists seem more dynamic. Almost nine out of ten households (85 percent) own at least one Bible,[35] which means that even the homes of many skeptics include a copy of God's Word. The typical household contains four copies of the Bible.[36] To be fair, despite its wide ownership, the household Bible ownership level has dropped from 92 percent in 1993.[37]

Americans have an array of views about what the Bible really is. A huge majority (80 percent) believes that it can be considered "sacred" or "holy" literature, although there is a slow demise of such thinking.[38] One-fifth (23 percent) contend that it is the actual Word of God, has no errors, and can be taken literally. Slightly more (30 percent) describe it as the inspired Word of God without errors but including passages that are symbolic rather than literal. Rounding out those who believe the Bible to be infallible, if not inerrant, are the 15 percent who say it is the inspired Word of God and does contain some factual and historical errors but may be trusted.[39] That represents nearly two-thirds of the public who accept the Bible as God's true and invaluable guidance to humankind. The remaining one-third of the population view the Bible either as a book by writers who conveyed their own understanding of God's ways and principles, those who contend the Bible is simply a book of popular stories that offer man-derived advice, and adults who have not yet figured out what they believe about the Bible.[40]

Of course, owning a Bible and using it are two different things. On a typical day about one out of five Americans will actually read the Bible of their own volition. About one-seventh (15 percent) read the Bible every day. The rest who peruse its pages on any given day come from segments such as those who read it several times a week (13 percent) or once a week (9 percent) or those who read the Bible anywhere from once or twice a month to once a year (27 percent). One-quarter of adults never read the Bible, and another 9 percent read it less than once a year.[41]

Those who spend time reading the Scriptures devote about a half-hour per sitting.[42] Since most of the people who invest any time reading the Bible are those who believe it is God's direct and purposeful message to His followers, it is curious that so little time is allocated to studying that content. To place this in context, realize that time-use studies show that Americans spend more time doing a dozen other things than absorbing God's words to us. Those include activities such as watching television, talking to friends and family, listening to music and the radio, surfing the Internet, dealing with texts and e-mails, managing household chores, attending to personal hygiene, eating, and so forth. Why don't we devote more time to reading His message? Apparently because we do not really believe it will produce a sufficient return on our investment of time and energy. A minority believes the Bible contains everything we need to know to live a meaningful life—and even that minority is declining in size.[43] And consider how few adults are interested in gleaning wisdom from the Bible on the kinds of issues that we find most perplexing. Only one out of four Americans are interested in receiving input on parenting (22 percent), family conflict (24 percent), or dealing with illness or death (28 percent).[44] In some cases, such as grasping what the Bible has to say about politics, most people don't even want to know (54 percent).[45] And, of course, our lack of commitment to the Bible also has to do with the fact that only one in three adults is convinced that the Bible is completely accurate and reliable in the principles that it teaches.[46]

BELIEFS ABOUT GOD'S ACTIVITY

Most Americans do not pay much attention to the supernatural realm during the course of a typical day. Given our relative lack of knowledge about the content of the Bible—our most reliable source of understanding the nature, purposes, and work of God—it is not surprising that we don't focus too much on spirituality. When we reflect on spiritual matters, we tend to fall back on many traditional beliefs that we do not fully understand.

A prime example is the controversial topic of creation. The debate over the genesis of the universe and life—that is, whether the world was created by God or through a "big bang" and whether people were created by God or evolved from lower life forms—has been hotly contested. Perhaps the clearest example of evolution is found by tracking the change in Americans' perspectives on these matters. Our views have swung from one end of the spectrum to the other and back. It seems likely that tens of millions of adults could be swayed one way or the other on a moment's notice.

There are few areas where the collision of science and faith are more evident than in opinions regarding the history of the universe. The most recent research notes that about half the nation believes that the complexity of the universe has led them to support the view that God must have created it; one-fifth embrace the big bang theory; and the remaining one-quarter have not yet reached a conclusion on the matter.[47]

As for beliefs about the history or origins of mankind, getting a handle on what we believe is more confusing than the fine print in an insurance policy. There are three obvious reasons for the confusion. The first is that people are torn between trusting the "facts" provided by science and relying on the teaching of the Bible. The second is how public opinion on this subject is measured. Various surveys approach the topic differently, providing data that is related but that measures disparate nuances of a complicated issue. The third factor to consider is peoples' anxiety concerning the public image they might be saddled with as a result of their beliefs on such matters. The combined result of these realities is that Americans are confused, fearful, ignorant, and rather disengaged on this matter.

Having said that, it seems likely that the largest share of adults— somewhere between 45 percent and 60 percent—believes that Darwin's theory of evolution is true.[48] Darwin is gaining greater public support, as the number of Darwinian adherents has slowly grown over the past two decades. Likewise, there seems to be greater support for the theory of evolution than there is for the creationist view (which is held by probably somewhere between 35 percent and 40 percent of Americans).[49] Caught between the conflicting views, some people try to blend the two approaches. One-quarter of the public believes that God guided the evolutionary process to enable humanity to emerge from less advanced life forms He had already created.[50]

Regardless of the exact statistics related to people's views on both the history of the universe and of humankind, the relentless tug-of-war that people experience on those seminal issues reflects the struggle Americans have to take the Bible at face value. The age of information overflow has caused most Americans to build protective walls around their heads and hearts in order to avoid "analysis paralysis"—that is, being incapable of making decisions and taking action because there is too much information to sift through, organize, understand, interpret, and act upon. As a result, we are continually reprioritizing what matters to us in order to focus on the things that we assume are necessary to personally survive and grow. The debates over creationism and evolution generally do not make the "Must Figure Out" list of most Americans. That, in itself, speaks volumes about the significance of God, Christianity, the Bible, and faith in our lives.

Things are only a bit less convoluted regarding other facets of God's work. For instance, seven out of ten adults believe God currently performs miracles.[51] However, whether physical healings that were specifically prayed for constitute a miracle or an act of medicine and science continues to baffle most Americans. About four out of ten adults have prayed to God for a healing of some sort, and seven out of ten of those people described praying for that outcome to be personally helpful, if not medically successful.[52] Empirical studies designed to evaluate the effectiveness of prayer on individual health have proved to be inconclusive, although various studies report that those who prayed may have experienced a more positive effect than the person they were praying for.

In fact, the entire matter of prayer confounds most people. While slightly more than three-fourths of the population prays to God during a typical week, praying has declined from nine out of ten people doing so just three decades ago.[53] Once again, though, those who pray are divided as to whether their prayers move God, primarily change themselves, or are simply an exercise in futility.

The marketplace provides additional evidence of people's confusion about spiritual matters. Despite the recent efforts to create greater awareness of God in the workplace, most adults continue to perform their appointed occupational tasks without much thought about or intentional inclusion of God or biblical principles. Just one out of every four adults regularly views their work as a mission from God.[54] About one-third takes the Colossians 3:23 admonition to heart—to "work willingly at whatever you do, as though you were working for the Lord rather than for people"—and pursues excellence in the work performance because they see the fulfillment of those duties as an act of faith or as serving God.[55]

BELIEFS ABOUT ETERNITY AND SALVATION

One of the most controversial aspects of Christianity in contemporary America relates to salvation. In a culture obsessed with tolerance, notions such as sin and judgment offend millions of citizens. However, the idea of a holy God judging—and saving—people has been such an ingrained part of our culture for so long that many people possess contradictory views on eternal life, wrestling with the competing views of a secular culture and a traditional Protestant interpretation of the Bible. American Catholics have struggled with the additional challenge of mediating the traditional Roman view of salvation (i.e., eternal life awarded due to a winning combination of grace and works) against the more recent papal views emphasizing grace alone.

Heaven has become a hot topic in recent years, thanks to a slew of books and movies purportedly describing what heaven is like. Most of those stories are based on the views of people who allegedly died, visited heaven, and returned to life. If nothing else, those efforts have helped to sustain a remarkably high belief that heaven exists: nearly nine out of ten Americans (85 percent) believe heaven is real.[56] (Notice that we are more likely to believe in heaven than to accept the idea of a personal God who inhabits heaven or a Savior who was resurrected from the dead to return to heaven.) To a nation whose foundational document—the Declaration of Independence—talks about the pursuit of happiness, the idea of heaven is a winner. Heaven is almost universally seen as a happy place.

What about the idea of personal judgment by an omnipotent God? It's not so popular—and it's losing altitude. During the past two decades, we have dropped from 81 percent who believed that everyone will answer to God for their sins on Judgment Day to 76 percent who hold that view.[57] More recently, we have declined from 83 percent to 76 percent who maintain that there are clear guidelines of good and evil that apply to everyone, regardless of their circumstances.[58] A similar proportion (75 percent) believes that there is such a place as hell.[59] Interestingly that number has remained pretty constant over the last two decades.

Satan, aka the devil, has long been an enigma to Americans. While most have accepted the narrative of good and evil battling for people's affections and God has typically been assumed to be the face of goodness, Americans have struggled to embrace the idea of a completely evil being who is God's enemy. We are divided into three groups when it comes to the existence of Satan. Roughly equal numbers—about one-quarter of adults—either believe that Satan is a real, living being who can influence people's lives in ways that oppose the work and desires of God or that Satan is not a living being but is simply a symbol of evil.[60] The other half of the country is in the mushy middle, uncertain what to believe about Satan. (However, as a sign of the times, people lean by a 2:1 margin toward believing that Satan is a symbol, not a living and active enemy of God.)

So, in a nation founded largely by Protestants for the purpose of religious freedom and the practice of their biblical beliefs, where do contemporary Americans stand on the matter of eternal destiny? Once again, diversity of belief is evident. Currently, one-third of the adult public (36 percent) might be described as what evangelicals consider to be "saved" from the "wages of sin" and assured of eternal life with God in heaven.[61] These are people who have made a personal commitment to Jesus Christ, have confessed their sins to God, and have accepted Christ as their Savior. That proportion has dropped by nine percentage points since 2006.[62] In some ways the Protestant Reformation is still being fought in the United States.

The largest counter to the notion of salvation by grace alone is the idea that salvation is based on being good or doing good works. That perspective is maintained by another one-third of the public. The remaining one-third of adults are evenly split between those who do not believe there is any type of afterlife and those who simply profess confusion about what's coming.[63]

Over the years, we have consistently found that very few Americans believe they will go to hell (usually 1 percent to 3 percent).[64] And even though very few adults (2 percent) have adopted Eastern or pantheistic religions, such as Buddhism or Hinduism,[65] a surprising number of Americans associated with Christianity (as well as some skeptics) believe in reincarnation. Currently about one-fourth of the population (24 percent) believes they will return to the earth in some other life form after they die.[66]

MORALITY AND WORLDVIEW

The patchwork of beliefs related to moral behavior is a direct outgrowth of the doubts, confusion, and resistance people have to the truth of the Bible and the clear moral precepts that it lays out for humanity.

Overwhelming majorities of people, regardless of their perspective on the veracity of the Bible, believe that the Bible provides understandable teaching on most of the moral issues of our day. Pornography? Two-thirds say the Bible discourages its creation and exposure. Gambling? Three-quarters argue that the Bible discourages humans from engaging in it. Homosexuality and same-sex marriage? Again, three-quarters contend that the Bible warns people not to go there.[67]

So, knowing that the Bible provides guidance on these and other urgent moral issues relevant to the world today, what proportion of American adults believes that specific behaviors are morally acceptable?

+ 69 percent—getting a divorce

+ 67 percent—an unmarried woman having a baby

- 66 percent—a sexual relationship between an unmarried man and woman

- 65 percent—medical research on stem cells obtained from human embryos

- 64 percent—gambling

- 63 percent—enjoying sexual thoughts or fantasies about someone you are not married to

- 63 percent—living with someone of the opposite sex without being married

- 61 percent—the death penalty

- 58 percent—gay or lesbian relations

- 52 percent—doctor-assisted suicide

- 47 percent—using marijuana for recreational purposes

- 44 percent—using profanity

- 43 percent—looking at pictures that display explicit sexual behavior

- 42 percent—having an abortion

- 34 percent—getting drunk

- 32 percent—sex between teenagers

- 19 percent—committing suicide[68]

While this profile bears no resemblance to what the Bible teaches—or to what the early Americans believed—it is a natural extension of the fact that only 34 percent of adults believe that there is any absolute moral truth.[69] When pressed as to where such truth can be found, we discover that only one out of ten American adults believe there is absolute moral truth and that it is found in the Bible.[70]

The survey data also shows that most of the moral behaviors listed that have been tracked in national surveys over the past decade have experienced significant increases in the percentage of adults who now describe that behavior as morally acceptable. The exceptions among the thirteen tracked behaviors are gambling, doctor-assisted suicide, and having an abortion. The largest swing in acceptability relates to homosexual relations, birth outside of marriage, and sex between single adults.

When Americans are pursuing their life goals, most of them do not worry about the moral acceptability of their choices and actions. Less than three out of ten adults say that when they make a moral choice they are striving to be consistent with biblical standards. The most common perspective is to make moral choices that feel right (four out of ten adults). The other one-quarter of the public claims they do not worry about the morality of a choice but simply do the best they can in any given situation.[71] That makes sense in a nation where half of the population reports that belief in God is not necessary to be moral.[72]

Young Adults and the Flow of Beliefs

As difficult as it may have been to read this summary of adults' beliefs, hold on to your seat: exploring the beliefs of our young people, which further indicates where the country is headed, will shake you up even more.

Adults under the age of twenty-five—a group whom the medical community tells us is made up of individuals who are still in the process of completing their brain development—have been assaulted by all kinds of theories and theologies as they have been developing their personal worldview. A side-by-side comparison of twenty religious beliefs between people eighteen to twenty-nine years of age and those who are thirty and older reveals that there is not a single instance where the younger adults reflect a more biblically orthodox position than do their elders. For eighteen of those twenty measurements there are statistically significant differences between the younger and older adults. Some of the highlights of that comparison include the fact that the young adults are:

- 29 percent less likely to say that their religious faith is very important in their life

- 18 percent less likely to own a Bible

- 42 percent less likely to believe the Bible is accurate in all the principles it teaches

- 34 percent less likely to read from the Bible during a typical week

- 59 percent more likely to never read the Bible

- 13 percent less likely to believe that the Bible is the Word of God

- 25 percent less likely to believe that God is the all-knowing, all-powerful Creator of the universe who still rules it today

- 23 percent more likely to believe that Jesus Christ sinned while on the earth

- 44 percent less likely to have confessed their sins and accepted Christ as their Savior[73]

When the beliefs of college students alone are considered, the picture is even more bleak. Among current college students, less than half believe that God exists; three-quarters accept evolution and Darwinism rather than creationism and intelligent design; just one in five believe the Bible is a perfect guide to morality and is relevant to today's world; and less than half believe that prayer is effective.[74]

Assuming that historical patterns hold true, the good news is that we can expect the views of the young adult group to change over the next decade or two—although not by very much. The bad news is that the changes will probably not move them in a direction that will increase the vitality of the Christian faith in America.

HISTORICAL PERSPECTIVE ON AMERICAN BELIEFS

Americans have never been a perfect people by biblical standards—no nation has been (or ever will be), and therefore Jesus came to save all of humankind. Ever since the colonists first arrived on America's shores, there has been an ebb and flow to the faith of Americans. Two patterns are noteworthy, though.

First, several major waves of change affecting America's faith—such as the First Great Awakening, the Second Great Awakening, the turn-of-the-century revivals, and so on—have successively moved the nation in a positive direction. The First Awakening produced an awareness of individual responsibility, an institutional separation of church and state that secured the rights of conscience and religious noncoercion in the civil arena, and Christian cooperation among denominations rather than the physical conflict that previously had been common. The Second Awakening secured the belief in human equality among God's creation without regard to race. The turn-of-the-century revivals produced the end of institutional child abuse and slavery.

Yet commensurate with these good changes, heterodox movements also sprang up within each spiritual wave. Thus, from the First Awakening emerged a strong unitarianism, restorationism, and primitivism; from the Second, universalism and transcendentalism; and from the turn-of-the-century revivals, an isolationism and false pietism that rejected interaction with the culture, as well as a social justice gospel that replaced Bible-centered teachings with a man-centered humanism. In short, with each genuine spiritual renewal, there also occurred what Jesus described in Matthew 13:25—that along with the good crop, the enemy came in and also planted weeds. So in each case, after the initial positive impact of the spiritual revival faded, the median public point for religious values and beliefs frequently ended up moving further away from biblical principles and truth than when that wave started.

Second, the waves of spiritual change away from biblical principles are now coming faster and occurring more rapidly than at any time in the past—the frequency of the cycle has both increased and intensified. This is one way of saying that we are moving away from biblical lifestyles and beliefs faster than ever, and there are no signs of an imminent reversal of this pattern.

Originally America was intentionally founded, more so than any other modern nation, to secure spiritual principles and values. In fact, Americans are generally in agreement, despite the revisionist historians who have argued differently, that a major reason for the founding of America was to give people of all faiths the freedom to believe and practice whatever religion they chose to follow. More than nine out of ten adults (95 percent) believe that to be true.[75] What *has* changed more dramatically than the shifts in our understanding of the genesis of this nation is the nature of the religious faith that people have chosen to adopt and practice. Most of us have no sense of the massive gap that exists between early American beliefs and contemporary American beliefs. Surveying this gap is instructive as we attempt to understand how far we've strayed and what it might take to restore sanity, righteous purpose, and moral order to a nation gone wild.

In order to better grasp the comparison between the past and present, recall that currently:

- In a nation that largely professes itself to be Christian, and where a supermajority of citizens profess to be Christians, traditional biblical beliefs are now in wide dispute or disfavor.

- Most Christians today perform their daily tasks without much thought about or intentional inclusion of God or biblical principles.

- Not only does a profile of current moral beliefs bear little resemblance to what the Bible teaches, but most Americans do not worry about the moral acceptability of their choices and actions when pursuing their life goals.

◆ Praying is on the decline, and only one-third of Christians believe there is any absolute moral truth.

◆ Biblical notions such as sin and judgment now offend millions of Christians, and the idea of personal judgment by an omnipotent God is widely rejected.

Sadly any objective examination of the current status of biblical faith in America certainly affirms its unhealthy state. A comparison of America's religious beliefs and values today with those of two centuries ago further attests to our debilitated condition, and the difference is well summarized by Jesus's statement to the church at Ephesus to "consider how far you have fallen!" (Rev. 2:5, NIV).

Early Americans believed that God's Word applied to *every* aspect of daily life—a fact documented by any perusal of early sermons. If something important was in the news, then it was also covered from the pulpit with a biblical perspective. Consequently, it is easy to find countless early sermons on numerous topics never covered today, such as earthquakes, fires, droughts, and hurricanes;[76] the execution of murderers;[77] solar eclipses, the sighting of a comet, or the discovery of a new planet;[78] national defense and foreign affairs;[79] the duties of civil rulers and of citizens toward government;[80] the issues associated with aging;[81] immigration;[82] education;[83] medicine and medical issues;[84] economics and taxation;[85] and other practical topics. As John Adams affirmed, "It is the *duty* of the clergy to accommodate their discourses to the times...how much soever it may move the gall [the critics]."[86] Ask today's Christians to name a single verse on any of these topics and the most common response will likely be a blank stare followed by complete silence.

Additionally, from the seventeenth until the twentieth century, state legislative sessions often began with the civil leaders gathering in a joint assembly with religious leaders from across the state and having a minister address the lawmakers in what was called the annual "Election Sermon." As affirmed by an early historian:

The clergy were generally consulted by the civil authorities; and not infrequently the suggestions from the pulpit, on election days and other special occasions, were enacted into laws. The statute-book, the reflex of the age, shows the influence.[87]

In the judicial branch hundreds of court rulings can be invoked to demonstrate that the influence of Christianity and the Bible was keenly felt, with countless Bible verses referenced and cited in these decisions. And if a defendant was sentenced to death by a jury, it was common for the judge, whether at the federal or state level, to deliver a salvation message to the defendant in the courtroom.[88]

Even the political rhetoric of our national leaders was abundantly populated with scriptural quotations. For example, in Patrick Henry's famous "Give Me Liberty or Give Me Death" speech, he quoted directly from eight different Bible phrases.[89] In Benjamin Franklin's famous address to the Constitutional Convention, he quoted eight different Bible phrases in only nine sentences.[90] In a letter from George Washington to Revolutionary War hero Marquis de Lafayette, Washington quoted seven different verses in only four sentences;[91] and in a letter to a Hebrew congregation, in only two sentences he quoted nine Bible phrases.[92]

Significantly, when modern political scientists examined fifteen thousand representative Founding Era writings from the realms of politics, government, journalism, sermons, literature, and education, they found that the single-most-cited source throughout those diverse works was the Bible, with 34 percent of the quotes taken from the Bible.[93]

The values and beliefs of the much more biblically informed culture of previous generations stand in stark contrast to those of today's largely biblically illiterate culture. One obvious difference is their widespread and publicly expressed conviction that God hated sin and that it was therefore the duty of all citizens to flee wickedness and seek God's mercy and forgiveness.

Consequently, during the American Revolution, Congress publicly called on Americans to "confess and bewail [their] manifold sins and transgressions, and, by a sincere repentance and amendment of life, appease his righteous displeasure, and, through the merits and mediation of Jesus Christ, obtain his pardon and forgiveness."[94] Such public calls to recognize God, forsake sin, and pursue personal holiness were such a regular emphasis in early America that by 1815, some 1,020 calls to public days of humiliation, fasting, and repentance had been issued—792 by governmental bodies and leaders, with an additional 238 by church leaders.[95]

Earlier generations also believed that citizens being God-conscious produced responsible behavior, both individually and collectively. In fact, Founding Father John Adams openly avowed that it was the intimate awareness of his own personal accountability to God that provided all the incentive he needed as a political leader to stay on the straight and narrow:

> Such compliances [compromises]...of my honor, my conscience, my friends, my country, my God, as the Scriptures inform us must be punished with nothing less than hellfire, eternal torment....The duration of future punishment terrifies me. If I could but deceive myself so far as to think eternity a moment only, I could comply [compromise] and be promoted.[96]

Thus, public affirmations of the awareness of one's personal accountability to God regularly appeared in America's early governing documents—such as the original 1776 constitution of Pennsylvania (written with the help of Benjamin Franklin)[97]—that openly declared:

> And each member [of the legislature], before he takes his seat, shall make and subscribe the following declaration, viz: "I do believe in one God, the Creator and Governor of the universe, the rewarder of the good and the punisher of the wicked..."[98]

In fact, the standard form of indictment for a common-law crime (such as murder, rape, assault, arson, robbery, and so forth) routinely stated, "John Smith, *not having the fear of God before his eyes*, did willfully commit murder" (or whatever the crime was).[99]

In short, early American policy affirmed the biblical teaching that when people were God-conscious, their values and beliefs—and thus their outward behavior—were improved. Perhaps this is why Founding Father James Kent, a "father of American jurisprudence" and the highest ranking judicial official in the state of New York, noted that in his state courts, he had only eight murder convictions in a total of sixteen years![100]

But early Americans understood not just that individuals but also nations were accountable to God. As Founding Father George Mason affirmed at the Constitutional Convention of 1787:

> As nations cannot be rewarded or punished in the next world, so they must be in this. By an inevitable chain of causes and effects, Providence punishes national sins by national calamities.[101]

The Bible taught, and Americans in previous generations widely believed, that public policies had spiritual consequences and brought either God's blessings or judgment directly upon a nation. Unlike today's Americans, who disapprove of God's job performance in handling natural disasters, citizens in earlier generations widely embraced the Bible's teachings that weather calamities and disasters were often a product of our own public sins and wickedness rather than any failure of performance on God's part.

Consequently, when the nation experienced devastating weather patterns, it was common to do exactly what the Massachusetts legislature did on July 4, 1776: call on its citizens that "with devout and importunate [unending] supplications to implore Almighty God that the frowns of His Providence, manifested by the severe drought wherewith some parts of the land have been visited, and all the humiliating events which have lately taken place in America, may, under the Divine influence, produce a sincere repentance and thorough reformation among all orders and degrees of persons."[102]

And because these more biblically literate generations of

Americans so thoroughly understood accountability to God, they were cognizant that they individually would answer to God Himself for their personal stewardship of what He had given them, which included their life, their family, their material possessions, *and also their government.* Consequently, even one-half century after the American founding, political races still had a 99 percent voting participation.[103] Founding Father Samuel Adams had captured the heart of this belief when he reminded citizens, "Let each citizen remember at the moment he is *offering his vote* that he is...executing one of the most solemn trusts in human society for which he is *accountable to God*" (emphasis added).[104]

They also understood their duty to serve others above themselves. Therefore, if a citizen was asked to serve others by running for office, then he was not at liberty to say no. As Declaration signer Benjamin Rush explained:

> He [a citizen] must love private life, but he must decline no station, however public or responsible it may be, when called to it by the suffrages [votes] of his fellow citizens.[105]

Why? Because, as Rush explained, the Bible specifically taught that "none liveth to himself" (see Romans 14:7) and therefore our life "is not our own property. All its fruits of wisdom and experience belong to the public."[106]

It is a biblical truth that those who are best suited for public office are frequently the ones who don't want to be there (see Judges 9:8–15); it is the self-promoting who make the worst leaders. The best leaders (e.g., George Washington, Patrick Henry, John Adams, and so many others) much preferred and sought private life to public life but always sacrificed their own preferences in order to fulfill the request to serve others. As Martha Washington affirmed, George had taught her "never to oppose [her] private wishes to the public will."[107]

Unlike the current generation, previous ones did not suffer from our modern compartmentalization, by which faith is placed into a nice, neat box and then set aside on a shelf so that it does not "contaminate" any other aspect of personal life, living, thinking, or behavior. The belief of earlier generations was well summarized by John Quincy Adams, who declared:

> With regard to the history contained in the Bible..."it is not so much praiseworthy to be acquainted with as it is shameful to be ignorant of it."[108]

In their day a thorough knowledge of the Bible and its teachings was so much the norm that to be well acquainted with it was not particularly noteworthy; however, to not know the Bible was considered shameful. Today, the societal default position is certainly reversed.

In recent years as America has increasingly rejected the Bible's teachings, the adverse statistical effects upon the nation and its people has become evident. Current world rankings now show that America's status is plummeting in numerous categories (e.g., falling economic freedom,[109] rising government corruption,[110] declining educational performance,[111] deterioration of national ethics and morality,[112] etc.) Of course, America's fall as a nation is nothing more than a reflection of the aggregate fall of individuals within the nation; but regardless, by no measurement is the overall spiritual and moral trajectory of the nation now moving in a positive direction.

Chapter 3

OUR RESPONSIBILITY AS CITIZENS

A S PREVIOUSLY DEMONSTRATED, because of America's changing values, we have become less conscious and supportive of facilitating the well-being of others and of preserving historical habits and customs. This is especially evident regarding individual involvement in community, state, and national life. Not only is there a disturbing lack of knowledge about the most elementary facts concerning the civic sphere, but also participation in exercising what was once considered the most sacred privilege of an American (the right to elect our own leaders) has tumbled.

More than nine out of ten residents of the United States who are eighteen or older have the right to vote. Amazingly, less than three out of every four register to do so. And in presidential elections, when turnout is highest among registered voters, one out of four don't bother to cast a ballot.[1] That means four out of every ten adults qualified to participate in the process that made this country uniquely great refuse to do so! More specifically, in the 2012 presidential election, nearly ninety million adults who were qualified to vote made a conscious decision not to participate. Placing these numbers in context, when you take into consideration the fact that recent presidential candidates have been elected by slim margins,[2] the mathematics are a bit disturbing: with just six out of ten qualified adults bothering to register and vote and the victorious candidate drawing support from about half of them, our nation is regularly being led by men who have the backing of less than one-third of the adult population.

Voter turnout is even worse in nonpresidential state and federal elections (called "off-year elections"), when an average of only 39 percent of the two-thirds of registered Americans vote. This means that in nonpresidential elections, only about one in four Americans vote to choose their federal congressmen and senators and state legislators and governors.[3] And since only a majority of that one-fourth is necessary to select the winners, this means essentially seven out of eight Americans do not vote for those who become their governors, senators, and representatives. (This helps to explain why the public approval rating for Congress hovers around 12 to 14 percent[4]— generally the same percentage as those who vote for the winners.)

For other elections, the numbers are even lower, including:

> ...five percent voter turnout in a recent Dallas mayoral election. Six percent in Charlotte, 7.5 percent in San Antonio. Seven percent in Austin. Seven percent in Tennessee's congressional primaries, 6 percent for a statewide gubernatorial primary in Kentucky, 3 percent for a U. S. Senate primary in Texas, and 3 percent for a statewide runoff in North Carolina.[5]

These figures are embarrassingly abysmal. In fact, consider the North Carolina race: based on the national voter trends, 3 percent of those registered voted, which means that only 2 percent of adults voted. In other words, it took a mere 1 percent of the public's consent to choose the winner—support from just 1 percent of the people to bestow statewide power and authority on a single individual!

Some public officials have turned to humor to draw attention to the appalling lack of interest in the political process. Eric Garcetti, mayor of Los Angeles, described his victory after a campaign in which more than $19 million was poured into advertising and he participated in forty debates, saying, "I got 33% of the 20% turnout of the 49% of the population registered to vote. I had a landslide with 2.6% of the population."[6]

Uninvolved and Uninformed

Americans will spend whatever time is necessary to check consumer ratings and consult with their friends to learn about the best smartphones, restaurants, or movies, but they refuse to apply anywhere near the same level of care and diligence when it comes to selecting those who will exercise extensive control, and even the power of life and death, over them. In fact, in the 2012 presidential election, one of the most popular Internet searches *on Election Day* was "Who is running for president?"[7]—and this question was being asked despite nearly $2 billion having been spent in advertising and marketing for almost a year to promote the names of the candidates.[8]

America's governmental system was designed as a limited government to protect our liberties, and it became the best government in the history of the world. But it has now become one that micromanages virtually every aspect of American life and living. Yet there is little current interest in learning about either what our government was originally or what it is now. For example:

♦ Two-thirds of Americans cannot identify the three branches of government (legislative, executive, judicial);[9] three of four do not know what the judiciary branch does;[10] and eight in ten cannot name even one of the federal government's powers.[11]

♦ Seven in ten do not know that the Constitution is the supreme law of the land.[12]

♦ Eight in ten cannot name even two of the rights listed in the Declaration of Independence,[13] and 44 percent are unable to define the Bill of Rights.[14]

♦ Only one in four can actually name one fundamental freedom protected by the First Amendment,[15] and just one in one thousand can name all five freedoms protected by it (speech, religion, press, assembly, petition).[16]

51

- ◆ Nearly 60 percent cannot name even one of the six-teen presidential cabinet-level departments, and only 4 percent can name as many as five.[17]

- ◆ Two-thirds cannot name a single member of the US Supreme Court, and only 1 percent can name all nine.[18]

- ◆ Two-thirds cannot identify the type of economic system that made the United States the most pros-perous country in the world (an unregulated, free-market, free-enterprise, capitalist system).[19]

Earlier generations believed that to pay no attention to one's country was the ultimate act of selfishness. Such disinterest demonstrated a flagrant callousness and lack of concern for the well-being of others. How so? As explained by evangelical Founding Father Benjamin Rush:

> Patriotism is as much a virtue as justice, and…is both a moral and a religious duty. It comprehends not only the love of our neighbors but of millions of our fellow creatures, not only of the present but of future generations.[20]

If one really cares about others and wants what is best for them, then a principal means by which that care can be exercised is through responsible stewardship of the country. To strive to secure the best government possible—to maintain a just government that will be a blessing and not a burden, a servant and not a master—is to demonstrate concern and seek what is beneficial for every person in the nation. Not being involved through at least a minimum of knowledgeable and informed voting shows a personal disdain for the welfare of others as well as the well-being of posterity.

Across the generations the pulpit was bold in expounding this biblical truth. As the famous Rev. Henry van Dyke declared:

> The true patriot is he who maintains the highest ideal of honor, purity, and justice for his country's laws and rulers and actions. The true patriot is he who is willing to sacrifice

his time and strength and prosperity to remove political shame and reform political corruption.... The true patriot is he who works and votes with the same courage that he would fight, in order that the noblest aspirations of a noble people may be embodied in the noblest rulers.[21]

This belief that caring for others involved the responsibility to vote for the best possible leaders was carefully inculcated into our young across the generations. As the famous Christian statesman Daniel Webster affirmed:

Impress upon...children the truth, that the exercise of the elective franchise is a social duty, of as solemn a nature as man can be called to perform; that a man may not innocently trifle with his vote; that every free elector is a trustee, as well for others as himself; and that every man and every measure he supports has an important bearing on the interests of others, as well as on his own.[22]

This certainly is not a topic of instruction for most schools today, or even for most families, but it was just the opposite in previous generations. In fact, Benjamin Rush, known as "the father of public schools under the Constitution," avowed that the primary purpose of public education was threefold: to teach students (1) to love and serve God, (2) to love and serve their country, and (3) to love and serve their family.[23]

Notice the order: God, country, family. These days few people would prioritize these responsibilities in that order. In fact, most would argue that involvement with civil activities detracts from the time necessary to build a strong family. But in reality it is just the opposite, for when government is neglected, whether through the inattention or the apathy of its citizens, history demonstrates that it will become filled with officials whose policies are hostile to the values, beliefs, and practices essential to the formation of strong and stable families. Even a cursory examination of America's family problems over recent decades affirms that government policies and programs regularly have lain at the root of, or exacerbated, those troubles.

Understanding this principle, Samuel Adams exhorted:

> Every citizen will see—and I hope be deeply impressed with a sense of it—how exceedingly important it is to himself, *and how intimately the welfare of his children is connected with it*, that those who are to have a share in making as well as in judging and executing the laws should be men of singular wisdom and integrity.[24]

Recall that Benjamin Rush not only placed duty to country above that to family, but he also placed duty to God as the first and foremost of citizen responsibilities. But God is no longer the primary influence in the lives of most Americans today, including most Christians. However, this is not surprising, for in order to know one's duty to God, one has to know God's Word, and the serious teaching and study of the Bible is definitely no longer a high priority in the lives of most Christians.

One indication of this departure from God's Word is the assertion of many Christians that the Bible does not support citizen involvement in the governmental arena. But such a pronouncement merely confirms the biblical illiteracy of those making that claim. In fact, ask most Christians today to name a mere half-dozen Bible verses that address government, and be prepared to wait perhaps years for an answer. Yet in John Locke's 1690 *Two Treatises on Government*, on which the Founding Fathers so heavily relied,[25] he invoked the Bible in 1,349 references in his first treatise and 157 times in his second one. Clearly, then, the Bible is neither silent nor neutral on civil government.

In fact, on three separate occasions in Romans 13:4–6, those in civil government are described as "God's ministers" (NKJV)—certainly not secular terminology, nor expressing a disapproval of the civil arena. But why should God view it negatively, for He Himself established government, and it is just as much a God-ordained institution as is the Church or the family.

Additionally, in Hebrews 11, called the "Faith Hall of Fame," most of the heroes listed in verses 22–34 were known for their involvement in civil government. Why would God hold up these champions of biblical faith for our emulation if He thought it was wrong to be involved in the civil sphere?

And 1 Timothy 2:1–2 directs us to pray "first of all" for all people, especially for leaders and those in authority. Thus, the command is to make praying for governmental leaders a top priority, right along with (if not before) praying for our families, churches, jobs, or ourselves. There is nothing else in the Bible that God directs us to pray for "first of all," thus indicating the importance that He Himself places on the governmental arena.

Then, in Jesus's parable in Luke 19, the master calls his servants together and gives them all a *mina*—a trust, a stewardship. He departs and then later returns to take account of their stewardship. One servant has increased his holdings by tenfold and another by fivefold, so the master rewards the first by making him a ruler over ten cities and the second a ruler over five cities. Most contemporary Christians do not think that being placed into civil government is a reward from the Master—which shows why it is time to rethink our beliefs about civil government based on what the Bible says rather than what secularists, including secular-thinking Christians, say.

There are scores of other verses, including the once-familiar Proverbs 14:34, which declares that "righteousness exalts a nation, but sin is a reproach to any people" (NKJV). Numerous Bible passages make clear that on the one hand, a nation will be blessed only when its public policies are such that God can approve, and on the other, that if God opposes a nation's public policies for their lack of righteousness and conformity to His general principles, then that nation will begin to decline and lose its stability, prosperity, freedoms, and other national blessings.

So if righteous policies are what exalt a nation and thus cause God's blessings to come collectively on every inhabitant of that nation, then how can such policies be enacted? Proverbs 29:2 answers that question, explaining that when leaders are righteous, citizens rejoice, but "when the wicked rule, the people groan" (NIV). Placing God-fearing people in office is the best means to ensure that policies will be enacted that God can bless. But in America, the only way in which competent, God-fearing people will be put into office at any level is if God-fearing citizens elect them—yet this is currently what most Christians refuse to do.

Whenever the wrong types of leaders make it into office, then a nation's laws and form of government, no matter how good they have been previously, are in dire jeopardy of becoming absolutely worthless. Consider Israel as an example. Did any nation in the history of the world have better civil laws? Certainly not, for God Himself had written their laws. Yet how good were those laws under rulers such as Ahab and Jezebel, or Manasseh, Jeroboam, Rehoboam, and other wicked leaders? Even though their laws had come directly from God, they were disregarded when placed in the hands of corrupt and deficient leaders.

Early Americans fully understood this truth, which is why Christian leaders such as William Paterson (a signer of the Constitution who was placed on the US Supreme Court by President George Washington) openly reminded citizens:

> When the righteous are in authority, the people rejoice [Proverbs 29:2, NKJV].[26]

This Bible verse, and the core principle it represents, was a topic of frequent discussion by Bible-minded ministers,[27] and across the generations, Christian civic duty and participation was an area of heavy emphasis from the pulpit.[28] Typical of this focus was the charge of the Rev. Mellish Irving Motte to his hearers:

> You should deposit your vote for office, with a religious sense of accountableness, like that which makes you so serious when you handle the emblems of the Savior's body and blood.[29]

Voting was to be considered just as sacred as the sacrament of Communion? Today that would be dismissed as heresy! But in making such a bold statement, Rev. Motte had the Scriptures on his side. In addressing Communion, 1 Corinthians 11 directs that the partaker is seriously to examine and judge himself and his motives—that Communion is a somber responsibility, not to be taken for granted or participated in with a haphazard or careless attitude, and that because of the gravity of the event, time was to be spent in preparation before God. This same sober-mindedness and sense of individual accountability to God was likewise to precede and accompany citizen voting.

Also addressing the religious solemnity of voting, the Rev. Willard Spaulding likewise declared:

> The pulpit should teach the people not to forget their religion while acting the part of citizens. Singular as it may seem, there are many men who stand well in the church but who are a disgrace to the state. They pray well but they vote infamously.... There are multitudes of the most moral and religious members of community who thus neglect their civil duties. Hence our elections in many cases are carried by the selfish and debased.[30]

And the Rev. Mathias Burnet had similarly admonished:

> Look well to the characters and qualifications of those you elect and raise to office and places of trust.... Think not that your interests will be safe in the hands of the weak and ignorant; or faithfully managed by the impious, the dissolute and the immoral. Think not that men who acknowledge not the providence of God nor regard His laws will be uncorrupt in office, firm in defense of the righteous cause against the oppressor, or resolutely oppose the torrent of iniquity.... Watch over your liberties and privileges, civil and religious, with a careful eye.[31]

Even the Rev. Charles Finney, the renowned revivalist and church theologian of the Second Great Awakening whose writings have transcended the generations and even the centuries, pointedly warned Christians:

> The church must take right ground in regard to politics....The time has come that Christians must vote for honest men, and take consistent ground in politics, or the Lord will curse them....Christians have been exceedingly guilty in this matter. But the time has come when they must act differently....God cannot sustain this free and blessed country, which we love and pray for, unless the church will take right ground. Politics are a part of a religion in such a country as this, and Christians must do their duty to the country as a part of their duty to God. It seems sometimes as if the foundations of the nation were becoming rotten, and Christians seem to act as if they thought God did not see what they do in politics. But I tell you, he does see it, and he [God] will bless or curse this nation, according to the course they [Christians] take [in politics].[32]

There are countless additional examples, and they all attest to the solemn reality that the current condition of our country and its government is simply a reflection of the action—or, more specifically, the lack thereof—by the God-fearing community. Where America finds itself today is well exemplified by the parable in which Jesus described a man who had a good field, growing wheat, but awakened one morning to find the wheat intermingled with weeds. How did it change from good to bad? In Matthew 13:25 Jesus identified the problem: while the good men slept, the enemy came in and planted the weeds. Jesus never faulted the enemy for doing what he did; the problem was that the good men went to sleep.

ASLEEP AT THE WHEEL?

Are Americans—and especially American Christians—awake today? For several decades political scientists have been flaunting research that suggests our political process is floundering because most voters are asleep at the wheel. Among the findings from some of these studies are:

♦ Voters can name some current issues but possess little depth of understanding about those matters. For instance, a recent study by the Pew Research Center demonstrated that only one-third of adults might be deemed "high knowledge" voters, with another one-third possessing moderate knowledge and the final one-third being largely clueless about public affairs. The survey showed that large numbers of people could not correctly answer a wide range of simple questions. For instance, one-third could not name either the vice president of the United States or the governor of their state. Two-thirds could not name the president of Russia. Roughly two-thirds did not know the basic elements of pending changes in the minimum-wage law. Three-quarters were ignorant of Senate action regarding a major military course of action.[33] Other surveys discovered that while most Americans had strong opinions about major government programs, such as the Affordable Care Act (aka Obamacare) and the Troubled Assets Relief Program (TARP), people had little understanding of the substance of those laws or the process by which those laws operate. And even though a majority of voters has consistently cited the economy as the most important issue facing the country, a declining proportion of the electorate can provide any insights into such integral components of the economic morass, such as the national trade deficit or where the federal government's enormous spending goes.[34]

♦ The public is generally outraged at the poor performance of Congress yet continually reelects more than 80 percent of incumbents. Studies designed to explain that seeming contradiction indicate that voters do not retain information about their representatives' past actions, do not pursue information about those officials' performance, are likely to vote on the basis of superficial characteristics (e.g., appearance, likability, name familiarity), and fall prey to campaign rhetoric and marketing without grasping the truth of such claims or the substantive differences between candidates.[35]

♦ Political scientists have exhaustively shown that the problem is not that voters cannot get enough information to make informed choices. Rather, voters are too distracted by other matters and too disinterested in the workings of their government to invest themselves in becoming sufficiently informed.[36]

After studying the electorate intensively, a pair of respected political researchers from Yale and Stanford concluded that despite the incredible increase in and accessibility of information available to Americans, "The political sophistication of American voters, measured by how much they know about politics and how well they think about what they know, has not changed much in the last 50 years."[37] Professors Jonathan Bender and John Bullock noted that "if most voters were Brookings-level policy wonks, the performance of the system would be quite different."[38] But they acknowledged that such a transition in the electorate is unlikely: "Today, just as in the 1950s, most Americans are unaware of the existence of most issues, perforce oblivious of parties' stands on those issues, ignorant of most of the basic rules by which government operates, and unfamiliar with all but the most important handful of events in the nation's history."[39]

Shame on us.

Only when citizens remain awake and exercise their role as active stewards can they keep the weeds from taking over, but that choice is totally ours. As President James A. Garfield (a gospel minister in the Second Great Awakening) bluntly affirmed:

Now, more than ever before, the people are responsible for the character of their Congress. If that body be ignorant, reckless, and corrupt, it is because the people tolerate ignorance, recklessness, and corruption. If it be intelligent, brave, and pure, it is because the people demand these high qualities to represent them in the national legislature....If the next centennial does not find us a great nation, with a great and worthy Congress, it will be because those who represent the enterprise, the culture, and the morality of the nation do not aid in controlling the political forces.[40]

This articulation of this biblical truth remained a heavy emphasis across American culture for generations. In fact, Founding Father Noah Webster, one of America's leading educators, specifically addressed this biblical responsibility in one of his most famous public school texts, telling students:

When you become entitled to exercise the right of voting for public officers, let it be impressed on your mind that God commands you to choose for rulers, *just men who will rule in the fear of God* [Exodus 18:21]. The preservation of a republican government depends on the faithful discharge of this duty; if the citizens neglect their duty, and place unprincipled men in office, the government will soon be corrupted; laws will be made, not for the public good, so much as for selfish or local purposes; corrupt or incompetent men will be appointed to execute the laws; the public revenues will be squandered on unworthy men; and the rights of the citizens will be violated or disregarded. If a republican government fails to secure public prosperity and happiness, it must be because the citizens neglect the divine commands, and elect bad men to make and administer the laws.[41]

In another text Webster also advised young voters:

In selecting men for office, let principle be your guide. Regard not the particular sect or denomination of the candidate—look to his character....It is alleged by men of loose principles, or defective views of the subject, that religion and morality are not necessary or important qualifications for political stations. But the Scriptures teach a different doctrine. They direct that rulers should be men *who rule in the fear of God, able men, such as fear God, men of truth, hating covetousness* [Exodus 18:21].... It is to the neglect of this rule of conduct in our citizens that we must ascribe the multiplied frauds, breaches of trust, peculations [white-collar larceny] and embezzlements of public property which astonish even ourselves; which tarnish the character of our country; which disgrace a republican government.[42]

Declaration signer Samuel Adams likewise warned citizens:

He who is void of virtuous attachments in private life is, or very soon will be, void of all regard for his country. There is seldom an instance of a man guilty of betraying his country, who had not before lost the feeling of moral obligations in his private connections.... "The public cannot be too curious concerning the [c]haracters of public men."[43]

And signer and penman of the Constitution Gouverneur Morris charged:

There must be religion. When that ligament is torn, society is disjointed, and its members perish. The nation is exposed to foreign violence and domestic convulsion. Vicious [ungodly] rulers, chosen by a vicious [ungodly] people, turn back the current of corruption to its source. Placed in a situation where they can exercise authority for their own emolument [benefit], they betray their trust. They take bribes. They sell statutes and decrees. They sell honor and office. They sell their conscience. They sell their country.... But the most important of all lessons is, the denunciation of ruin to every state that rejects the precepts of religion.[44]

John Witherspoon, a gospel minister and a signer of the Declaration, similarly admonished:

> Those who wish well to the State ought to choose to places of trust men of inward principle, justified by exemplary conversation. Is it reasonable to expect wisdom from the ignorant, fidelity [faithfulness] from the profligate [unfaithful], assiduity [diligence] and application to public business from men of a dissipated [careless] life? Is it reasonable to commit the management of public revenue to one who hath wasted his own patrimony [inheritance]? Those, therefore, who pay no regard to religion and sobriety in the persons whom they send to the legislature of any state are guilty of the greatest absurdity and will soon pay dear for their folly.[45]

The message was clear: if citizens became negligent in electing competent, godly leaders to office, government would become corrupt. Voting was therefore stressed as one of the most important of Christian responsibilities, never to be taken lightly.

To have been given this great power through our vote and then not to use that power (or to use it unwisely) is reminiscent of the servant described by Jesus who received a trust from his master and decided to do nothing with it. (See Matthew 25:24–28; Luke 19:20–24.) Significantly, none of the servants had asked for the stewardship they received, but the master bestowed it on them anyway and then held them directly accountable to him for what they did with the trust he gave them.

In like manner, none of us asked to be born in America, nor did we ask that its government be placed in our hands, but the reality is that the Master has put it in our keeping and will call us to account for our management of it. Each of us will one day individually stand alone before the great judgment seat to be held accountable for everything we did—and did not do. And when the Almighty asks us, "And what did you do with that government I entrusted to you? What did you do with that vote I placed in your hands?" what will be our reply? Answers such as "I chose to keep myself unsoiled by the rough-and-tumble nature of politics" or "I let the professionals deal with it" will be unacceptable.

What legacy will we leave the next generation? Sadly too many Christians do not think about legacy, often excusing their current inactivity by asserting that what happens in the future is not their concern—that Christ will return before they have to worry about any legacy. And as we become a more narcissistic society, we seem determined to "live in the moment" without regard for how our current choices will influence our and other people's future.

But in taking this approach, we simply adopt the outrageous egocentricity expressed by King Hezekiah who, when he learned of the trouble, difficulty, and destruction that was coming upon the nation and his own children and grandchildren, took solace in the fact that at least it wouldn't come upon him. (See 2 Kings 20:16–19.)

For anyone today to guide their actions and reactions solely by the imminent return of Christ is to ignore the Bible itself, for Jesus Himself pointedly told His followers, "Occupy till I come" (Luke 19:13, KJV). He even delivered a teaching that blasted those who so focused on the imminent return of the Master that they neglected their earthly responsibilities. (See Matthew 24:45–51 and Luke 12:42–48.) Sound biblical eschatology will never lead to civic inaction, for that would be a direct violation of Christ's unequivocal command to His followers to remain engaged until His return.

When the argument was raised two centuries ago that because the civil arena had no eternal consequence then time spent in the pursuit of our civil duties was time wasted, the Rev. John Witherspoon promptly responded:

> Shall we establish nothing good because we know it cannot be eternal? Shall we live without government because every constitution has its old age and its period? Because we know that we shall die, shall we take no pains to preserve or lengthen our life? Far from it, Sir: it only requires the more watchful attention to settle government upon the best principles and in the wisest manner [so] that it may last as long as the nature of things will admit.[46]

The fact that something may someday pass away does not release Christians from exercising their duties of stewardship over that responsibility. After all, it is also inescapable that every one of us will someday die, so why prolong our time here by visiting doctors, engaging in physical exercise, or being watchful of our diet? Go ahead and smoke twelve packs a day, eat everything that can be crammed into your mouth, and avoid exercise at all costs! The reason we don't do this is that a mature person understands present responsibility; so too with our obligation toward civil government.

We must heed the warning delivered two centuries ago by the Rev. Matthias Burnet, when he charged citizens:

> Finally, ye...whose high prerogative it is to...invest with office and authority or to withhold them and in whose power it is to save or destroy your country, consider well the important trust...which God...put into your hands. To God and posterity you are accountable for them [your rights and your rulers]....Let not your children have reason to curse you for giving up those rights and prostrating those institutions which your fathers delivered to you.[47]

The responsibilities facing God-fearing citizens are somber, and the potential repercussions from our actions—or lack thereof—are both far-reaching and long-lasting. Whenever citizen selfishness and complacency rules, wrong principles and policies will abound, and when it comes to sound government, the enemy is seldom "them" but instead is almost always citizen apathy. It is time for Christians to reengage in civil stewardship from a biblical viewpoint—a viewpoint that was long understood by previous generations and that must be re-embraced by this current one.

Chapter 4

THE SEARCH FOR GOOD GOVERNMENT

W ITH DECLINING CITIZEN participation and stewardship, American government has undergone fundamental transformations. These changes, occurring both in the type and the function of government, have adversely affected the daily lives of Americans.

To understand the scope of the changes, there must be a standard for measurement and comparison, so let's begin by identifying the seven primary forms of government:

1. **Theocracy:** a government run by immediate representatives of God who claim to act directly at His behest on every issue. Many Islamic nations throughout the Middle East and Asia are theocracies, often ruled by an ayatollah or imam.

2. **Monarchy:** a government headed by an unelected king, queen, or emirate.

3. **Anarchic or revolutionary:** a government in which written laws are largely meaningless and where the supreme power rests with each individual, who does whatever he wishes or has the power to do. Founding Father John Quincy Adams described this as having "no other law than that of the tiger or the shark."[1] This is also described in the Bible as a government in which

"every man [does] that which was right in his own eyes"
(See Judges 17:6; 21:25; Deuteronomy 12:8.)

4. **Democracy:** a government in which absolute power
   resides solely in the people, who exercise the lawmaking power through direct majority votes or refer-
   endums rather than through elected representatives.
   Because this government is based on the popular sen-
   timents of the people at any given point in time, selfishness and popular passions often prevail over reason
   and deliberation. It is therefore an unstable and fluc-
   tuating government. Founding Father John Adams's
   term "mob rule" as well as Benjamin Rush's "moboc-
   racy" aptly describe this type of government.

5. **Totalitarian:** a highly centralized government that
   restrains freedom, enforces conformity, and has little
   toleration for individualism or differences of opinion.

6. **Oligarchy:** a government in which power resides in
   the hands of a few, who are largely unaccountable to
   the people.

7. **Republic (and constitutional republic):** a government in which power is exercised through representatives elected by the people. A weak form of a republic
   is a parliamentary system or representative democracy,
   in which those elected by the people become the sovereign power until the people select new representatives. The highest form of this type of government is
   a constitutional republic, in which the representatives
   elected by the people are not sovereign but instead
   are subordinate to a higher law—a written constitution. The result is what Founding Father John Adams
   described as "a government of laws, and not of men."[2]

Where does America fit within these general categories? America
has never been a theocracy. For a short time, it participated as part of

the British monarchy but then declared independence and become the seventh type of government on the list: a constitutional republic, where it remained for centuries. Today, however, the country has begun adopting key elements from the third, fourth, fifth, and sixth forms described above. As a result, where we are now is quite different from where we were just a few decades ago.

America today is commonly described as a democracy, and our textbooks and political leaders frequently tell us it is, but the US Constitution declares otherwise, expressly stipulating that:

> The United States shall guarantee to every state in this union *a republican form of government*...[3]
>
> —EMPHASIS ADDED

Thus, we pledge allegiance to a republic, not a democracy. Our Founders had an opportunity to establish a democracy in America and deliberately chose not to. Their reasons for rejecting it were abundant:

> Democracies have ever been spectacles of turbulence and contention; have ever been found incompatible with personal security or the rights of property; and have, in general, been as short in their lives as they have been violent in their deaths.[4]
>
> —JAMES MADISON

> Remember, democracy never lasts long. It soon wastes, exhausts, and murders itself. There never was a democracy yet that did not commit suicide.[5]
>
> —JOHN ADAMS

> A democracy is a volcano, which conceals the fiery materials of its own destruction. These will produce an eruption, and carry desolation in their way.[6]
>
> —FISHER AMES
> Framer of the Bill of Rights

A democracy is not only a very bad form of government, but as John Adams explained, it often leads downward to even worse forms:

> Democracy will soon degenerate into an anarchy, such an anarchy that every man will do what is right in his own eyes, and no man's life or property or reputation or liberty will be secure and every one of these will soon mold itself into a system of subordination of all the moral virtues and intellectual abilities, all the powers of wealth, beauty, wit, and science, to the wanton pleasures, the capricious will, and the execrable [abominable] cruelty of one or a very few.[7]

By selecting a republican form of government, America had chosen to follow the example of ancient Israel as explained in Exodus 18:21: choosing its own leaders, but only after having first established a fixed framework of higher laws to govern the nation and its leaders.

In America our Declaration and Constitution provided that framework. In the Declaration of Independence the Founders described its higher law as the "the Laws of Nature and of Nature's God," which also included approximately two dozen God-given inalienable rights. Every citizen and leader was subject to that higher law. Our documents then established that the primary purpose of American government was first and foremost to secure to every individual the open practice of his God-given rights, which included, among others, the rights of life, liberty, property, self-defense, religious worship, the selection of one's own occupation and profession, the right to increase one's wealth, justice in legal proceedings, freedom of association and movement, and others. These inalienable rights are never subject to a vote—ever—and by thus preventing government from taking control over these spheres of human activity, our documents instituted what is called a limited government. Within this framework of fixed higher laws, citizens choose leaders to represent them at the local, county, state, and federal levels.

THE SCOURGE OF LAWLESSNESS

While a constitutional republic constantly produces the most pros-perous and stable form of government enjoyed by man, it also requires the greatest amount of care and maintenance. But this care has not been exercised in recent years, and the result is that America is no longer what John Adams described as "a government of laws, and not of men." Due to the steady incorporation of key elements from the democratic, oligarchic, anarchic, and totalitarian forms into our system, America has now become a nation where the personal opinions of leaders supersede fixed laws. The result is gov-ernment lawlessness, and the evidence of it is abundant.

When we were a constitutional republic, federal laws could be enacted *only* by cooperative action among the federal government's three elected entities of the House, Senate, and president. But today laws passed in that method have become the exception and no longer the rule.

In 2012 more than 3,800 new federal laws were added to the books, but only 127 of them went through Congress in the traditional manner specified by the Constitution; the rest were passed by federal agencies without any direct action by Congress.[8] Some 38,000 such laws have been enacted in the past decade,[9] and 81,000 since 1993.[10]

The current cost to comply with these bureaucrat-written federal laws (which even impose fines and jail time on the noncompliant) is a staggering $1.8 trillion per year,[11] which costs each American family $14,678 per year, or about one-fourth of its annual income.[12] The massive power now held by federal agencies and bureaucrats has caused them to be termed the Fourth Branch—a branch com-pletely repugnant to our republican form of government.

Two centuries ago Founding Father Samuel Adams summarized the central problem with this system we have now adopted when he explained:

> If the public are bound to yield obedience to the laws, to which they cannot give *their* approbation, they are slaves to those who make such laws and enforce them.[13]

Not only do unelected bureaucrats (who are often egocentric and tyrannical) write federal laws imposing their will on Americans, but those bureaucrats are also largely unaccountable—there is almost no action so egregious that it can cause them to be fired.[14] This fact has been repeatedly demonstrated in recent years.

For example, in May 2014 it was revealed that numerous military veterans had died from the incompetence and deliberate neglect they received in hospitals under the direct control of the federal government. The supervisors over some of the worst perpetrators among the staff in those hospitals were quickly identified, and since firing them (or any other federal employee) was almost impossible, the US House promptly passed a bill (by the lopsided margin of 390–33) to change the process so that bad supervisors could finally be dismissed. But the Senate refused to even take up the measure, choosing instead to continue protecting bureaucrats from accountability.[15]

Likewise, the extensive IRS abuse of power revealed in January 2013 that had illegally targeted innocent individuals for unprecedented government harassment not only resulted in no firings but also many of the violators actually received performance bonuses.[16] A similar absence of accountability accompanied the June 2013 revelation of the National Security Administration (NSA) scandal in which the federal government was found to be engaged in a secret campaign to eavesdrop on virtually every technology-aided private conversation that takes place in America.

On rare occasions a government leader or politician becomes so corrupt or lawless that he is finally targeted for removal, but even then government unions and civil service process can keep those officials on the payroll for years (and even decades) after their wrongdoing was prosecuted. There are hundreds of readily available examples; notice a few from Connecticut:

♦ Former juvenile probation officer Richard Straub, convicted of sexually assaulting underage boys he oversaw, still collects a government payment of $55,030 annually.[17]

♦ Former Connecticut governor John Rowland, who spent ten months in federal prison after pleading guilty to corruption charges, still receives $50,000 annually.[18]

♦ Former state Rep. Jefferson Davis, on the state's sex offender registry for conviction of inappropriate sexual activity with a young boy, collects $5,706 annually.[19]

♦ Former state Sen. Ernest Newton, who served prison time for pleading guilty to accepting a bribe, still receives $7,983 annually.[20]

♦ Former Bridgeport mayor Joseph Ganim, convicted of using his office for personal gain, still receives $13,652 annually.[21]

Similarly, in New York City some eight hundred government-payroll educators "accused of breaking rules, abusing kids—or simply failing to provide students with a decent education" were to be paid $22 million by the city in 2012 *for doing absolutely nothing*. Astonishingly, these incompetent or lawless teachers were kept in "the infamous 'rubber rooms' where as many as 800 teachers languished—sometimes for years—awaiting disciplinary hearings."[22]

Across the country, government rewards itself for bad behavior and protects its own incompetence. As long as government employees remain unaccountable for their ineptness, they and their agencies will continue to be callous, deaf, indifferent, inefficient, and hard-fisted—characteristics commonly associated with a totalitarian government.

But it is not just government bureaucrats who regularly display lawlessness; the judiciary does as well. They hold themselves to be the makers of law—and consequently above it. In fact, on public tours of the US Supreme Court, tour guides regularly announce to assembled groups, "This is the building from which all the law in the land emanates." The law of the land comes from judges? Really? Then what are those tall, round-domed buildings where legislators meet? Apparently what goes on in those structures means little to today's judiciary.

Under our original republican form of government, the Constitution had made clear that the courts were *not* permitted to make public policy. The Founders' decision to withhold this policy-making power from the unelected judiciary had been deliberate and was abundantly reaffirmed across the decades in the most public and vocal means possible.[23]

Today the judiciary scorns its constitutionally limited role. In fact, some judges now so disdain their oath to uphold the Constitution that in recent decisions they have even declared, literally, that the Constitution itself is actually unconstitutional![24] Striking down legal strictures that limit them, judges simply legislate from the bench, seeking to force all citizens to conform to their personal beliefs and values[25]—characteristics common to an oligarchic form of government.

The president is certainly not exempt from this nationally increasing lawlessness. In fact, like a river spilling over its banks in a flood, lawlessness now openly flows from the executive office.

For example, the Constitution explicitly requires that presidential appointees for powerful government posts (such as the czars who exercise extensive power and authority) be approved by the Senate before they can serve. This prevents a president from loading government with mere political hacks seeking to line their own pockets and impose their own will on the people they are supposed to serve.[26] But the president openly scorns this requirement and has ignored the required Senate approval for 80 percent of the powerful czars he has appointed.[27]

Similarly, although the president takes an oath that "he shall take care that the laws be faithfully executed," he has openly announced his refusal to execute literally scores of federal laws—all because they do not align with his own personal beliefs.[28] In fact, when Congress fails or refuses to enact national policies he seeks, he simply enacts them through his autocratic use of executive orders. Executive orders were intended to be a management tool to give clarifying instructions to direct employees on how to carry out their constitutionally assigned duties, like an interoffice memo from the CEO of Walmart (or Home Depot or any other company) to his employees, explaining how they should handle certain situations.

But what if the CEO of Walmart begins telling Macy's, Kohl's, Dillard's, Sears, and all other stores what their policies must be? That would be an illegitimate use, and even an abuse of power, but this is what the president regularly does. He has unilaterally and unlawfully created national policies to implement his own personal views on things ranging from education to law enforcement, religious liberties to the environment, gun regulation to welfare policy, immigration to abortion, health care to student loans, and many other areas.[29]

Imagine any citizen picking and choosing which laws he will obey or making up personal policies he imposes on all others. No officer subject to the rule of law would permit such individual anarchy, yet the president haughtily does what he allows no other citizen to do, simply because he can—because he has the force and the position to do so, which are characteristics common to an anarchic government.

Congress also practices lawlessness—as when it passes onerous laws to restrict and regulate the people but then exempts itself from those laws. For example, federal law requires that whistle-blowers who report violations of laws, gross mismanagement, waste of funds, or abuse of authority be protected from any retaliation by their employer, yet that law doesn't apply to Congress. Congress similarly excludes itself from onerous and heavy-handed OSHA (Occupational Safety and Health Administration) laws as well as workplace requirements of the Civil Rights Act, the American With Disabilities Act, the Age Discrimination Employment Act, the Fair Labor Standards Act, the Equal Pay Act, the Family and Medical Leave Act, the Freedom of Information Act, antidiscrimination training, and so many others.[30]

Congress also uses complicated omnibus bills to hide unpopular and often oppressive acts from the people. *Omnibus* is taken from a Latin term that means "for everything." Thus, an omnibus bill is one that covers everything—a single law that combines numerous subjects that are completely unrelated. Because so many different items—often hundreds of them—are tucked away in such a bill, each receives little or no public scrutiny or debate. Omnibus bills are therefore used to pass controversial and even disliked measures that would never survive if they were to be considered individually.

For example, when a bill giving preferential treatment to homosexuals was introduced in Congress, it was defeated five consecutive times after receiving public scrutiny.[31] Unable to pass the bill because of widespread public opposition, Congress simply rolled that bill (along with hundreds of other unconnected measures that had *nothing* to do with military issues) into the massive omnibus military spending bill. By that means, that unpopular measure, hidden deep within that enormous bill, became law.[32] In like manner, almost 80 percent of what was included in the massive recent Farm Bill had *nothing* to do with farming.[33] Clearly, much of what occurs in government is deliberately hidden from the people, lest they find out and object.

AN INTEGRITY DEFICIT

In all three branches of government individuals now seek their own good rather than the good of others or of the nation. Long ago John Adams warned that the transformation of government brought about by this type of selfish behavior would be deleterious:

> The interest of the people is one thing—it is the public interest; and where the public interest governs, it is a government of laws, and not of men. The interest of [an individual], or of a party, is another thing—it is a private interest; and where private interest governs, it is a government of men, and not of laws.[34]

Not surprisingly the current lawless attitudes of our public officials mirror a measurable decline in their integrity. For example, in 1970 there were only thirty-two officials convicted of public corruption, but statistics from the most recent year (the government stopped compiling these numbers in 2011) show that the number had soared to 785 convicted officials[35]—an increase of over 2,400 percent.

The reason for this integrity deficit was given nearly two centuries ago by Justice Joseph Story (appointed to the US Supreme Court by President James Madison), when he explained:

> To secure integrity, there must be a lofty sense of duty and a deep responsibility to future times as well as to God.[36]

Integrity is the product of being God-conscious and of having a sense of accountability to God and to posterity. But polling clearly affirms that both the personal conviction of individual answerability to God as well as a deep sense of selflessness and service is no longer part of the DNA of Americans.

As lawlessness has increased and integrity has waned, the strength of the nation has visibly deteriorated. Thus, America has now dropped out of the list of the most economically free nations of the world for the first time since such records have been kept, being surpassed by what were long considered third world and weaker nations, such as Chile, Singapore, Hong Kong, Australia, Switzerland, New Zealand, Canada, Mauritius, Ireland, Denmark, and Estonia.[37]

The United States has also fallen in its ranking as a corruption-free government. It now ranks nineteenth in the world for clean government, tied with Uruguay and being surpassed by nations such as Barbados, Denmark, New Zealand, Great Britain, and Singapore.[38]

Our growing national mediocrity is further affirmed by the measurements of those who have been through our education system. In an assessment of twenty-three nations America ranks near the bottom in adult problem-solving in technology, near the bottom in adult math skills, and in the bottom half of nations in adult literacy.[39] Overall America finished sixteenth of the twenty-three, being topped by countries such as Finland, Denmark, Norway, Estonia, the Czech Republic, and the Slovak Republic; America only barely beat out Cyprus, Poland, Ireland, and France. We spend more money per person on education than any other nation in the world,[40] but under the current system of government-controlled education, that money is largely wasted.

Americans clearly do not like what is currently happening or where the country is headed. In fact, they now believe that the government violates and endangers their rights rather than protects them.[41] Thus:

- In the past five years the percentage of those who hold a favorable view of the federal government has plunged to only 28 percent.[42]

- Over the past decade the public approval of Congress has likewise plummeted: only 5 percent now view it favorably.[43]

- Three-fourths of Americans now believe that courts make decisions based on their individual views rather than the law or the Constitution,[44] and therefore in the past fifteen years public approval of the Supreme Court has also fallen dramatically.[45]

Current governmental behavior is viewed unfavorably, but it is nevertheless generally tolerated for two reasons: (1) widespread citizen disinterest in public affairs and (2) America's changing beliefs and values.

Concerning the latter, two-thirds of Americans currently reject any notion of absolute truth or fixed moral standards,[46] so their only binding criterion for what constitutes right and wrong has become their own personal views. Ironically, while citizens themselves now regularly "do what is right in their own eyes," they don't like it when their government officials do the same.

Chapter 5

THE FADING INFLUENCE OF INSTITUTIONS

HAVING READ ABOUT the values, morals, and political behaviors of our nation, you may be wondering how we got here. Why do we hold the values that shape our lives? What formed those moral standards that drive our choices and actions? How did we decide to distance ourselves from a political process that has delivered such freedom and opportunity to us?

The answer lies in America's primary institutions. These are entities that provide perspective, energy, and structure to our thinking and behavior. Some institutions are formal (e.g., military, government) while others are informal (e.g., family, traditions, social norms). They provide stability to our relationships, our worldview, and our daily practices. That stability provides opportunities for growth—personally, culturally, and organizationally.

Institutions are not just organizations or large-scale entities that wield power and operate in bureaucratic ways. Institutions have patiently and diligently molded the foundations of the nation and have capably guided us through good times and bad for more than two centuries. Without the unique contributions of a broad array of integrated world-class institutions in place, the United States would be more like a struggling third-world nation than the trendsetting world power it has been for so long.

Though they get limited attention and even less credit, institutions play a significant role in our lives. They provide numerous irreplaceable benefits for our nation. In essence their cumulative effect is to shape our sense of life's meaning and purpose by integrating and processing information, resources, relationships, and goods and services. Perhaps the ultimate product attributable to our institutions is a widely accepted worldview. It is that multifaceted perspective on life, drawn from so many contributors, that determines the nature and character of a nation. That worldview is displayed and applied by what we know as culture: the traditions, norms, customs, and dreams of a society.

By adding their voice to the choir of culture, each institution provides a modicum of leadership in the society it seeks to influence. Esteemed historian Samuel Huntington believed that the genius of the American system lies more in the contributions of its institutions than in its reliance upon an elective republican form of government.[1] Given that institutions not only provide perspective, but also define, provide, and protect our rights, he may be right. Many nations have tried to operate within an elective framework; only the United States has succeeded with such astonishing longevity and solidarity.

Recognizing the importance of institutions in American society did not originate with Huntington's crystalline analysis. Alexis de Tocqueville traveled here from France in 1831 to explore the genesis of the greatness of the United States. His classic analyses, *Democracy in America*[2] and *American Institutions and Their Influence*, concluded that while democracy was critical to the nation's success, institutions played an indispensable intermediary role between individuals and the government. De Tocqueville wrote that the nation's freedom was largely due to the interstitial presence of those institutions, a preferable substitute for heavy-handed and intrusive governance, societies' natural tendencies toward barbarism and forced servitude, and a tendency to degenerate into tyranny. Institutions, he argued, facilitate levels of liberty, justice, balance, and equality that otherwise would not emerge. In the United States he identified several institutions in particular—family, churches, charitable organizations, and the rule of law—that he deemed especially crucial in the American context.[3] Little has changed in this regard since his profound treatises were published more than one hundred seventy years ago.

But few Americans these days give a second thought to the institutions that give our nation its heartbeat. Perhaps it is because we take them for granted. We have never known a time when our core institutions were not shaping our minds and hearts. Among the hallmarks of our nation has been our adherence to the rule of law—which has been facilitated by the consensus among our institutions in the goodness and necessity of that adherence. And we have passed off the capacity of America to solve complex problems as a reflection of our national appreciation for creativity, our entrepreneurial spirit, and even a free-market system that enables the best ideas to gain credence and traction. But we ignore the role that our institutions play in nurturing creativity, encouraging and funding the entrepreneurial spirit, and protecting the free-market system from the constant threat of regulation and limitation.

As a couple of guys who have traveled and worked around the world, we have seen firsthand how imperfect the American system is—and yet how much better it works than any other system around. Why? Because our institutions insist on doing what they do to the best of their ability for the common good.

- ♦ You flip a switch, and you expect your lights to instantly glow—and they do. (Based on personal experience, that outcome is not guaranteed in many nations, especially during the summer months.)

- ♦ You turn on the faucet, and you expect to enjoy an endless supply of clean, safe water—and you get it. (Dozens of the world's nations cannot match this service.)

- ♦ You frantically plow your way through traffic to get to the airport because you know your airplane is likely to leave on time and transport you safely to your desired destination. (You're probably not interested in an additional chapter of frustrating and harrowing flight stories drawn from our experiences overseas, but suffice it to say that on-time departures are an infrequent luxury in many countries of the world.)

♦ If you lose your passport in the United States, there is a standard process to follow that produces a replacement passport within a reasonable time frame for a known fee. Make the same blunder in a developing nation and you are likely to enter the Bribery Zone. (Been there, done that; not recommended.)

♦ When you drop off your child at school, you are confident that a qualified teacher will be in the designated classroom to teach your child information and skills deemed valuable for success in our culture. If you drop your child off at a public school in many developing nations, you wonder if you will ever see him again, much less whether a qualified teacher will be waiting for him with a game plan in mind. (Sponsor a child in such a country, then visit him and listen to the stories their parents tell about the anxiety that the simple act of engaging in public education can cause.)

♦ As we write this, more than a dozen nations of the world are currently under the control of military leaders who staged a coup. The United States has never had a military uprising of that nature and is not likely to experience such a perilous demonstration of power. (Having been face-to-face with a crazed and armed military man in a developing nation—saved only by our language barrier—one comes to appreciate the training, supervision, and commitment of America's soldiers.)

Without our core institutions, American life would not be what we know it to be today.

ADDING VALUE

Day after day our news reports contain stories about the thousands of efforts people and organizations make to grow. Whether it is economic growth, social growth, intellectual growth, spiritual growth, or any other form of growth, that development is made possible by the work of institutions. How? By insisting upon transparent and accountable leadership, adhering to the rule of law, and maintaining standards that implement penalties for corruption and disruption.

Institutions play a kind of cultural parenting role in our society. In essence, they are in charge, and they dictate the rules and standards. To gain voluntary compliance with those rules and standards, they offer incentives and disincentives for specific behaviors. The consistency with which they dispense such rewards and punishments enables them to establish and maintain order, trust, and hope—which, in turn, facilitates growth. It takes an extensive and complicated web of laws, covenants, rules, codes, and relationships, along with commonly held beliefs, social norms, traditions, and codes of conduct for it all to work smoothly.

That is one of the unique attributes that makes America so special.

WHY THE DECLINE?

So when you think about the values, morals, and behaviors alluded to in the previous chapters and wonder what kept them so viable for so long, the answer is that our core institutions upheld the foundations that produced such ways of life. And when you ask the natural follow-up question—why are those values, morals, and political behaviors changing so dramatically now?—the answer is that our institutions are dissipating so rapidly and dramatically that we are losing the ability to sustain the greatness that once characterized America.

The central issue involved in the transition of our values, morals, and behaviors relates to trust. In order for a society to remain stable and developing, its institutions must be trusted. The public must have sufficient confidence in the competence and the objectives of those institutions to comply with their demands.

What has happened, of course, is that our trust has shifted from institutions to individuals—that is, from "them" to "me."

This transition began in the 1950s. Our population was booming, the economy was expanding, and our institutions were stretched in ways they had never been stretched. A small percentage of the population, primarily young adults, began to question rules and authority and to cut corners, changing traditions, customs, and even morals ever so slightly. But cultural change is a war that is won or lost after millions of tiny, sometimes imperceptible battles have been fought to a conclusion. The small gains made by the rebels of the fifties opened the door to increasingly larger shifts in our thinking and behavior.

By the time the antiwar rallies of the midsixties took flight, young people around the country were being regularly accosted with alternative philosophies. University professors and drug enthusiasts argued that young adults should never trust anyone over thirty. Feminists pecked away at male-female relationships, marriage, modesty, sexuality, vocational rights, and more. The civil rights movement highlighted the bigotry and injustice that resided in the hearts and lifestyles of millions. Antiwar activists challenged the right of the United States to "invade" other countries for no apparent reason, to jeopardize the lives of young men thrust into combat, to create bombs with unprecedented power to kill, and to approve federal budgets that poured untold billions of dollars into the "destructive war machine."

Protestants belittled Catholics, with the presidential nomination of John Kennedy serving as the match that set flame to that bonfire. Churches were denigrated for being out of touch, while new religious perspectives and practices were borrowed from pop culture and Eastern mysticism. The recent battles over same-sex marriage were birthed during this same era, with the "gay liberation movement" paving the way for the numerous victories that the LGBT community has won in the early twenty-first century.

The result of the thousands of little battles that were fought each year was diminished trust in our venerable institutions.

+ The family was in a shambles after being accosted by feminists and others. Cohabitation, communal living, serial marriage, no-fault divorce, sexual liberation, "open" marriages, birth outside of wedlock, civil ceremonies—all of these new approaches began their march toward being adopted as normative.

+ The government has never fully recovered the confidence of the public that was shattered during the era of turbulence. The stature of the presidency was diminished by the disgraceful events that led to Richard Nixon's resignation, followed by four disastrous years of Jimmy Carter's well-intentioned but incompetent leadership. The Supreme Court was lambasted by the Right for allowing abortion and eliminating school prayer. Congress began a slow downward spiral that continues to this day.

+ Christians began to question all manner of religious tradition and purpose, causing churches to unsteadily respond to criticism about irrelevance and insensitivity. For better or worse, the emergence of the Jesus movement led to further questioning of the institutional church, upsetting the sense of ritual and stability that had for so long been a feature of organized Christianity.

+ Businesses were caught in the cross fire, derided as capitalists, traditionalists, tax avoiders, and greedy, with many other epithets hurled at them.

+ Banks were accused of being institutions of corporate greed, racism, and manipulation, exploiting the poor through redlining and other discriminatory practices.

◆ Law enforcement and the military were widely chastised for representing law and order at a time when anarchy and chaos seemed like a more pleasing way to millions. People employed in the police or military were deemed warmongers, violent, unjust, and heavy-handed.

By the end of the counterculture years every major institution in America had been thoroughly trashed in the public psyche. It has been said that disco swept the nation in the eighties because people just wanted to dance. Why wouldn't they? Everything that had been held dear and sacred regarding the world's greatest modern civilization had been attacked and ravaged during the past quarter century. The American people needed a time to cool down, rethink meaning and purpose, and restore stability to a disheveled society.

But the greatest carnage was the tarnished trust and confidence that people had in the institutions that had made the nation great. It was as if Pandora's box had been opened, a social tornado of unprecedented proportion escaped it and swept everyone off their feet, and by the time it had run its course everyone needed to push the reset button. Except that's not how cultures work.

Luke 11 contains a passage that describes what happens when an evil spirit leaves and the person who has been freed from that bondage does nothing to reclaim the spirit's former territory and prevent its return. In the aftermath, the passage notes, the evil spirit returns with a team of other spirits more vicious and riled up than ever. The result is a worse catastrophe.

> He [Jesus] knew their thoughts, so he said, "Any kingdom divided by civil war is doomed. A family splintered by feuding will fall apart.... Anyone who isn't with me opposes me, and anyone who isn't working with me is actually working against me. When an evil spirit leaves a person, it goes into the desert, searching for rest. But when it finds none, it says, 'I will return to the person I came from.' So it returns and finds that its former home is all swept and

in order. Then the spirit finds seven other spirits more evil
than itself, and they all enter the person and live there. And
so that person is worse off than before."

—LUKE 11:17, 23–26

That situation is analogous to what has happened to America.
After a couple of decades of hard-fought battles over values, morals,
and political direction, the public wanted a break. They elected
Ronald Reagan to guide the country back to a healthier and saner
place. But too much damage had already been done, and the wheels
of regress had been set in motion, pushing America toward the
precipice.

How Bad Is It?

There is a public relations principle that says once a person's reputation has been tarnished, it can never be fully restored. With that
in mind, one of the most common strategies deployed by political
campaign advertising in hotly contested races is to carpet bomb an
opponent's reputation. During the height of the campaign season,
it is hard to escape advertising that features negative judgments,
character-bashing lies, and innuendo against an opponent with no
regard for truth, civility, respect, or righteousness. It is a win-at-all-
costs tactic that has proven to be effective in winning elections—
and destroying the public's trust in the political process as well as
in the men and women who wish to serve their country through
that process.

So once the 1970s came to a close, Americans turned skeptical of
the institutions that had served them so faithfully for two centuries.
It has gotten so bad that now there are few institutions left standing.
The Gallup Organization has been studying national confidence in
institutions since the 1970s. To provide a glimpse of what has been
happening, examine the data in Table 5-1.

The damage that has been done to people's confidence in America's
core institutions is both dangerous and disheartening. Given the
paramount role these institutions play in the shaping of our lives,

you would hope that people would possess "a great deal of confidence" in these entities. It was the possession of such a high level of trust in our core institutions that facilitated the unprecedented and virtually unbroken record of national prosperity and development over the years. Such an unshakable belief in those institutions is what most impressed learned observers who evaluated the strength of the nation, such as de Tocqueville and Huntington.

In the absence of such a high degree of trust in core institutions we have no choice but to turn to alternatives for insight and guidance—and chief among those options is ourselves. De Tocqueville was one of the first to recognize the natural tendency of humans to turn inward when the external foundations crumble; the isolationist tendency signals the beginning of the end of a great society. That is what we are experiencing today in America. The radical individualism that was identified in earlier chapters is a direct result of the decline of our trust in these life-shaping institutions.

Table 5-1

CONFIDENCE IN AMERICAN INSTITUTIONS[4]

How much confidence in institution?			Great deal + quite a bit of confidence			
A great deal	Quite a bit	Little/ none	Average over the decade			
Institution	*2013*	*2013*	*2013*	*2010–13*	*2000–09*	*1990–99*	*1980–89*
Military	43%	33%	6%	76%	73%	67%	57%
Church/ organized religion	25	23	19	47	51	56	60
Presidency	19	17	35	36	43	49	n/a
Public schools	14	18	26	33	37	39	49
Supreme Court	13	21	23	36	42	46	50
Banks	10	16	28	23	43	38	49
Congress	5	5	52	11	22	23	26

The Gallup data presented in Table 5-1 shows that the highest-rated of these institutions is the military—but even at that, only four out of ten adults have "a great deal of confidence" in our military. Next highest are churches and organized religion, but only one out of every four adults has a high level of trust in our religious institutions. Only one out of every five adults has the highest degree of confidence in the presidency, one out of seven adults has such confidence in public schools, and one out of eight in the US Supreme Court. A mere one out of ten have a great deal of confidence in banks, and only one out of every twenty adults shares such a degree of trust in the central lawmaking body of the land (the Congress).

Additional information can also be gleaned from the table:

◆ Today there is not a single institution among these core entities in which even half of the nation has "a great deal of confidence." But over the course of the 1980s, three of the seven entities averaged 50 percent or more and two others were right at that level.

◆ With the exception of the military, our confidence in these institutions continues to erode, decade after decade.

◆ Four of these seven institutions—the presidency, Congress, public schools, and our chief financial institutions (banks)—have as many or more people who say they have "very little" or "no" confidence in them as say they have "a great deal" or "quite a bit" of confidence.

Other companies also track the public's confidence in our core institutions. A different context is provided by research conducted for the Edelman Trust Barometer, which compares the general or overall trust of core institutions across nations. The Edelman research examines trust levels in government, nonprofit organizations, business, and media. In its most recent surveys, done in twenty-three nations, the United States ranked fourteenth in institutional confidence.[5] That places us squarely among a group of nations categorized as "distrusters"—those countries where most of the people are suspicious of their leading institutions. That's not exactly what you would expect from the world's reigning "superpower."

A few other research findings might bolster our understanding of how America's confidence levels deflated so quickly. For instance:

♦ Most of our sense of what is happening in the world and how to assess both national and local conditions comes from information and perspectives delivered by the media. However, 60 percent say they have "little or no faith" in the media to report the news "accurately and fairly." In fact, ever since Gallup began asking that question in 1997, a majority of the public has admitted that they cannot trust the media to give them the straight scoop.[6]

♦ Often, the only "news" we receive about institutions and their leaders is bad news. For instance, a recent national survey confirmed that two-thirds of adults (68 percent) say most of the news they receive about teachers is negative.[7]

♦ A study among members of the nation's second-largest Protestant denomination found that its pastors don't trust the denomination's officials, perceiving them as judgmental and self-serving. The pastors don't trust other pastors in the denomination, either, feeling unable to openly share in confidence with their peers and acknowledging the unspoken competition among pastors. They also distrust the people in their congregation, criticizing them for being selfish and having unrealistic expectations.

Meanwhile the laity associated with the denomination generally do not trust or respect their pastors, believe that denomination officials don't really care about the laity, and are even wary of the motives of other congregants. The denomination's leaders, who commissioned the study, were found to distrust the pastors they lead and are dissatisfied with the seminaries that produce the denomination's pastors.[8]

♦ A majority of adults (53 percent) say they do not trust government leaders to tell the truth—"at all." Not just "sometimes" or "most of the time," but they do not trust them to tell the truth ever![9]

♦ It is not just institutions that are viewed askance by the public, but also the leaders of those institutions. Another Gallup tracking study reveals that few institutional leaders are highly rated by the public. When asked to gauge how much they trust a list of such professionals, less than half of all adults said they have high levels of trust in clergy (47 percent), judges (45 percent), bankers (27 percent), business executives (22 percent), and members of Congress (8 percent).[10] Realize that these are the people responsible for guiding and protecting our spiritual and moral development, our justice and liberty, our financial stability and security, our commercial productivity and lifestyle resources, and the creation and evaluation of our laws.

♦ A tracking study by the Harvard Institute of Politics found that our young adults are more cynical than ever, more cynical than older adults, and reflect declining levels of trust in our cultural leaders.[11]

When you put all of this together, it is not a pretty picture. The result of our declining trust is that we are turning inward, becoming more self-reliant and skeptical as time goes on. We feel increasingly betrayed and misunderstood. We are less interested in pursuing the common good because we feel that those who should be leading us in that direction are instead pursuing their personal good. We have built up a wall of resentment toward those in power, assuming that they are abusing their position and power to advance their own agenda or, at the very least, the agenda of a small segment of the public.

Our research reveals that Americans may subconsciously know that institutions matter, but they consciously argue that the original, laudable purpose of institutions—to serve people better—has been usurped by a new outlook, that of seeking the benefit of the institution itself. With that assumption in mind, the public then focuses upon abuses that are consistently reported by the media, and a self-perpetuating cycle of demise spins out of control, to the ultimate detriment of our nation.

So today we find ourselves in a society that has developed a new worldview. It is a perspective that has limited hope for a better tomorrow and little heart for the institutions that could foster better outcomes. Without strong, visionary leaders of integrity who can reshape institutional performance, improve public communication regarding our reality, and engage people in a restorative process, this is the destiny we are accepting.

Chapter 6

AMERICA'S FAMILY MAKEOVER

T HE CHANGES IN family life over recent decades have been no less tumultuous than those throughout the rest of the culture. As already noted, Americans now prefer personal isolationism, which means spending increasingly less time in involvement with others, including even their own family members.[1]

For generations family counselors and psychologists have recognized and affirmed that both quantity and quality time spent with family members are the bases for a successful family life. For millennia one way that this had been implemented was through a parent working outside the home to provide sustenance and protection for the family and the other working inside, nurturing, shaping, and training the children of the rising generation.

In 1940 this was still the practice for 60 percent of American families,[2] but in recent decades this view of the family has come under attack as antiquated and sexist. Parents are instead encouraged to pursue even greater involvement outside the home and away from the children. By 1969 the percentage of stay-at-home mothers with young children had fallen to 44 percent; in 1979 it was down to 34 percent; in 1989 25 percent;[3] and currently only 12 percent of families reflect this traditional family structure.[4] In fact, there has been an 85 percent increase in working mothers who say they would like to spend even more time working, which would leave them with even less time to spend with their children.[5]

Interestingly, mothers who work outside the home rate themselves as better parents than those who spend full time with their children,[6] but ironically they are less satisfied with their own lives. Only 31 percent of working moms say they are "very happy," compared to 45 percent of nonworking moms who say the same.[7]

Much of the change in the family structure may be attributed to America's growing secularism. Even Wikipedia, which largely mirrors the secular leanings of our culture, acknowledges that the concept of the historic traditional family is rooted in "creation myths"[8] and that the Judeo-Christian model comes from the Bible Book of Genesis.[9] It is apparent that the more that American society moves away from biblical knowledge and acceptance, the more strongly it rejects the traditional family.

Secularism, defined as an "indifference to or rejection or exclusion religion and religious considerations,"[10] is on a rising trajectory in America, even among millions of professing Christians. In 1952 some 75 percent of Americans said religion was very important in their lives, but that number has fallen to 56 percent today,[11] and weekly church attendance has likewise decreased from almost half of Americans to its current 39 percent.[12] In 1958 only 14 percent of Americans felt that religion was losing its influence in American life, but today that number is at 77 percent.[13] Additionally, just under 20 percent of Americans (the highest percentage ever recorded—and a sharp increase from just five years ago) now affiliate with no religion at all and say they are not even interested in finding a religion—none at all—that might be right for them.[14]

This new group is called the "nones" because they affiliate with no religious group. They are not only the fastest-growing religious segment in the country, but also they are having a dramatic impact on the cultural landscape. For example, 72 percent of them support abortion and 73 percent same-sex marriage[15]—a percentage of support dramatically higher than in the general population at large.

CHILDREN AT RISK

As a result of the religious, and therefore the moral, changes of recent decades, there has been a corresponding change in public policy regarding the family, and that change reflects a steady movement away from traditional biblical teachings. The negative societal consequences of this change are measurable.

There are at least three groups in which the effects of children not growing up with a father and a mother can be readily assessed: (1) children born outside of marriage and raised in single-parent homes, (2) children from divorced homes, and (3) children from homes where one or both parents are absent because of incarceration.

Among the first group, children born outside of marriage and raised in single-parent homes:

- Educational attainment is significantly lower than that of children from traditional families,[16] and children from single-parent homes are almost twice as likely to repeat a grade in school and more than twice as likely to be suspended or expelled from school.[17]

- Young men from these homes are twice as likely to end up in jail as those who come from traditional two-parent families.[18]

- These children are seven times as likely to be delinquent[19] and almost twice as likely to have pulled a knife or a gun on someone in the past year.[20]

- Gang involvement is almost twice as high.[21]

- 90 percent of the increase in violent crime between 1973 and 1995 was committed by those born out of wedlock and raised in a single-parent home,[22] and 75 percent of juvenile criminals come from those homes.[23] In fact, an increase of only 1 percent in out-of-wedlock births produces a corresponding increase of up to 5 percent in murder rates.[24]

- Children in single-parent households have less family income and are more likely to be poor than children in married-parent households.[25]

♦ The annual average income of a traditional family is $101,000 but of a single-mother family is $35,000.[26]

Children pay a high price for the rejection of the traditional family structure by their parents. (By the way, single mothers also pay a high price, especially through the feminization of poverty.)

Another public policy change of recent years that has accommodated the increased selfishness of parents is that of no-fault divorce, whereby after two adults have made a lifelong commitment to each other, either can walk away from the marriage for any cause, or even for no cause. (Strikingly, more than 80 percent of no-fault divorces involve one spouse abandoning a relationship that the other wants to keep alive.)[27] As a consequence of these modern laws (in place largely since the early 1980s),[28] divorces have soared—and this provides the second measurable category: children from divorced homes.

Among this second group, we find the following:

♦ Children from divorced homes experience lower scores in school, higher absenteeism, and a dropout rate of 31 percent, compared to only 13 percent for children from intact homes.[29]

♦ Children who have experienced a divorce are 50 percent more likely to develop health problems.[30]

♦ Children of divorce suffer higher rates of depression, addiction, and arrest.[31]

♦ Eleven percent of boys from divorced parents end up in prison before they are age thirty-two, compared with only 5 percent of boys from intact homes.[32]

♦ Thirty-three percent of girls of divorced parents become teen mothers, compared with only 11 percent of girls from intact homes.[33]

♦ Both divorced women as well as daughters of the divorced have higher incidents of poverty.[34] (Some 30 percent of single-mother families live in poverty, but only about 6 percent of married couples with children are poor.[35])

♦ Additionally, "adult children of divorce tend to have: lower paying jobs and less college than their parents; unstable father-child relationships; a history of vulnerability to drugs and alcohol in adolescence; fears about commitment and divorce; and negative memories of the legal system that forced custody and visitation."[36]

♦ The adult children of divorce are 89 percent more likely to divorce than those raised in intact families.[37]

♦ While 79 percent of the children of married parents felt emotionally safe when growing up, only 44 percent of children of divorced couples felt the same.[38]

♦ The lifespan for children of divorce averages five years less than those who grew up in intact families.[39]

Disrupting the traditional combination of a father and a mother in the home harms children. (The exception to this is in homes where genuine abuse occurs,[40] but this is not the majority of cases.) In describing the current policy of no-fault divorce, one former family court judge explained, "It is easier to divorce my wife of 26 years than to fire someone I hired one week ago. The person I hire has more legal clout to sue me than my wife of 26 years."[41]

Significantly, the divorce rate has fallen from its high of about 50 percent in 1980 to around 40 percent today.[42] But much of this fall may be attributed not to strengthened marriages but rather to a growing practice of cohabitation, which increased tenfold between 1960 and 2000.[43] This should come as no surprise, for adults who experienced divorce as children are 61 percent more likely to agree that it is a "good idea for a couple who intend to get married to live together first."[44] Sadly divorce takes a toll not only on the lives of those who experience it, but also on future generations.

The third category with measurable statistics is children of incarcerated parents, where one or both parents are absent from the home as the children are being raised. This now directly affects nearly three million children,[45] with nearly ten million more having a parent who is or was under correctional supervision (such as parole).[46] These children:

♦ Have greater physical health problems, including elevated rates of cancer, high cholesterol, asthma, migraines, HIV/AIDS, obesity, and diabetes[47]

♦ Have increased rates of mental health problems, including depression, anxiety, and withdrawal[48]

♦ Have higher rates of educational difficulties, including cognitive delays, behavioral problems, and school failure[49]

♦ Have greater levels of material hardship as well as family instability (frequent moves, divorce, introduction of unrelated parental figures, etc.)[50]

♦ Are "40 percent more likely to have an unemployed father, 34 percent less likely to live with married parents, 25 percent more likely to experience material hardship, and four times more likely to face contact with the child welfare system"[51]

♦ Have higher rates for "abuse of drugs and alcohol, engaging in antisocial behavior, dropping out of school or experiencing a decline in school work as well as having high levels of truancy, aggression, and disruptive behaviors"[52]

♦ Are more likely to be incarcerated (70 percent will themselves end up in prison)[53]

A solution for these problems is to break the cycle of parental criminal behavior so that the parents can be with their children rather than separated from them in a prison. Statistically speaking, one of best means of doing this is through faith-based programs.

Currently in government-run prisons (state or federal) the average recidivism rate is 68 percent (meaning that within three years of release from prison, that person commits a crime that returns him to prison);[54] but the recidivism rate is only 8 percent in faith-based prisons[55]—a 90 percent more effective approach than that of secular prisons. Similarly, the average cure rate in government-run drug rehab programs (state or federal) is under 20 percent,[56] but in faith-based drug rehab programs such as Teen Challenge, the cure rate ranges from 62 percent to 84 percent.[57] Faith-based programs dramatically reduce the number of parents reentering prison, thus more quickly breaking the family cycle of crime, thereby reducing future crimes and crime victims as well as increased criminal justice expenditures.

THE BEST MODEL FOR FAMILIES

The statistics regarding children from these three atypical family structures (out of wedlock, divorced, and incarcerated) makes a strong case that the best arrangement for all involved is what is called the "nuclear family"—that is, a family built around a central nucleus of a father, mother, and children.[58] Statistics regarding the typical traditional family arrangement make the case for this proposition even more airtight. For example:

- ◆ Married adults have better health, including fewer accidents or injuries, have less depression, live longer, and enjoy greater happiness.[59]

- ◆ Married women have lower domestic violence rates and are victims of fewer acts of violent crime.[60]

- ◆ Children from intact families have higher literacy and graduation rates, lower teen pregnancy and juvenile offender rates, and higher rates of marital success.[61]

♦ Children from intact homes are five times less likely to live in poverty.[62] Significantly, only 22 percent of children in married households experience one year of poverty in their lives compared with 81 percent in other households.[63]

♦ Nearly all of the increase in child poverty since the 1970s can be attributed to family breakdown,[64] and its direct public costs now exceed $112 billion a year.[65]

♦ In traditional intact families, children are *less* likely to:
  • Be abused
  • End up in jail as adults
  • Suffer depression
  • Be expelled from school
  • Repeat a grade
  • Have behavior problems
  • Use drugs
  • Carry weapons
  • Be sexually active[66]

♦ Statistically speaking, "If the United States enjoyed the same level of family stability today as it did in 1960, the nation would have 750,000 fewer children repeating grades, 1.2 million fewer school suspensions, approximately 500,000 fewer acts of teenage delinquency, about 600,000 fewer kids receiving therapy, and approximately 70,000 fewer suicide attempts every year."[67]

The statistics are clear and unequivocal. The modern experiments to change the traditional family ignore the well-being of those involved, especially children and mothers, and thus weaken the long-term strength and health of the culture.

Not surprisingly, as the traditional family has now been largely rejected in preference for other arrangements, the definition of family has correspondingly changed. In law dictionaries at the beginning of the twentieth century, *family* was defined as a "father, mother, and children"[68] (the traditional nuclear family). But by the start of this century, a family had come to mean "two or more people who share goals and values, have long-term commitments to one another, and reside usually in the same dwelling place."[69] A father, mother, or children are no longer necessary in this new arrangement, which is now known as the postmodern family.[70]

As late as 1990, some 65 percent of Americans still believed that children were an important part of a happy marriage, but that number has declined to only 41 percent;[71] and with the growing de-emphasis on children, the fertility rate has declined by nearly half since 1960.[72] Significantly, the fertility replacement rate for the nation is 2.1—that is, families must average 2.1 children if the national population is to remain constant and not decline,[73] but the American rate has dropped to 1.9 (an all-time low)[74] and is continuing downward. As one expert noted, "There are no cases of peace and prosperity in the face of declining populations."[75]

What do these new trends concerning faith and its formerly positive influence on the family mean for the future of American culture? This question can be answered by examining the beliefs of the rising generation, such as millennials (generally considered as those born in the 1980s and 1990s).

While the "nones" (those who have and want no religious affiliation) are at an all-time high of 20 percent (and still rising) among the general population, for millennials, that number jumps to a startling one-third (34 percent).[76] And 74 percent of them were raised *with* a religious affiliation[77] but have now rejected it.

Clearly many parents of these younger adults failed to transmit to them a vibrant and useful faith, which was largely because the parents themselves lacked a vibrant and useful faith. As proof of this, although eight out of ten Americans claim to be Christians, only 9 percent of these Christians agree with six of the most elementary nonnegotiables of the Christian faith.* So poorly equipped

---

* These six include the beliefs that: (1) absolute moral truth exists; (2) the Bible is totally accurate in all of the principles it teaches; (3) Satan is a real being or force, not merely symbolic; (4) a person cannot earn his or her way into heaven but

are Christian young people by their minimally believing Christian parents that 61 percent of Christian youth who now attend college abandon their faith as a result.[79]

With the current lack of a biblical view of Christian faith, it is not surprising that there is also an accompanying failure in biblical morals. Hence, as the Barna Group has previously documented, "Of more than 70 other *moral* behaviors we study, when we compare Christians to non-Christians we rarely find substantial differences."[80]

So too with millennials. While they say they are indeed tempted by porn, lying, cheating, alcohol and drug abuse, and outside sexual involvement (and tempted at a rate much higher rather than are either their parents or grandparents),[81] the real problem is that "millions of Millennials do not see temptation as something to be avoided."[82] Consequently, nearly half of millennial mothers have had *all* of their children outside of marriage, and nearly two-thirds had at least *one* child out of wedlock; only one-third had all of their children within marriage.[83] Additionally, the already exploding cohabitation rate noted previously rose by an additional 88 percent between 1990 and 2007,[84] and most of this increase involved millennials.[85] The adverse consequences to be experienced not only by these mothers and their children but also by the culture itself have already been documented.

Significantly, any objective examination of the problems currently existing with the family results in the only logical recommendation possible: readopt what the Bible originally established (and what America long embraced) as the basis for the family—the lifelong union of one man and one woman. (Obviously the same-sex marriage issue has also had a dramatic effect on the conversation about what constitutes a "family," and that issue will be addressed in the following chapter.)

---

rather it comes by God's gift of grace; (5) Jesus lived a sinless life on earth; and (6) God is the all-knowing, all-powerful Creator of the world who still rules the universe today.[78]

Chapter 7

LAWS AND POLICIES THAT DEFINE THE NEW AMERICA

DESPITE THE FACT that roughly eight out of ten Americans regularly describe themselves as Christian,[1] Americans' current beliefs about what is "moral" bear little resemblance to traditional Christian teachings and clear-cut biblical directives.

For example, we now consider the following behaviors to be "moral":

- Homosexuality (58 percent) [2]

- An unmarried woman having a baby (67 percent)[3]

- Divorce (69 percent)[4]

- Destroying human embryos for research (65 percent)[5]

- Sex between an unmarried man and woman (66 percent)[6]

The Bible, in unequivocal language, teaches that each of these things is *not* moral.

Historically in America morality could not be determined apart from religious teachings, specifically those from the Bible. As President George Washington reminded the nation:

> And let us with caution indulge the supposition that morality can be maintained without religion.... Reason and

experience both forbid us to expect that national morality can prevail in exclusion of religious principle.[7]

Across the next century this continued to be the standard, for as President Zachary Taylor affirmed, "A free government cannot exist without religion and morals, and there cannot be morals without religion, nor religion without the Bible."[8] And then in the following century President Teddy Roosevelt still avowed:

> The teachings of the Bible are so interwoven and entwined with our whole civic and social life, that it would be literally—I do not mean figuratively, I mean literally—impossible for us to figure to ourselves what that life would be if these teachings were removed. We would lose almost all the standards by which we now judge both public and private morals; all the standards toward which we, with more or less resolution, strive to raise ourselves.[9]

But it was not just the executive branch that was forthright in its declarations that morals must be drawn from the Bible; the judicial branch was just as forceful. For example, Judge Zephaniah Swift, author of the first American legal text, avowed that "moral virtue is substantially and essentially enforced by the precepts of Christianity."[10] And Justice John McLean, placed on the Supreme Court by President Andrew Jackson, similarly affirmed:

> The morality of the Bible must continue to be the basis of our government. There is no other foundation for free institutions.[11]

Even the US Supreme Court, in a unanimous 1844 decision, rhetorically queried, "Where can the purest principles of morality be learned so clearly or so perfectly as from the New Testament?"[12] And when the American Medical Association adopted its original code of medical ethics in 1847, it too acknowledged that religion and morality were also the foundation of medical principles.[13]

But as America has become increasingly secular and more

biblically illiterate, the less the Bible has retained its place as the standard for morality—a fact affirmed by the changing definition of that word. Originally *moral* was defined as that which is "good or evil, virtuous or vicious" according to "the law of God,"[14] but today's definition no longer has any mention of God or His law.[15] The current standard is now the one thrice denounced in the Bible as "every man doing that which is right in his own eyes." (See Deuteronomy 12:8; Judges 17:6; 21:25.)

Part of what is perplexing about the current moral condition of America is not that we have so quickly abandoned and completely reversed positions long held to be moral but that we embrace the new morals even though there is abundant objective scientific and public-policy evidence demonstrating their harmfulness to ourselves and to our society. We seem bent on committing societal suicide, if not national parricide.

The Bible assures us that all of God's commands are given for *our* benefit, so that *we* can prosper and be successful. (See Deuteronomy 6:24; Joshua 1:8.) Societal statistics in numerous categories repeatedly prove the accuracy of this truth, so that even if someone held a completely secular viewpoint, then solely on the basis of public-policy evidence he or she would arrive at the same positions the Bible announces to be moral. But this not what is happening.

HOMOSEXUALITY

Consider homosexual behavior. The Bible explicitly condemns it,[16] but biblical morality aside, the scientific evidence on this subject is also unequivocal. As an example, based purely on medical evidence and not morals, the Centers for Disease Control (CDC) and the Food and Drug Administration (FDA) prohibit men who have sex with other men (MSM) from donating blood[17] because MSM:

> ...have an HIV prevalence (the total number of cases of a disease that are present in a population at a specific point in time) 60 times higher than the general population, 800 times higher than first time blood donors and 8,000 times

higher than repeat blood donors.... [They] also have an increased risk of having other infections that can be transmitted to others by blood transfusion. For example, infection with the Hepatitis B virus is about five to six times more common and Hepatitis C virus infections are about two times more common in [MSM] than in the general population.[18]

Furthermore, even though homosexuals comprise less than 4 percent of the population,[19] they account for 63 percent of all syphilis cases.[20] And statistics show that HIV/AIDS is almost exclusively a homosexual disease. In fact, when it was originally identified in 1982 by the Centers for Disease Control, it was named GRID (gay-related immunodeficiency), also called gay compromise syndrome or gay cancer.[21] When it subsequently spread into the heterosexual community through transfusions of infected blood that had been donated by homosexuals and by women having sex with bisexual men who had previously had sex with other men, the name of the disease was changed to AIDS. The scientific evidence is unequivocal,[22] and homosexual leaders openly affirm that HIV/AIDS is indeed a homosexual disease.[23] Significantly, it is increasing *only* in the homosexual community and decreasing in all others. According to the FDA:

> Men who have had sex with other men represent approximately 2% of the US population, yet are the population most severely affected by HIV. In 2010, MSM accounted for at least 61% of all new HIV infections in the U.S. and an estimated 77% of diagnosed HIV infections among males were attributed to male-to-male sexual contact. Between 2008 and 2010, the estimated overall incidence of HIV was stable in the U.S. However the incidence in MSM increased 12%, while it decreased in other populations. The largest increase was a 22% increase in MSM aged 13 to 24 years.[24]

Clearly there is a conspiracy of silence about these types of scientific facts in the media, education, and political arenas.

But beyond the direct health dangers of homosexual behavior, there are also substantive economic consequences. For example, in 2014 alone the White House budget designated $29.7 billion to deal with the consequences of this "gay disease" (and this does not include state and local expenditures).[25] In fact, the lifetime medical treatment cost just for the new cases diagnosed annually is projected at $16.6 billion,[26] and that cost is repeated for each year's new diagnoses. Additionally, $12.5 billion of the taxpayer-funded Medicare and Medicaid expenses this year was for HIV/AIDS,[27] and the average expense for an HIV/AIDS patient is much higher than for other patients, including even seniors, who are often represented as being the biggest economic drain on such programs. For example, concerning Medicaid, "Enrollees with HIV were significantly more expensive than their non–HIV positive counterparts, with per capita [annual] costs almost five times greater ($24,867 compared to $5091)."[28] Indisputably both the taxpayer-born economic costs as well as the societal consequences of this behavior are inconsistent with a healthy culture and sound public policy.

HOMOSEXUAL MARRIAGE

So too with homosexual marriage. Nearly three dozen foreign countries currently grant marital rights to homosexual individuals,[29] and statistics from those countries provide clear warnings to America.[30]

Only a small percentage of individuals are homosexual. Just as less than 4 percent of Americans are homosexual,[31] Wikipedia, which is very positive toward homosexuality and homosexuals, reports the same generally low incidence in other countries that keep such statistics (e.g., 1 percent of the population in Great Britain, 1 percent in New Zealand, 4 percent in Ireland, 2.5 percent in Australia, 1 percent in Canada, etc.).[32] But not only are the numbers of homosexuals very low, the statistics from those other nations also show that only a very small percentage from within that small group marry when given the opportunity.[33]

For example, according to statistics from Iceland, while there are some 315,000 citizens in that nation, in 2011 only thirty-six homosexuals in the entire nation married, and ten homosexuals divorced.[34] These low numbers are not that unusual, for in all nations allowing homosexual marriage, the percentage of homosexual marriages falls below the percentage of homosexual representation in that country.[35]

Additionally, "While a high percentage of [traditional] married couples remain married for up to 20 years or longer…the vast majority of homosexual relationships are short-lived and transitory.…A study in the Netherlands, a gay-tolerant nation that has legalized homosexual marriage, found the average duration of a homosexual relationship to be one and a half years."[36] And lesbians seemed particularly inclined toward a lack of commitment, for although only 44 percent of homosexual marriages involved lesbians up to the year 2010, 62 percent of homosexual divorces did.[37] (By the way, lesbians experience a rate of domestic violence forty-four times greater than that of traditionally married women.)[38]

Furthermore, "While three quarters or more of [traditional] married couples remain faithful to each other, homosexual couples typically engage in a shocking degree of promiscuity. The same Dutch study found that 'committed' homosexual couples have an average of eight sexual partners (outside of the relationship) per year."[39]

So for citizens in the countries witnessing such casual arrangements whereby a "committed" homosexual marriage involves so many extramarital partners and ends so quickly, the conclusion is inescapable that marriage itself is generally meaningless. Consequently:

> Marriage is slowly dying in Scandinavia. A majority of children in Sweden and Norway are born out of wedlock. Sixty percent of first-born children in Denmark have unmarried parents. Not coincidentally, these countries have had something close to full gay marriage for a decade or more.[40]

Similarly, since Great Britain adopted homosexual marriage, the marriage rate has now hit its lowest levels since measurements began in 1862.[41]

Some homosexual activists and leaders candidly acknowledge that their ultimate goal is the elimination of all marriage and that homosexual marriage is merely a first step toward that objective.[42] Regardless of whether or not such an agenda is reflective of homosexuals in general, the overall effect has nevertheless been a rapid and precipitous movement away from marriage of any type. Statistics from other nations clearly demonstrate that weakening heterosexual marriage increases out-of-wedlock births, and the extreme adverse societal consequences of children being raised outside of a home with a father and a mother were extensively documented in the previous chapter.

Thus, the 5,500-year-old definition of marriage has been rewritten, and cultures have been completely upended and restructured merely to accommodate the wishes of a small percentage from within a small percentage of the population. That accommodation has not resulted in so-called marriage equality but rather a destruction of marriage for traditionals. This is a radical cultural change simply to accommodate the personal inclinations of a tiny fraction of the population. By the way, *inclination* is deliberately used here to indicate a personal choice, for science continues to affirm that there is *no* homosexual gene,[43] so the oft-heard claim of "I can't help being homosexual, just as a person can't help being black, female, or tall" is fallacious and not backed by scientific evidence.

It is perplexing why America embraces and encourages behavior that indisputably weakens and undermines its culture, and it is astonishing how quickly such behavior has become mainstream and "moral." After all, it was only a decade ago that the Supreme Court first struck down laws limiting homosexuality[44] and that the first state permitted homosexual marriage.[45] But today, just a few short years later, civil courts not only protect homosexuality but also openly enforce punitive penalties against those who refuse to affirm and celebrate it.[46] In fact, scores of cities have now adopted policies like that in San Antonio, Texas, which places a $500 per day fine and a permanent exclusion from ever running for public office on any citizen who criticizes homosexuality or homosexual marriage.[47] What a difference a decade makes! But such rapid change is possible only when there is no firm foundation of biblical convictions, especially among the eight out of ten Americans who profess Christianity.

ABORTION

Similarly surprising is the national position on the abortion issue. The Bible not only teaches that life in the womb is created by God,[48] but it also condemns the shedding of such innocent blood.[49] Nevertheless, only 29 percent of Americans would like to see *Roe v. Wade*, the decision that legalized abortion, overturned, and 63 percent do not want to see it end.[50] Specifically, 76 percent of white mainline Protestants, 65 percent of black Protestants, and 63 percent of white Catholics (and nearly 40 percent of Christians overall) want to see abortion protected and continued,[51] and 65 percent of abortions (or about six hundred fifty thousand annually) are performed on professing Christians,[52] with two hundred thousand each year on born-again Christians.[53]

PHYSICIAN-ASSISTED SUICIDE

Just as unborn life is no longer viewed as a gift from God, neither is life outside the womb. Instead, it is adjudged to be the personal property of each individual, who is then free to do whatever he wants (or doesn't want) with his own life. As a consequence, physician-assisted suicide is on the rise in America.

By the way, physician-assisted suicide, also known as Physician Aid in Dying (PAD), differs from euthanasia. With the former, the doctor (rhetorically speaking) gives a gun to the patient and says, "Here—shoot yourself!" But with the latter, the doctor himself holds the gun and pulls the trigger.

Significantly, a core tenet of the Hippocratic oath (at the heart of the medical profession since 400 BC) is "I will give no deadly medicine to any one if asked, nor suggest any such counsel."[54] Despite this binding oath by physicians, PAD is now legal in Oregon,

Washington, Montana, Vermont, and New Mexico and has been introduced in many other states as well. The growth of this new policy, which is the consequence of rejecting God as the author of life, is not surprising given current citizen beliefs. Today nearly 70 percent support PAD—including 48 percent of those who attend church weekly and 74 percent of those who attend church multiple times a month.[55]

For previous American generations, there were two problems with physician-assisted suicide: first, *physician-assisted*, and second, *suicide*. Consider the latter first.

Suicide is a Latin term that means "self-murder,"[56] and murder was a violation of both biblical law (as in the sixth of the Ten Commandments, "Thou shall not murder") as well as the common law (incorporated into the Constitution through the Seventh Amendment in the Bill of Rights). The Bible records numerous accounts of suicide and presents it in a negative light.[57]

Man was *not* to murder anyone—not even himself. It is Christ, not individuals, who holds the "keys of hell and of death" (Rev. 1:18, KJV). The Bible affirms that everyone has an appointed time of death, and that time is set by God, not chosen by the individual (Heb. 9:27). As Ecclesiastes 7:17 queries, "Why should you die before your time?" (NKJV).

Interestingly, the most famous law book in the American founding (Blackstone's *Commentaries on the Law*) discussed suicide in a manner that any reader of the Bible Book of Esther could easily grasp. In Esther, when Mordecai urged Queen Esther to go present herself before the king, she reminded him that it was a deadly offense for anyone to show up before the king uncalled for. (See Esther 4:10–11.) Blackstone alludes to this practice, explaining not only that "no man hath a power to destroy life, but by commission from God, the author of it" but that those who committed suicide were guilty of "invading the prerogative of the Almighty, and rushing into his immediate presence uncalled for."[58]

As America becomes more secular, the less it holds to the biblical position of Jeremiah 10:23: "Lord, I know that peoples' lives are not their own; it is not for them to direct their steps" (NIV).

GUN CONTROL

For generations and centuries so many things in America had never become an issue but now are; this includes gun control. The right of individuals to own, carry, and use guns was traditionally unquestioned, being a practice firmly rooted in history, law, and the Constitution—specifically the Second Amendment, which guarantees to every individual the indisputable right to "keep and bear arms" in defense of themselves and others.

Significantly, this right was drawn from the Bible. Exodus 22:2 forms the basis of what became known as the "Castle Doctrine," a doctrine explained by Founding Father James Wilson, a signer of the Declaration and the Constitution and an original justice on the US Supreme Court:

> Homicide is enjoined [required], when it is necessary for the defense of one's person or house....Every man's house is deemed, by the law, to be his castle; and the law, while it invests him with the power, [places] on him the duty of the commanding officer [of his house]. "Every man's house is his castle...and if any one be robbed in it, it shall be esteemed his own default and negligence."[59]

Thus, if you were robbed in your home, it was not the police's fault but your own, for God made *you* the commander of your "castle"—hence, the "Castle Doctrine."

Other Bible verses affirm the biblical right of self-defense,[60] and thus it was therefore considered an inalienable, or a God-given, right. Significantly, the Founding Fathers established American government with the primary purpose of securing to every individual the right to practice his or her inalienable rights. As the Declaration of Independence affirms:

> We hold these truths to be self-evident, that all men are created equal, that they are endowed by their Creator with certain unalienable rights.... That *to secure these rights*, governments are instituted among men.[61]

The purpose of government was to protect God-given rights, which included that of self-defense. But as with so many other areas today, that original purpose has now been turned backward. For example:

- ◆ In New York a man watched a group of young thugs approach his home. Suspecting they were members of the notoriously violent MS-13 gang, he instructed his wife to call the police while he retrieved his gun. He went outside and asked them to leave, but they approached him and threatened to "kill [his] family and [his] babies." When nearly two dozen rushed him, the man fired four warning shots into the ground. For attempting to defend himself and his family, he was arrested and charged with a felony.[62]

- ◆ In South Dakota when a woman saw a club-wielding attacker come onto her family's property and assail her husband and son-in-law, she fired a warning shot into the ground, causing the assailant to flee. The police found the attacker, club and all, but arrested only the wife for firing a warning shot into her own property to protect her family.[63]

- ◆ In Georgia the manager of a store where there had been string of robberies was himself confronted by an armed robber who pepper-sprayed him, put a gun to his head, and threatened to kill him unless he opened the safe. When the manager drew his own gun from his pocket and fired at the would-be thief, the company fired him.[64]

♦ When a man in Washington DC saw three pit bull-dogs attack an eleven-year-old boy, he went inside his home and retrieved a gun, shooting one of the dogs. For saving the boy's life, he was subjected to a criminal investigation by the city.[65]

♦ In New Hampshire a gas-station clerk was confronted by a knife-wielding man who attempted to rob the store. When the clerk pulled a gun and the would-be robber realized he had brought a knife to a gunfight, he promptly fled. For defending himself, the clerk was fired.[66]

♦ In Washington state two university students confronted an intruder—a six-time felon attempting to illegally enter their apartment. At his aggressive behavior, they brandished a gun, causing him to turn and flee. For defending themselves, their guns were taken, and the university placed the two students on probation.[67]

Sadly to defend your own life or the lives of others around you can now subject you to direct punishment or even arrest.

Debt

Another moral issue about which the Bible is exceedingly clear is that of avoiding debt.[68] But not only do we no longer heed that guidance, leaders now encourage just the opposite—that elevated spending, and thus increased debt, actually creates prosperity.[69]

Apparently many Americans agree, for the average debt per American family has increased nearly 40 percent just since 2000, while family net worth has fallen 16 percent during the same time.[70] Citizen debt, which includes things such as mortgages, car loans, and student loans, is now at $11.4 trillion.[71] The average mortgage debt is roughly $148,000;[72] auto loan debt is nearly $31,000;[73] student loan debt is $35,200;[74] and credit card debt is $15,000 (usually spread over three cards).[75]

Debt has now become the standard order of business in many families, and so too in the nation. In the past decade, the national debt has swelled to more than $17 trillion[76]—the highest in the history of the country. That number is too large for most to visualize, so compare it to something that is a bit easier to imagine: the total value of *all* goods and *all* services produced by *all* individuals and *all* businesses in the entire United States in a single year. This is called the gross domestic product (GDP). Certainly, the annual national income produced by millions of businesses and services is massive.

To help understand the almost unfathomable size of the debt, experts have created what they call the *debt ratio*, which compares the national debt to the annual GDP. Using this ratio, each percentage point indicates that one year is necessary for the normal economic effect of the total output of national individual and business productivity to pay off the national debt (as long as no new debt is incurred).[77] Thus, the lower the percentage, the fewer the years needed to retire the debt.

In 1980 the debt ratio was 32 percent of the GDP,[78] meaning that it would take thirty-two years for the economic effects of the full production of the US economy to pay off the debt as it existed at that point. But since 1980 the debt ratio has burgeoned to 103 percent of the GDP,[79] meaning that it will now take 103 years for national productivity to pay off the debt. And because so much more debt has been (and is still being) added every year, the GDP ratio will be 190 percent by 2038,[80] meaning that it will then require 190 years to pay off the debt. The numbers are moving rapidly in the wrong direction—a direction dangerous to the future health of the country.

On a more practical level debt reduces freedom by limiting the number of options for what individuals or nations can do with their income. That is, the greater the debt, the less freedom those in debt have with how they use their own resources; others (specifically, their creditors) will determine how their resources will be used. This is why the Bible declares in Proverbs 22:7 that "the borrower is servant to the lender" (KJV).

For this reason God commanded His nation Israel to avoid debt, explaining that if Israel was the lender, then she ruled the others, but if she was the borrower, then others ruled her. (See Deuteronomy 15:6.) Our Founding Fathers understood this. As Thomas Jefferson explained:

> To preserve their [the people's] independence, we must not let our rulers load us with perpetual debt. We must make our election [choice] between *economy and liberty*, or *profusion and servitude*.[81]

Notice the sequences: frugality produces liberty, but spending produces slavery. So to enjoy liberty, practice frugality; but if you don't mind being in bondage and under oppression, then spend away.

So strongly did the Founders oppose debt that Jefferson declared:

> I...place economy [frugality] among the first and most important of republican virtues, and public debt as the greatest of the dangers to be feared.[82]

Alexander Hamilton, the nation's first secretary of the treasury, likewise explained:

> Nothing can more interest the national...prosperity than...extinguishing the present debt, and to avoid, as much as possible, the incurring of any new debt.[83]

President George Washington agreed:

> [The] progressive accumulation of debt...ultimately [endangers] all governments.[84]

Debt destroys freedom and prosperity and produces taxation, servitude, and oppression. Servitude is what Americans are unwisely choosing today, and not for themselves only, but also for their children. A child born in 2014 owes the government $39,500 as his or her part of the federal debt, but by 2032, when that child is eighteen, his portion will be $90,000, and by 2038, when that child becomes twenty-four, he will owe $142,000.[85]

This is immoral. In no other arena of life do we allow this practice. I cannot obligate someone else to pay my mortgage or my car loan or my personal debt, but we regularly do this to future generations, and we do it without their consent.

The Founding Fathers viewed this practice as reprehensible, which is why Thomas Jefferson declared:

> No generation can contract debts greater than may be paid during the course of its existence.... Neither the representatives of a nation, nor the whole nation itself assembled, can validly engage debts beyond what they may pay in their own time, that is to say, within thirty-four years of the date of the engagement.... Succeeding generations are not responsible for the preceding.[86]

He therefore concluded:

> The principle of spending money to be paid by posterity, under the name of funding, is but swindling futurity on a large scale.[87]

George Washington agreed, sternly warning that we were to work at "avoiding occasions of expense...avoiding likewise the accumulation of debt, not...ungenerously throwing upon posterity the burden which we ourselves ought to bear."[88] But right now, we are doing just the opposite, and because of our foolish self-indulgence today, our posterity for decades to come will pay a price they will be unable to bear.

Entitlement Programs

One of the most distressing aspects of America's massive debt is that it will *not* be substantially lowered anytime soon, for America has obligated itself to continue spending at very high levels for years into the future by means of entitlements. An entitlement is a "right" to participate in and receive benefits from a government program, such as welfare, unemployment compensation, food stamps, government housing, health insurance, Social Security, Medicare, and scores of others.

Originating largely in the 1930s, these programs were designed to be "safety nets" to provide temporary help to the needy and at-risk. But this once short-term and limited assistance has now grown into full-blown lifestyle opportunities, providing lifelong income possibilities that no longer even remotely reflect the original purpose of those programs.

Prior to President Franklin Roosevelt (who largely introduced the concept of entitlements), spending on such programs was inconsequential. But with his advent of the New Deal and its many new and unprecedented social programs, entitlement spending grew eight-fold. The second wave of entitlement programs was introduced by President Lyndon Johnson with his Great Society programs, and under Johnson, spending tripled from what Roosevelt had done. Then, under President Barack Obama and his new entitlements (such as health care and greatly expanded food stamps and welfare), entitlement spending once again exploded,[89] having grown from a mere 0.4 percent of the GDP in 1900 (and only 5 percent of the federal budget) to 18 percent today (accounting for 45 percent of the budget).[90]

Entitlements are no longer just temporary "safety nets," for today 49 percent of American households, involving some 148 million Americans,[91] receive a government entitlement check.[92] The government now sends $2 trillion annually to individuals through its various entitlement programs,[93] and money is given so freely and unconditionally that most Americans don't even realize they are getting a government check. In fact, up to two-thirds of those who currently receive an entitlement check say, "No, I have not used a government social program."[94] Clearly, Americans no longer recognize entitlements, and 60 percent of Americans now receive more government benefits than they pay in taxes[95]—certainly an unsustainable economic practice.

One of the "safety net" programs is the National School Lunch program, which was begun in 1946 to provide food at school for the poorest students. But today, 32 million—or two-thirds of all public-school students—participate in this program,[96] and the program has just been made available to *all* students, *regardless of family income*.[97]

And then there are food stamps. Originally designed to help put food on the table of the poor, currently 47 million Americans receive food stamps,[98] which are now used to buy lobster and gourmet cupcakes as well as menu items from Taco Bell, Kentucky Fried Chicken, and Starbucks.[99] They are likewise used for gambling, casinos, horse race tracks, lottery tickets, and amusement parks such as Disney World, as well as to purchase cigarettes and liquor.[100] They are also used to purchase lingerie and provide bail for convicted felons and are even exchanged for cold, hard cash.[101]

Not only does the food-stamp money continue to flow, but also President Obama is actively soliciting more Americans to receive and use food stamps, even paying bonuses for those states that sign up the most applicants the most quickly.[102] As a result, under President Obama the number of able-bodied adults receiving food stamps has doubled.[103]

With the reckless government spending of recent years, entitlement expenditures are now nearly one hundred times higher than they were in 1960.[104] At that time, entitlement spending was less than one-third of the federal budget,[105] but since then has been increasing by an average of 9.5 percent every year,[106] now comprising roughly two-thirds of the budget.[107]

With the current rate of growth, in only a generation from now the expense for these burgeoning entitlement programs (and the interest payment on the debt caused by them) will be so high that they will consume *all* the tax revenues for each year. That is, *all* the taxes paid to the government each year will be used in their entirety just to pay for entitlement programs, with no revenue remaining for national defense or any other item.[108] As one national media source noted:

Former Wyoming senator Alan Simpson said last week, "Entitlements are the engine on the train driving us to the cliff." He's right. Forget about fiddling with tax rates— there isn't enough money in America to pay for all this spending.[109]

Correlating to this never-ending cascade of ceaseless spending is a decline in public faith in the federal government, which now stands at an all-time low.[110] In the 1960s 80 percent of Americans said that they trusted the federal government to do what is right always, or at least most of the time;[111] today that number is 19 percent.[112]

WELFARE

Welfare, originally designed as a stop-gap for those who were unable to make economic ends meet because of poverty-level income, is one of the most recognizable of the many entitlement programs. It was a widely supported program, for Americans definitely want to help the poor. Americans are a generous people, and over the past year two-thirds say they volunteered their time for some charity and 83 percent say they donated money.[113] So strongly inclined are Americans to help others that 57 percent believe that dealing with the poor should be a top priority of the president and Congress.[114]

This desire to help the poor was behind President Lyndon Johnson's 1964 announcement, "I have called for a national war on poverty,"[115] because, he said, "for the first time in our history, it is possible to conquer poverty."[116] But welfare is no longer a safety net designed to keep people from slipping into poverty.

In more than a dozen states a family of three receiving welfare support can live on a middle-class salary—all while holding absolutely no job. In fact, in Hawaii a family of three would have to earn more than $61,000 to make it worthwhile to abandon their welfare benefits.[117] Furthermore, in eleven states welfare recipients make more than the starting salary for a schoolteacher, and in thirty-nine states they make more than the starting salary for a secretary.[118] Moreover, when all the money spent on welfare programs in 2011 was divided among those at or below the poverty level, it averaged $61,194 spent per household.[119]

The genuinely poor do indeed need to be helped, and there are scores of Bible verses admonishing us to help them. But significantly, nearly *all* of these verses are directed at individuals and the congregation. The only responsibility concerning the poor that government is charged with is to provide justice for the poor and maintain their rights whenever they utilize the civil process.[120] Government is *not* charged with meeting the material needs of the poor.[121]

This biblical pattern was understood and closely followed in early America. Founding Fathers such as George Washington and Thomas Jefferson therefore served as vestrymen in their respective churches, meaning they arranged care for the poor in their local communities. But in addition to the responsibility of the church to help the poor, individuals also had a biblical obligation to do the same. As Thomas Jefferson affirmed:

> I deem it the duty of every man to devote a certain portion of his income for charitable purposes; and that it is his further duty to see it so applied as to do the most good of which it is capable. This I believe to be best insured by keeping within the circle of his own inquiry and information the subjects of distress to whose relief his contributions shall be applied.[122]

George Washington felt the same personal duty (as should every Christian). When he was called away from Mount Vernon to serve as commander in chief of the Continental Army during the American Revolution (a demanding responsibility for which he took no paycheck throughout his eight years of service), he directed his business manager:

> Let the hospitality of the house, with respect to the poor, be kept up. Let no one go hungry away. If any of this kind of people should be in want of corn, supply their necessities, provided it does not encourage them in idleness; and I have no objection to your giving my money in charity.... What I

mean by having no objection is, that it is my desire that it should be done.[123]

God mandated that provision should be made to help the poor, but, significantly, work was required in exchange.[124] After all, the Bible commands, "If anyone will not work, neither shall he eat" (2 Thess. 3:10, NKJV). (Of course, the exception to this was orphans, widows, and the disabled, who truly were unable to work; if they physically could not supply for themselves, then charity was provided for them—but not by government.)

This biblical policy of work for welfare is what was adopted in America. In fact, when Benjamin Franklin was serving America overseas in London, he wrote a newspaper piece criticizing the English practice of providing for the poor by taxing citizens. He rebuked the British for that approach, explaining:

> I am for doing good to the poor, but I...think the best way of doing good to the poor, is not making them easy in poverty, but leading or driving them *out* of it. In my youth, I travelled much, and I observed in different countries, that the more public provisions were made for the poor, the less they provided for themselves, and of course became poorer. And, on the contrary, the less that was done for them, the more they did for themselves, and became richer.... In short, you offered a premium for the encouragement of idleness, and you should not now wonder, that it has had its effect in the increase of poverty.[125]

The Bible and the Founders both firmly supported a work requirement in order to receive welfare benefits, and Americans today strongly agree with this approach (although they are probably unaware that its origin is from the Bible). Currently, 80 percent of Americans believe that work is the best solution for poverty, and 83 percent favor some type of work requirement as a condition for receiving welfare.[126] It might therefore surprise Americans to know that a work requirement is no longer a precondition for receiving welfare benefits. By way of background, in 1960 two-thirds of low-income households were headed by persons who worked, but by 1991 that number had been cut in half, with only 11 percent working full time.[127] To reverse this trend of giving benefits without work, in 1996 a major welfare-reform bill became law, reinstituting a work requirement as a condition for receiving welfare payments. But President Obama unilaterally suspended that requirement.[128] Welfare spending is now the largest single-ticket item in the federal budget—larger than Social Security, Medicare, or even national defense.[129]

Significantly, since President Lyndon Johnson announced the War on Poverty in 1964, by 2004 roughly $9 trillion had been spent to defeat that enemy,[130] and it has now grown to nearly $1 trillion a year on the government's nearly eighty poverty programs—an increase of 32 percent just since 2008.[131] Despite that infusion of massive amounts of monetary resources, the poverty level has remained relatively unchanged.[132] This is because, as the Scriptures affirm, government is not the proper delivery system for this aid—a fact unequivocally affirmed by the American Institute of Philanthropy (AIP), also known as Charity Watch.

The AIP rates various organizations by calculating the percentage of donated income that actually makes it to the intended target. According to the AIP, a charity's effectiveness is "satisfactory" if 60 percent of what it collects reaches its intended mission.[133] Donors should avoid contributing to organizations where less than 60 percent of contributed funds reach the designated target.

So what percentage of every dollar collected by the government for the benefit of the poor actually reaches them? A dismal 30 percent.[134] The US government is quite possibly the nation's most inefficient mechanism for meeting the needs of the poor. No reasonable contributor would fund an organization where only thirty cents out of each dollar reached its target, but many today not only tolerate such malfeasance but also even encourage more government spending to fight poverty. Why? Just to see 70 percent of each additional dollar wasted? The most efficient means of taking care of the poor is through individuals, churches, and charities, but not government.

By the way, government officials often talk about the importance of fighting poverty in order to justify their own efforts to spend more, but significantly they fail to define what constitutes poverty. There is a distinct difference between what most citizens think of as "poor" and what the government considers it to be.

According to federal data, "The typical 'poor' American...receives medical care whenever needed, has an ample diet and wasn't hungry for even a single day the previous year."[135] In fact, "About 80 percent of poor families have air conditioning, nearly two-thirds have cable or satellite TV, half have a computer and a third have a wide-screen LCD or plasma TV."[136] Furthermore, three-fourths have a car or truck, more than half have Xbox or PlayStation, nearly half own their own homes, and just under half have Internet access.[137] And the living space of the average American poor family is *greater than that of the typical middle class in England, France, Sweden,* Germany, and elsewhere across Europe.[138]

Of course, this is not to say that real hardship and genuine poverty does not exist among some individuals in America; it does. But when the group collectively known as "America's poor" struggles to make ends meet, those struggles generally include paying for cable television, air conditioning, and a car, not just obtaining food. In fact, 96 percent of those classified as "American poor" say that their children experienced *no* hunger at *any* time in the previous year;[139] and while common health problems for the poor across the world include malnutrition, thinness, and physical underdevelopment, in America the most frequent health problem for the poor is obesity.[140]

President Ronald Reagan, having witnessed the inefficiency of the government in this area, insightfully quipped, "My friends, some years ago, the Federal Government declared war on poverty, and poverty won."[141] The original design may have been well-intentioned, but the endeavor has been no more effective than trying to use a screwdriver as a shovel, or a sponge as a hammer. Government simply was *not* designed by God to take care of the poor, and to use it for that purpose is a disservice not only to the genuinely poor but also to the citizens who are taxed at high rates in order to pay for these ineffectual programs.

PUBLIC SCHOOL EDUCATION

Another area where serious problems are readily apparent is government public education. Some of its obvious problems were mentioned earlier, but there are many others worth noting that are also highly disturbing.

By the way, American education originally had strong biblical origins, and for literally centuries public education operated under biblical standards and practices. In fact, across our history, countless biblical sermons were preached about education and how it was to be operated.[142] But in 1962–1963, through three US Supreme Court decisions, the long-standing inclusion of religious principles and practices was first repudiated and a new philosophy of public education decreed. The results are both tangible and measurable.

Significantly, education consumes a substantial part of government expenses, for over $12,000 per year is spent per student in elementary and secondary education, and across the course of a full public school education from grade one to grade twelve, this equates to well over $140,000 per student.[143] But America is certainly not getting its money's worth.

For example, America used to be number one in the world in high-school graduation rates but now finishes in the bottom quartile among leading industrial nations of the world.[144] In fact, 3 million American students now drop out of school each year, and in America's fifty largest cities, the dropout rate is over 40 percent. This is not inconsequential, for 75 percent of all crimes in America are committed by a high-school dropout.[145]

But America's educational standing in the world is not declining just in dropout rates; it is occurring in virtually every other academic measurement as well. For example:

♦ In international math testing among fifteen year olds, by 2000 America had already fallen to nineteenth in the world and by 2012 had further slipped to thirty-third, being surpassed by nations such as Vietnam, Singapore, Liechtenstein, Estonia, Iceland, and Portugal.[146]

♦ In international science testing among fifteen year olds, by 2000 America had dropped to fourteenth in the world and by 2012 had moved on down to twenty-fifth, being bested by nations such as Poland, Germany, Ireland, Slovenia, and Latvia.[147]

♦ In international reading testing among fifteen year olds, back in 2000 America had already fallen to thirteenth in the world and by 2012 had further fallen to twenty-second, being beaten by nations such as Korea, Estonia, Australia, the Netherlands, and Belgium.[148]

In fact, American education today is so bad that 19 percent of high-school graduates are illiterate[149]—that is, after twelve years of school and an average of $140,000-plus spent per student, one out of five graduates flat-out can't read! This is not a recently emerging problem, but it has been going on in public schools across recent decades. Back in the 1960s America was number one in the world in literacy but by 1991 had fallen to sixty-fifth.[150] As a result, there are now 32 million American adults who cannot read, and 21 percent cannot read above a fifth-grade level.[151] Not only is this personally tragic for those who experience these educational failures, but also illiteracy contributes to many costly social problems, including crime—evidenced by the fact that 63 percent of prison inmates are illiterate.[152]

Today there are many different forms of education in America. In addition to government-run secularist education, there is also private schooling (both religious and secular), parochial schooling, homeschooling, and charter schooling (which is a public school but with less government involvement and regulation). Significantly, in every one of these other educational approaches, academic scores surpass those of the government-run secularist public schools.[153] Nevertheless, we continue to fund that most which works least (we currently spend $632 billion each year on government education),[154] and we are even repeatedly told that what education needs—what will solve all its problems—is more money. Clearly, as proved by the other forms of education that get higher scores, that claim is simply not true.

IMMIGRATION POLICIES

Federal law currently allows 675,000 legal immigrants each year, and Congress and the president can set an additional number for special refugees.[155] Some 40,000 federal agents are paid to enforce these laws, but once again Americans are not getting what they pay for, for there are an estimated 11.7 million illegal immigrants now residing in America (up from 8.5 million in 2000).[156]

Significant problems have been created by many from within this group. For example, noncitizens make up 8.6 percent of the adult population but 26.4 percent of the federal prison inmates[157] and 25 percent of drug offenders.[158] Additionally, in 2013 alone Immigration and Customs Enforcement released 36,007 detained *criminal* illegal immigrants back into the country, including some 200 murderers, 400 rapists, 300 kidnappers as well as 16,000 convicted of DUI, 2,700 convicted of assault, 1,300 of domestic violence, and 1,300 of battery.[159] All told, those illegals released back into the community had been responsible for 88,000 crimes.[160]

In addition to the societal costs associated with crimes committed by illegals, there are other major economic consequences. For example, many illegal immigrants openly participate in government benefit programs, and the average illegal immigrant household receives $14,387 more in benefits than it pays in taxes.[161]

The Bible warns, "When a crime is not punished quickly, people feel it is safe to do wrong" (Eccles. 8:11). When the government refuses to enforce laws, it encourages more individuals to break the law and to do so on a more frequent basis. Laws should be enforced or they should be changed or repealed, but they should not be ignored.

BUSINESS REGULATION

With the rapid and uncontrolled growth of government, it has now expanded into nearly every arena of life and living, including those formerly considered out of bounds to its federal micromanagement, such as that of private business.

Historically the economic system in America that produced our unrivaled prosperity is known as a free-market, or free-enterprise, system. By definition this is a system in which "prices and wages are determined by unrestricted competition between businesses, *without government regulation.*"[162] It is "an economic system that allows supply and demand to regulate prices, wages, etc, *rather than government policy.*"[163] In other words, the free market is regulated by the people and their freely made choices, not by the government. Throughout world history the nations and peoples that have adopted this system have risen, while those who embraced government-regulated economic systems have consistently become poorer.

Central to this economic system is the profit incentive. If an individual sees that his hard work can be profitable, he will invest the time, skill, and labor necessary to produce and sell an innovative, life-improving product. But that profit will be made *only* if the consumer is convinced that the product he is considering purchasing will improve or better his life in some way. Thus, consumers are willing to exchange their hard-earned money in order to have an enjoyable car, a useful phone or computer, or a set of clothes or shoes they believe enhances their appearance. Those with bad ideas or who refuse to invest the time, energy, and capital necessary for success will invariably fail. It is the public (and not the government) that chooses winners and losers in business and bestows profits on the good ones.

The Bible teaches that profit-makers are to be economically rewarded, thus encouraging them to do even more. In Luke 19:11–26 Jesus tells a parable of how the master called His servants together and gave each of them an investment, telling them, "Do business with this until I come back" (v. 13, NAS). When the master later returned to check on their progress, the first reported a tenfold profit return and the second a fivefold; the third showed no profit at all but openly expressed his disgust in doing anything to make the money grow. Angered by the servant's lack of willingness even to try, the master took the investment from him and gave it to the one who had been the most productive.

The message of Jesus's story is clear: those who show increase and make a profit are to be rewarded, but the unproductive are not. But in America today it is just the opposite: the government uses punitive taxes to take profit away from profit-makers and then bestows generous benefits on the incompetent and unproductive. This unbiblical policy of taking from the productive to give to the nonproductive was vigorously opposed at the time of the American founding. As Thomas Jefferson explained:

> To take from one, because it is thought that his own industry and that of his fathers has acquired too much, in order to spare to others, who, or whose fathers have not exercised equal industry and skill, is to violate arbitrarily the first principle of association, "the *guarantee* to every one of a free exercise of his industry [hard work], and the fruits [profits] acquired by it."[164]

Founding Father Charles Thomson pointed out that taxing profits actually encouraged idleness, for if someone knew that the fruit of his own hard work was going to the government rather than himself, then what was his incentive to work harder, longer, or more? As he explained:

> When the quantity of the tax depends on the caprice [whim] of those who have the superiority [power]...what encouragement is there to labour or save? The wealth we thereby acquire, will be a new motive...to tax us anew. No wonder then if people will choose to live poor and lazy, rather than labor to enrich their task-masters [i.e., the government].[165]

As Benjamin Franklin attested:

> There cannot be a stronger natural right than that of a man's
> making the best profit he can.[166]

When people are allowed to retain their profits, they have an incentive to work harder and produce more. This infuses wealth into the entire community, for when individuals and businesses become profitable, they invariably broaden their efforts, hiring others to help them, which thus bestows the blessing of steady employment and income on the families of persons they employ. Furthermore, much of the money made by the employer (and his employees) is spent on local services and supplies, thus placing it back into the community.

But ignoring the lessons of the Bible, history, and common sense, America now taxes long-term profits (through what is called the capital gains tax) and does so at a rate higher than any other free country in the world. Currently the average capital gains tax for American business is 28.7 percent, but throughout the rest of the industrialized world, the rate is 18.2 percent.[167] This tax makes it more expensive for businesses to operate and takes from them the capital they need to expand and hire new employees. Thus, both productivity and employment fall when business capital is taxed.

Although the definition of a free-market economic system is one in which the people and their choices (and not their government) regulate businesses, the opposite has now become standard practice. For example, if you make a simple decision to hire your neighbor to work for you in a small business out of your garage—even if it is just a lemonade stand—that decision will place you under the authority of regulations such as the National Labor Relations Act, the Age Discrimination Act, the Equal Pay Act, the Civil Rights Act of 1964, the Equal Employment Opportunity Act, the Americans With Disabilities Act, the Minimum Wage Act, and many others.

In fact, the government has enacted 38,000 new federal regulations in the past decade,[168] and 81,000 since 1993.[169] It now issues a new regulation at the average rate of one every three hours—

twenty-four hours a day, seven days a week. Just for the first nine months of 2012, the cost to implement these regulations was $1.8 trillion.[170] So, what does this do to business, and thus to citizens and consumers?

For a small business of twenty or fewer employees (and these businesses provide 80 percent of American jobs), the average cost to comply with federal workplace regulations is $7,645 per employee.[171] These costs are passed on to consumers, thereby raising the price of cars, food, lodging, clothing, services, and everything else. Additionally, 83 percent of small businesses say that the cost of these regulations prevents them from expanding their operations and hiring more employees.[172]

Furthermore, in a time comparison spanning more than a decade, the least-regulated businesses experienced a 63 percent growth in output and a 4 percent decline in labor expenses, while the most regulated industries had only a 33 percent growth with a 20 percent increase in labor expenses.[173] This means that the goods produced by regulated industries were much more expensive for consumers than goods from other industries. (By the way, remember the nearly $1 trillion that the government spent in 2008–2009 to bail out the four private industries of insurance, real estate, banking, and auto? Significantly, those four were among the most heavily government-regulated industries; those that operated under a full free-market system did not need a bailout.[174])

Business regulations serve as a government tax on consumers, and this tax is often called a hidden tax, for consumers do not recognize how much less their goods and services would cost if employers were not forced to comply with so many onerous regulations. (For all practical purposes, businesses and corporations do *not* pay taxes; only consumers do, for all business costs, including the cost of business taxes and regulations, are passed on to the customer by means of higher prices for goods.) The amount of this hidden tax on consumers was nearly twice as large as the amount collected last year through visible income taxes.[175]

NATIONAL DEFENSE

The arena of national defense is yet another category that has experienced fundamental change over recent years. Currently only 20 percent of the national budget is spent for defense,[176] but that percentage was much higher in previous generations. For example, defense spending was 39 percent of the federal budget in 1795 under President George Washington; 70 percent under President James Madison in 1815; 47 percent under President John Quincy Adams in 1825; 57 percent under President Andrew Jackson in 1835; and so forth.[177]

This higher percentage was reflective of the belief of Americans that a primary purpose of government was protection—to protect citizens in their persons and also to protect their God-given and constitutional rights. Consequently, President George Washington reminded Congress that "providing [funding] for the common defense will merit particular regard."[178] Why? Because, as Washington explained, "To be prepared for war is one of the most effectual means of preserving peace."[179] A strong military is the best means of protecting citizens and preventing war, for potential brigands will always attack the least armed and least prepared.

And just as it was the responsibility of government to protect the borders and homeland of citizens, Thomas Jefferson also affirmed:

> The persons and property of our citizens are entitled to the protection of our government in all places where they may lawfully go.[180]

But today protecting America and the rights of its citizens appears to no longer be a primary purpose for government. Jesus affirmed in Matthew 6:21 that you can tell where someone's priorities are by where their resources are placed, and the president and Congress have decided to steadily shrink the defense budget year after year through coming years.[181]

So if not defense, then what does the government now see as its primary purpose? Simply follow the money to answer that question.

The federal government now spends more than twice as much on Social Security and health programs as it does on defense (20 percent goes to defense, and 41 percent goes to the other two); another 13 percent of the budget goes toward welfare programs, 6 percent toward paying the interest on the burgeoning national debt, and the remaining 21 percent scattered among a variety of other social programs.[182] The emphasis clearly is on social spending (which is increasing annually) and not on defense (which is decreasing annually).

The Bible affirms that God ordained government to protect citizens and to administer justice (see Romans 13:3–4, 6) but that He placed social programs firmly in the hands of the individual, the family, and the church—but not the government. From a biblical perspective, America now has its priorities completely reversed.

TAXATION

To finance the ongoing growth of government and its explosion of expensive (and increasing) spending on "benefit" programs is very costly. So where does government get the money to pay for this? It must borrow it and go into debt, or it can collect it through taxes and fees. Currently it can, and does, both. But as its expenses continue to skyrocket, so does both its borrowing and its taxation.

Concerning the latter, in 1913 the top tax rate was 7 percent and was reserved only for the wealthiest—those who made $500,000 or more (the equivalent of $11.6 million today).[183] By 1990 the top tax rate was 28 percent, and it too was reserved for the "wealthy"—which at that time had been lowered to include those making more than $32,450.[184] By 2013 the top 1 percent of the wealthiest Americans paid 30 percent of the total revenues collected from income taxes[185] —certainly far more than their "fair share." Government, in its attempt to garner more money to fund its spending addiction, keeps raising tax rates and dropping thresholds so as to place higher taxes on lower levels of income.

Sadly most Americans are unaware of how much they pay in taxes, for so many taxes are hidden, and others are spread among various collecting agencies and fees. One way of understanding the total amount paid is through what is called Tax Freedom Day. This is the day of the year when the nation, collectively, has earned enough money to pay its total tax bill (federal, state, and local) for that year. In 2014 Tax Freedom Day fell on April 21.[186] This means that for the entirety of every workday and work hour before April 21, the totality of what each individual made belonged to the government; only what was earned after April 21 belonged to the individual. (By the way, in 1900 Tax Freedom Day fell on January 22.)[187] Taxes were so high in 2014 that Americans spent more on paying taxes than they did on food, clothing, and housing combined.[188]

The steadily repeating cycle of increasing spending, increasing debt, and increasing taxes, followed by another round of more spending, more debt, and more taxes, and so forth, leads to the result predicted by Thomas Jefferson, who forewarned:

> If we run into such debts, as that we must be taxed in our meat and in our drink, in our necessaries and our comforts, in our labors and our amusements, for our callings and our creeds, as the people of England are, our people, like them, must come to labor sixteen hours in the twenty-four, give the earnings of fifteen of these to the government for their debts and daily expenses; and the sixteenth being insufficient to afford us bread, we must live, as they now do, on oatmeal and potatoes; have no time to think, no means of calling the mismanagers to account.... This example reads to us the salutary lesson, that private fortunes are destroyed by public as well as by private extravagance. And this is the tendency of all human governments. A departure from principle in one instance becomes a precedent for a second; that second for a third; and so on, till the bulk of the society is reduced to be mere automatons of misery, to have no sensibilities left but for sinning and suffering.... And the fore horse of this frightful team is public debt. Taxation follows that, and in its train wretchedness and oppression.[189]

In Summary

The more secular and biblically illiterate America becomes, the less is the genuine purpose of government being fulfilled, whether in the issues of morality, life, education, economics, business, self-defense, taxation, or any other. Government now regularly invades and usurps the responsibilities of the individual, the family, and the church, thus violating the jurisdictional line that Jesus Himself drew in Matthew 22:21. Significantly, a government will be limited only so long as it understands that there is a power greater than itself to which it must answer—God Almighty, who not only ordained government but also gave specific directives on how it was to operate. Whenever government becomes secular, it ceases to be limited, for it recognizes no power higher than itself and therefore becomes the supreme authority on all subjects and in all venues—as has now become the case in America.

THE CONDITION OF THE CHRISTIAN CHURCH

O NE OF THE indisputable reasons for the long-term strength of the United States has been the powerful roles that individual faith and religious institutions have played. People have traditionally drawn their sense of morality, values, and core beliefs from the religious teaching they received through the churches they attended. Core relationships were formed from the pool of people they met at their church. Their children received basic religious instruction from the church, reinforcing the values and morals taught in the home.

The pastor was often a respected public leader who would speak to the issues of the day from the pulpit, based upon the authority of God's Word. Churches took seriously their responsibility to help the needy and disadvantaged while also providing compassionate support for members who fell on hard times or encountered crises. The Genesis 12 principle of being blessed to be a blessing to others (vv. 1–3) was one of the hallmarks of the American Church, evident in how Church resources were distributed to serve members and nonmembers alike.

During the past quarter century, as American society shifted from being an other-centered to a self-centered culture, the Church has often acquiesced to the expectations of the culture rather than challenging those expectations and providing leadership during a transitional era. While the nation's churches are still among the most active organizations in helping people with material needs, the general mentality about the role of the Church in society has undergone a wholesale redefinition.

Over the past thirty years we have witnessed a major shift in how Americans articulate their perception of the purposes of the organized Church. For an institution that so many millions of Americans have accepted as part of their life for the duration of their life, surprisingly few people have thought much about what they expect the Church to be and to do—either at the local, congregational level or as the Church universal. Most people think simplistically about the idea of "church," noting that churches provide teaching, religious events, programs, and support services but little beyond that.

An example of the lack of focus directed toward churches comes from a recent Barna Group survey that asked people to identify the most important thing their local church needed to do in order to make a positive contribution to people's lives and to the life of the community. The most common answer was "I don't know," offered by three out of ten respondents.[1] Only five other activities were listed by at least 3 percent of the public. Those efforts included addressing poverty (mentioned by 29 percent), cultivating biblical values (14 percent), serving families and their children (13 percent), providing recovery programs and support for addicts (10 percent), and helping people to deal with workplace and financial issues (7 percent).[2]

What makes that list so interesting is that it is significantly different in nature from the way the Bible describes the ultimate purposes of the Church (that is, the aggregate body of believers in Jesus Christ, not simply a local gathering that meets in a building for events under the direction of a paid clergyman). The Scriptures seem to suggest that the primary purposes of the Church are to worship God; to guide and prepare people to become vibrant disciples of Christ; to serve people by addressing their needs; to love God and people in consistent and tangible ways, including through sharing the hope of the gospel; and to obey God's commands, as conveyed through the Bible. Obedience, in particular, covers a lot of ground, since the Bible contains so many principles and commands relayed by God to His people.

Another way of understanding what the Church should look like is to examine the early Church as described in the Book of Acts. In that narrative, especially in the first eight chapters, we see the followers of Jesus engaged in worship, evangelism, discipleship, stewardship, community service, and mutual-care relationships among the believers.

If some combination of these objectives form the ultimate purpose of God's Church, how is that body of people doing in America in the early twenty-first century?

MEASURES OF HEALTH: RELIGIOUS ACTIVITY

One way we could assess the health and vitality of the Church in our society is to examine what Americans do related to their faith, recognizing that about eight out of ten adults consider themselves to be Christian.[3] We can explore that in two ways: where things stand today and how things have changed over the past decade.[4]

Most of the Christian churches in the United States track certain measures of the spiritual health of the congregation. We mention this because the behaviors they track are a great example of the truism that "you get what you measure." Barna Group studies among Protestant pastors found that the five measures used by most churches are worship service attendance, dollars donated, number of programs offered, number of staff people hired, and square footage of the facilities available for ministry use. If you consider the implications of these five measures, it becomes clear why America has become obsessed with growing "megachurches." In the type of ministry that results from satisfying these criteria, quantity is more important than quality in ministry.

Most importantly, these standards are inadequate because they do not reflect the reason God sent Jesus to our planet. Yes, these are measurable behaviors, but the outcomes they provide are not very meaningful. Jesus did not die to fill auditoriums, raise money, offer religious programs, hire employees, and build more extravagant campuses. If He had, these would be the perfect measures of the "success" of a church. Because that was not His mission, we need to evaluate other kinds of behaviors and beliefs.

Even with that caveat in mind, it is instructive to examine some of the most frequently studied religious activities, such as church attendance and Bible reading. There have been substantial drop-offs in both of those activities in the past decade. Church attendance has declined from 43 percent to 36 percent.[5] Bible reading undertaken other than when a person is at a church event has dropped even more, from 44 percent to 33 percent.[6]

Given the slide in church attendance, it is unfortunate but not surprising to discover that the proportion of adults who are "unchurched"—that is, who have not attended a church service or event in the past six months other than a special event, such as a wedding or funeral—has climbed from 34 percent to 47 percent in ten years.[7] Notice that the unchurched figure is now dangerously close to the 50 percent mark—indicating that half of American adults avoid church life.

Some of the "peripheral" religious activities have fared no better. For instance, both adult Sunday school attendance and small-group participation have been halved in the past ten years. Only one out of ten adults is found in a Sunday school setting on any given weekend, down from 21 percent in 2004. Just 9 percent of adults are presently active in a small group, compared to 20 percent ten years ago.[8]

Praying has dropped noticeably, from 83 percent in 2004 to 78 percent now. That's not a huge reduction, but it is certainly movement in the wrong direction. Even in a society where increasing numbers of people describe themselves as "spiritual but not religious" and where spontaneous spirituality is often preferred to planned religious engagement, prayer seems to be an ideal fit in the desired religious agenda. However, prayer is on the decline.

If the adage "You can tell where a person's heart is by how they spend their money" has any validity, then the Church is in bigger trouble than many people realize. In 2004, slightly less than two-thirds of adults (64 percent) contributed money to a church during the prior year. In 2014, though, that statistic fell all the way to 45 percent—less than half of the public! The amount of money donated to churches leaves much to be desired too. In 2003 the median annual household giving to churches was $1,362 (in 2013 dollars). In 2013 the household median had risen by just twenty-four dollars to $1,386—an increase of less than 2 percent after a decade. The typical household that donates to a church gives less than 3 percent of its annual income to churches and other religious causes.[9]

Table 8-1
RELIGIOUS ACTIVITY 2004–2014[10]

Activity	All adults		Born again	
	2004	2014	2004	2014
Attended church, in past seven days	43%	36%	60%	60%
Read the Bible, other than at a church event, in past seven days	44	33	67	60
Attended adult Sunday school in past seven days	21	10	37	22
Attended small group in past seven days	20	9	33	17
Volunteered at a church in past seven days	24	12	36	24
Prayed to God in past seven days	83	78	98	98
Attended church, read Bible, and prayed to God in past seven days	28	28	48	48
Donated to a church in past year	64	45		
Shared faith in Jesus Christ with a nonbeliever in past year	n/a	n/a	55	37
Unchurched (no church attendance past six months)	34	47	15	20

One other religious behavior we have tracked for years is what we labeled "active faith," referring to a combination of attending a church service, reading the Bible, and praying to God during the same week. Amidst the fall in every other religious behavior we have measured, it is intriguing to find that the proportion of adults who engage in all three of these efforts in a given week has remained stable since 2004. In other words, there is a segment of roughly one out of every four Americans who are deeply committed to a religious routine that includes those three endeavors, regardless of how the culture around them is changing and people's religious life is being redefined.[11]

MEASURES OF HEALTH: RELIGIOUS BELIEF

In the past ten years there has been a lot of change in people's religious beliefs too. Unlike the changes in people's religious behavior, some of the belief shifts have moved more people toward a more biblical understanding of certain matters of faith.

For instance, while the proportion of adults who are firmly convinced that Jesus Christ lived a sinless life has remained steady in the past decade, the proportion that is convinced that He did not live a sinless life has declined slightly (from 27 percent to 19 percent).[12] In like manner, the percentage of adults who are strongly persuaded that Satan is real has remained virtually unchanged since 2004, but the percentage that strongly believes Satan is just a symbol of evil but not a living entity has actually fallen substantially (from 42 percent to 29 percent).[13] Likewise, there has been no change in the number of people who firmly reject the idea that you can earn your way into heaven (28 percent), while the percentage that strongly agrees that such a means to eternal salvation exists has dropped from one-third to one-quarter of the public.[14]

It is worth noting that about one-third of the population falls somewhere between these positions on each of those measures. In other words, they may lean toward one answer or the other but remain unconvinced. Of course, the absence of strong or firm convictions on such seminal spiritual matters usually means that they give little thought and attach limited significance to whatever the "correct" answer might be on such questions.

Unfortunately, not every theological perspective has experienced such positive change. There has been a huge drop in the percentage of people who strongly affirm that their religious faith is very important in their life today, declining from almost three-quarters of adults in 2004 to just half today.[15] Fewer people now have an orthodox, biblical perception of the nature of God—omnipotent, omniscient, Creator of the universe, engaged with the world—than was true ten years ago (a seven-point reduction, to about six out of ten Americans).[16]

The Bible remains a bit of a mystery to millions of Americans. Two-thirds of adults believe the Bible is the actual or inspired Word of God, a drop from three-quarters less than a decade ago.[17] In fact, there has been a concurrent eight-point rise in the percentage of adults who now argue that the Bible is not holy literature at all but rather a book of "good teachings" composed by men based on their own ideas and experiences.[18]

The percentage of evangelicals and born-again Christians has also remained relatively flat over the course of the past decade. Evangelicals—defined by answers to ten theological questions, not a self-description—are now just 6 percent of the population.* Born-

---

* The ten questions we ask to identify someone as an evangelical are: (1) Turning to a different topic now, do you consider yourself to be Christian, Jewish, or of some other religious faith? (Appropriate answer: Christian.) (2) Do you agree or disagree (response probed: Is that strongly or somewhat?)? The Bible is totally accurate in all of the principles it teaches. (Appropriate answer: strongly agree.) (3) Do you agree or disagree? You, personally, have a responsibility to tell other people your religious beliefs. (Appropriate answer: strongly agree.) (4) Do you agree or disagree? Your religious faith is very important in your life. (Appropriate answer: strongly agree.) (5) Do you agree or disagree? The devil, or Satan, is not a living being but is a symbol of evil. (Appropriate answer: strongly disagree.) (6) Do you agree or disagree? If a person is generally good or does enough good things for others during his life, he will earn a place in heaven. (Appropriate answer: strongly disagree.) (7) Do you agree or disagree? When He lived on earth, Jesus Christ was human and committed sins, like other people. (Appropriate answer: strongly disagree.) (8) There are many different beliefs about God or a higher power. Which one of the following descriptions comes closest to what you, per-sonally, believe about God? (Appropriate answer: God is the all-powerful, all-knowing, perfect Creator of the universe who rules the world today.) (9) Have you ever made a personal commitment to Jesus Christ that is still important in your life today? (Appropriate answer: yes.) (10) I'm going to read some statements about what will happen to you after you die. Please tell me which one of these state-ments best describes your own belief about what will happen to you after you die. (After reading statements, ask) Which one of those comes closest to what you believe? (Appropriate answer: When you die, you will go to heaven because you have confessed your sins and have accepted Jesus Christ as your Savior.).

again Christians—a segment that includes evangelicals but is based on responses to two questions about life after death, not a self-description*—are down ever so slightly, from 38 percent a decade ago to 36 percent today.[19]

---

* The two questions posed to classify someone as a born-again Christian are: (1) Have you ever made a personal commitment to Jesus Christ that is still important in your life today? (Appropriate answer: yes.) (2) I'm going to read some statements about what will happen to you after you die. Please tell me which one of these statements best describes your own belief about what will happen to you after you die. (After reading statements, ask) Which one of those comes closest to what you believe? (Appropriate answer: When you die you will go to heaven because you have confessed your sins and have accepted Jesus Christ as your Savior.) Note: These two questions are part of the evangelical filter as well. Consequently, a person can be born again but not evangelical; a person cannot be evangelical but not born again.

TABLE 8-2

RELIGIOUS BELIEFS[20]

Belief	All adults		Born again	
	2004	2014	2004	2014
When Jesus Christ was on earth, He committed sins				
strongly agree	27%	19%	21%	14%
strongly disagree	39	37	61	62
Satan is a symbol of evil, not a living being				
strongly agree	42	29	39	22
strongly disagree	26	25	38	43
Have a responsibility to share my religious beliefs with other people who believe differently				
strongly agree	35	23	56	44
strongly disagree	44	33	72	63
My religious faith is very important in my life these days				
strongly agree	72	53	91	83
If a person is good enough or does enough good things for other people, he can earn a place in heaven				
strongly agree	34	25	25	18
strongly disagree	28	28	48	45
God is the all-knowing, all-powerful Creator of the universe who still rules the world today	69	62	93	92
Self-identified Christian	81	78	97	98
Evangelical Christian	7	6	18	16
Born-again Christian	38	36	n/a	n/a

BORN-AGAIN CHRISTIANS

Naturally, how you define a group of people goes a long way toward determining what you discover about that group. In the case of born-again Christians, testing by the Barna Group has revealed that if you define them by using a self-identification approach in surveys—that is, simply asking survey respondents whether or not they consider themselves to be born again—you get a group of people who are reacting to the desirability of the label more than the content of their faith. Specifically, among people who call themselves "born again," roughly one-third also admit that they have no ongoing relationship with Jesus Christ. Meanwhile among those who do not embrace the self-identification of "born again," more than one-fourth of those people have an ongoing relationship with Christ, have confessed their sins to Jesus, and believe they will have eternal salvation solely because of what Jesus did for them on the cross. In response to that discovery, the Barna Group thus uses the two theological questions that get at commitment and perspective on salvation rather than rely upon the self-report that we know to be inaccurate. (See previous footnote for the actual questions used.)

However, even when using this refined approach, the profile of born-again Christians is disappointing. For instance, we know that in most instances, the attitudes, values, and behavior of born-again Christians are very similar to those of the non-born-again public. And in most cases, even when the absolute levels of a given behavior or perspective are distinct, the change patterns that have emerged over the past decade are virtually identical between the born-again and non-born-again populations.

For example, while a higher proportion of born-again adults than Americans in general read the Bible during any given week (60 percent), such reading is down by seven points since 2004.[21] Similarly, adults' Sunday school and small-group participation have only about half as many born-again participants now as was true in 2004.[22]

Tellingly, a majority of born-again adults had shared their faith in Christ with a nonbeliever during the six months prior to their interview back in 2004, but only one-third (35 percent) did so in 2014.[23]

When it comes to beliefs, the same reality is evident: higher percentages of born-again adults embrace biblical views, but those percentages are on the decline and are hardly indicative of a mass of people who have embraced the Bible's teachings as true. This was evident in their responses to questions about the accuracy of the principles taught in the Bible, the perceived responsibility to share their religious beliefs, and the importance of their religious faith.[24] As with the population at large, the beliefs of born-again adults were stable or slightly more biblical compared to ten years ago regarding the holiness of Christ, the existence of Satan, the nature of God, and ideas regarding the means to salvation.[25]

Losing Cultural Influence

Overall, then, the research indicates that most people who can be classified in some way as Christian are neither growing deeper nor more orthodox in their faith. Given that the best way to persuade people to follow Christ is by believers demonstrating what that looks like in action, the question then arises as to how well Christians are carrying out the religious beliefs they profess to believe.

First, we have to point out that while a large majority of Americans say they are either "religious" or "spiritual" people, focusing on their faith is not a significant priority in life. In fact, only one out of every eight adults (12 percent) says that their faith is their highest priority. The outcome is slightly better among born-again Christians (20 percent) but not enough to make a discernible difference.[26]

The limited energy people put into living their faith principles is further demonstrated by answers to a question regarding the most important goal in their life today. If it is true that we were created by God for the purpose of knowing, loving, and obeying Him, then everything we do ought to be subsumed under the challenge of first and foremost expressing complete love to God and devoting ourselves to knowing and obeying Him as completely as we are able. Yet when we ask Americans about their most important goals in life, most people's primary goal has little to do with God or faith. Instead, their attention revolves around personal accomplishments and possessions.[27] Specifically, a Barna Group study revealed America's goals to be as follows:[28]

Maintaining good health	20%
Getting a better job	15%
Being a good parent	10%
Taking care of family	8%
Surviving life's challenges/hardships	7%
Being a better Christian	6%
Experiencing greater happiness/fulfillment	5%
Reducing spending/debt	5%
Making more money	4%
Self-improvement	4%
Having a better relationship with God	2%
Going to heaven	2%
Having a good marriage	1%
Helping/serving others	1%

None of these goals is necessarily bad, wrong, or beyond the boundaries of what God would bless. But few of these goals reflect our primary life purpose of knowing and loving God. And if you were hoping that the research showed born-again adults had a different ranking of life goals, you would be disappointed. Born-again individuals were identical to the population at large in their responses with a single exception: they were twice as likely to list some aspect of becoming a better Christian as their main goal.[29] However, just 12 percent of the born-again segment listed that.[30] In total only one out of every six born-again people identified a goal related directly to faith as their top goal.[31]

How is it possible that so many Americans spend so much time, money, and effort associating with the Christian faith, only to emerge with their faith showing such little impact on their life choices? Much of the problem relates to their worldview. Every person has a worldview, regardless of age, educational achievement, nationality, faith of choice, or political ideology. A worldview is simply a mental filter that helps us to organize information about the world and our preferences in ways that help us respond to life's circumstances so that our behavior is consistent with what we believe to be true, right, and proper.

You could not make it through a day in this complicated world without a worldview to help you make sense of reality and respond in ways that are appropriate for who you are. A clear and coherent worldview minimizes the chances of you possessing contradictory views as well as reducing the likelihood of behaving in ways that are at odds with what you truly believe or value. An intentional and well-conceived worldview allows you to reduce your internal stress and to have greater impact by communicating and acting in ways that are consistent and relevant.[32]

While every person's worldview is unique, we all share some pivotal perspectives about the world and our place in it that enable us to identify a dozen or so common worldviews. One of those is often described as a "biblical worldview." As the name implies, this perspective is based upon accepting central precepts taught in the Bible as being true and significant. Among the elements that are found in a biblical worldview are these:

+ The God of Abraham is the one, true God. He is eternal, omnipotent, omniscient, loving, just, and good.

+ Everything that exists was created by God and exists to fulfill His will.

+ The purpose of peoples' lives is to know and love God, which implies worshipping and obeying Him, as well as serving Him and other people.

+ Jesus Christ came to the earth to be a sacrifice to God the Father for our sins. He lived on the earth, taught truth, died an unjust and painful death on our behalf, was resurrected from death, and is alive today.

+ Satan is the enemy of God and has been given temporary influence over the world. While he wishes to and believes he will one day overthrow God, he is incapable of that act.

♦ God exists in three unique but indivisible persons: God the Father, God the Son, and God the Holy Spirit.

♦ God knows and loves every person intimately and desires for each person to constantly and continually seek a deeper, interactive relationship with Him.

♦ The Bible is God's inspired and infallible guide for humankind; we are to know and obey His commands and live in accordance with His expressed principles. It is the only tangible source of absolute moral and spiritual truth.

♦ Every human being has sinned against God and therefore needs a savior; Jesus Christ is that Savior, and we can have an everlasting relationship with God, even beyond our years on the earth, only through our confession of sin and embracing the forgiveness of those sins by Jesus Christ.

♦ All resources and material things were created by God and belong to Him. We may be granted temporary use of those resources for the purpose of advancing His agenda.

♦ All of the true followers of Jesus Christ constitute the Church. God desires for those followers to live and work in unity with one another, to pursue God's plans, and to bring as many people as possible into a personal relationship with Him through His Son Jesus.

There are more components that can be added to a biblical worldview—indeed, by definition, the entirety of scriptural truth forms a complete biblical worldview—but the points listed here provide a viable summary of many of the crucial truths that are foundational to such a perspective. The importance of these views is that they form a cohesive understanding of life and shape our response to daily circumstances. The failure to adopt any of these points of view—or a belief that they do not matter—causes responses that are out of sync with God's plan and desires.

Millions of dollars are spent annually tracking what we buy, where we buy it, what celebrities we like, which politicians we would vote for, what TV shows we watch, and how much money we will spend on nonessentials. When the Barna Group created a survey about fifteen years ago to track the prevalence of a biblical worldview, it was a novelty. Since that measurement process began, the results have consistently shown that few Americans possess a biblical worldview. Today just 4 percent of American adults and only 10 percent of born-again Christians possess a biblical worldview.[33] In a society as driven by pop trends as ours, the likelihood of behaving like a biblical Christian without the guiding force of a biblical worldview is slim to none.

Shockingly, there has been little overt concern about the lack of a biblical worldview of Americans. Part of the reason for that is the primary religious teachers of Christians are their pastors—and only half of Protestant pastors possess a biblical worldview.[34] Pastors cannot and would not teach others what they do not know or believe. And they certainly will not make a fuss about the absence of a biblical worldview among their congregants because it would reflect poorly on their own teaching and leadership abilities. Surveys among pastors have shown that about three out of every four Protestant pastors believe that their church "intentionally and continually assists people in developing a biblical worldview,"[35] and more than nine out of ten pastors contend that their church is effective in that work.[36] They are either being coy or they are seriously misinformed. Of course, when half of the pastors do not have a biblical worldview, they certainly are incapable of providing for others what they do not have for themselves. Among the other half, the development of a biblical worldview rarely emerges as a critical ministry objective, so those pastors may be providing accurate information: their church is being as effective as necessary in developing something they do not hold as a high priority.

If American society is to make a U-turn and regain cultural

health and stability, our population must be aware of what a biblical worldview is and be committed to integrating such a life perspective into its minds and hearts. Possessing a correct biblical worldview is central to cultural change because we do what we believe. If we do not believe the principles and precepts communicated in the Bible, we will not live in harmony with them. Instead, we will pursue actions that are consistent with what we really believe—the things that matter to us. Thus, there is a disconnection between people's faith and lifestyle. People say that their religious faith is very important, because having a slate of religious beliefs gives us a feeling of completeness and righteousness, but usually that faith has nothing to do with how we live. That wall of separation between intellectual faith and personal action is exactly what has placed the United States in the predicament we have been describing in this book.

Despite our separation of professed faith and actual biblical application, millions of Americans have a sense that something is wrong. Two-thirds of American adults—and four-fifths of born-again Christians—are concerned about the moral condition of the nation. Three-quarters of all Americans are worried about the future of our nation. Two out of three adults are discouraged by the direction the country is moving. Three-quarters of us believe the country is more divided now than at any moment during our lifetime. Four out of five citizens argue that most voters—perhaps including themselves?—do not know enough about what is going on in the country to be informed voters.[37] But what are we going to do about it?

Perhaps nudged into discomfort by the Holy Spirit, most Americans are uneasily seeking to reconcile their faith and lifestyle. Six out of ten adults—including three-quarters of all born-again adults—say they would like to know how faith and spirituality relate to current issues they are facing in life.[38] Further, three-quarters of all adults—born again or not—say they want to figure out how to live a more meaningful life.[39] It is this persistent unease that gives us hope that the situation can be turned around. Without that internal nagging to keep searching for a better understanding of truth and purpose, America would be dead in the water, resigned to becoming just another secularized society with a dead soul and dark future.

So when more than four out of every five adults say they have a vibrant, meaningful, satisfying, growing, and important relationship with God,[40] it is hard to take that seriously. Have Americans completely deluded themselves into believing they have an intimate and authentic relationship with the living, holy God of creation while at the same time being completely ignorant of what that relationship could and should be? Or are they simply marking time while they await an experience or insight that will more fully enlighten them and deepen their connection with Him?

CULTURAL INFLUENCE

One of the difficulties facing Christian leaders these days is the desire for them and their churches to be popular and accepted rather than biblically obedient. Genuine leadership is about helping the greatest number of people possible by doing what is morally right. It takes inner strength and deep conviction to be an effective leader. Pandering to public tastes and preferences is a quick road to disaster, since a public without a biblical worldview is susceptible to the latest and greatest arguments.

As a case in point, realize that when adults were asked to identify the greatest failures and negative contributions of the Christian Church to American society in the recent past, the public has no lack of ideas to share. Among the most common criticisms are that churches have become too political, have opposed same-sex marriage, have been intolerant and bigoted, believe that Jesus is the only means to forgiveness and eternal salvation, and have opposed abortion.[41]

The response of the organized Church has largely been one of silence or apology. While there have certainly been instances where a given leader's words or tactics are indefensible, in a far greater number of cases the greatest offense has been the unwillingness of Christian leaders to provide a biblically appropriate response.

An increasingly secularized culture has been challenging the Church for several decades—and, emboldened by victory after victory in the public square, that culture is increasingly defiant and disrespectful toward the fundamental principles that built this nation. Consider the turnabout that has occurred in the past quarter century in this culture war.

Our public, taxpayer-funded schools, where education was based upon and friendly toward the Christian faith and its Scriptures, now disallow prayer, Bible reading, religious gatherings, and moral teaching. Millions of our schoolchildren are medicated in order to control them, taught that they evolved from apes, told that all faiths are equal (except Christianity, which is portrayed as an inferior, undesirable faith), and trained to believe that there are no absolute moral truths. A substantial portion of school budgets are now funded through gambling proceeds.

Our Christian homes, which were once considered the heart of Christian teaching and accountability, are now restricted by increasingly intrusive laws that preclude parents from disciplining or from defending the rights of their children, sometimes going so far as to separate children and families that do not meet government approval. Marriage has been redefined and overtaken by the state, millions of children have been legally killed in the womb, and divorce has been legally minimized.

The government has reduced religious freedoms, substituted federal policies and programs for parental guidance and responsibility, and replaced God as the defender and provider for the American people. Moral challenges have been labeled "hate speech," and "intolerance" is backed by onerous government sanctions and penalties. The threat of the IRS hovers over churches that dare to speak, the executive branch uses "executive orders" that skirt the need for legislative approval and accountability, and the unelected judicial branch unilaterally makes laws that are similarly unalterable by the people or any elected official.

The entertainment industry produces a flood of immoral content that seduces our children, inflames the lust of our adults, and dulls the minds of the population. Celebrities are held up as virtuous and worthy of worship while Jesus Christ is questioned and devalued. The biblical worldview is mocked while alternative worldviews based on individual feelings and distortions of biblical truth are elevated. New technologies are adopted that overwhelm people's minds and hearts with garbage while censorship, licensing, and fines are used to minimize public exposure to biblical truths.

WHERE IS THE LEADERSHIP?

In the face of these attacks on religious liberty, freedom, and biblical truth, literally nine out of ten Christian pastors, by their own admission, have retreated to the safety of their church grounds, refusing to take up the battle and to equip their people for that battle.[42] In the ultimate irony the demise of our culture is often used in these pastors' sermons as the motivation proposed for people to spend more time in the Scriptures—so they will better understand the destruction of our nation and its people as it takes place before their very eyes. There is no call to action to the people in the sanctuary beyond satisfying the typical measures of church success: attending regularly, giving generously, and enabling the organization to expand.

There is no acknowledgment that the failure of the Christian body to do as both the Bible and the US Constitution encourage— that is, to stand up for righteousness and freedom—will result in a nation where Christianity itself could one day be outlawed as an intolerant, exclusive faith system that is detrimental to the health and well-being of the country, where preaching the Word of God is construed as "hate speech," and where the Bible is banned because of its politically incorrect teaching. Instead, the expectation is that churched people will know the Scriptures better and eagerly wait for God do something miraculous—without recognizing that the Scriptures they are studying consistently demonstrate that God always uses His genuine followers to change the world, regardless of how many are available.

Waiting for God to show up and do the miraculous sounds like a demonstration of faith, but it is really a flawed, unbiblical strategy. God does not call upon His followers to wait for miracles to change the world. Instead, He is waiting on us to get moving and bring forth those changes.

When a majority of the senior pastors of Protestant churches proclaim that there must be a separation of religion and politics and that it is unacceptable for pastors to use the pulpit to incite people to "political" action[43] (that is, to exert any biblical influence on public policy and thus shape the culture), we are a nation in grave danger. Who else besides our pastors would be the protectors of biblical truth and action? Why would we not expect our spiritual leaders to guide our public policy reflections based upon biblical exegesis? What does leadership mean if not motivating, mobilizing, resourcing, and directing people to pursue a strategic course of action to bring our society in line with the purposes and precepts of a loving and almighty God?

Earlier we noted that the proportion of adults who are unchurched has been steadily rising to the point where nearly half of Americans are now without any regular church connection. Why is that number rising so dramatically? A major explanation is that in their eyes—and the eyes of millions of currently churched adults who are likely to join the ranks of the unchurched in the decade to come—the Christian church does not stand for anything signifi-cant, positive, or tangible. Sure, it may teach a bunch of ideas and stories, but a narrative that does not produce action or life change is simply entertainment. If that's the case, then the real challenge is who entertains best: Hollywood, Broadway, Disneyland, Nashville, or the local church? The answer might be a toss-up, but you can be sure "church" is not among the finalists vying for supremacy in that contest.

Essentially, we have reached the point at which it is indisputable that most church leaders are failing to lead, and most Christians are refusing to take their spiritual growth into their own hands but are waiting for someone else to do something. With our backs against the wall, it is time for the believers in America to clarify their beliefs and put them into action in order to save what is left of the freedoms that so many Americans have fought and even died for. To refuse to engage in the battle of the day is a rejection of their sacrifice and a repudiation of unequivocal biblical directives. To fail to energetically defend those rights and freedoms will produce a nation that has abandoned its heart and soul. To surrender the right to fight for the ways of God is a rejection of the God who provided the written instructions to pursue righteousness, in His name, at any cost.

Chapter 9

RESTORING THE GOVERNMENT

BY NOW YOU may have learned many new things—perhaps statistical measurements, perchance Bible positions on specific issues, or possibly facts about the current condition of the church or the government. The bad news is that all of this shows us exactly where we are at this moment, and it is not a pretty picture. In fact, the outlook is dismal if not outright bleak. But the good news is that it doesn't have to stay this way. This is what this book is all about.

The first step to substantive change—however simplistic it might sound—begins with securing correct knowledge. The apostle Paul taught the early Christians that the key to leaving old habits and adopting new ones is to be renewed in the mind (Eph. 4:22–24). This requires inputting the right information.

REDISCOVER THE BIBLE

The Bible tells us to seek sound knowledge,[1] and *seek* is a proactive verb that requires intentional activity by the individual. It takes deliberate effort to get the proper knowledge on any subject, and it rarely comes from the easy-to-access mainstream-media sources, whether print, broadcast, or online, for that profession has been documented as holding some of the most secular and antibiblical viewpoints of any in the nation.[2]

The first and most important of sources by which biblical citizens must shape their view of civil government is the Bible. This sounds like a religious cliché, but in this instance it is not, for to do this correctly will involve looking at the Bible in a manner very differently from the way it has been examined over the last half-century. Recall that in John Locke's 1690 work that had such a profound influence on the thinking of America's Founding Fathers, he invoked the Bible more than fifteen hundred times to illustrate the proper operation of civil government. In doing so, he indisputably demonstrated that the Bible is neither silent nor neutral on this subject.

But most Christians today know hardly any of these verses. They must therefore rediscover and relearn the Bible, approaching it with a distinctly fresh and open-minded viewpoint, uncontaminated by the modern biases of compartmentalized and narrow thinking. The Bible is as essential to a proper understanding of civil government as it is to every other area of life. As President Teddy Roosevelt affirmed:

> Almost every man who has by his life-work added to the sum of human achievement of which the race is proud, of which our people are proud, almost every such man has based his life-work largely upon the teachings of the Bible.... Among the very greatest men a disproportionately large number have been diligent and close students of the Bible at first hand.[3]

Founding Father Elias Boudinot, a president of Congress during the American Revolution and a framer of the Bill of Rights, reaffirmed the same truth, declaring:

> Were you to ask me to recommend the most valuable book in the world, I should fix on the Bible as the most instructive, both to the wise and ignorant. Were you to ask me for one [book], affording the most rational and pleasing entertainment to the inquiring mind, I should repeat, it is the Bible: and should you renew the inquiry, for the best philosophy, or the most interesting history, I should still urge you to look into your Bible. I would make it, in short, the Alpha and Omega of knowledge.[4]

Numerous other civil leaders reiterated this message:

> [The Bible] is a book worth more than all the other books that were ever printed.[5]
>
> —PATRICK HENRY

> All the miseries and evils which men suffer from vice, crime, ambition, injustice, oppression, slavery, and war, proceed from their despising or neglecting the precepts contained in the Bible.[6]
>
> —NOAH WEBSTER
> Schoolmaster to America

> The Bible is the best of all Books, for it is the Word of God, and teaches us the way to be happy *in this world* and in the next. Continue therefore to read it, and to regulate your life by its precepts.[7]
>
> —JOHN JAY
> Original Chief Justice of the US Supreme Court
> Coauthor of *The Federalist Papers*
> (emphasis added)

> The Bible contains more knowledge necessary to man in his present state, than any other book in the world.[8]

> By renouncing the Bible, philosophers swing from their moorings upon all moral subjects....It is the only correct map of the human heart that ever has been published.[9]
>
> —BENJAMIN RUSH
> Signer of The Declaration

> The Bible is the best book in the world.[10]
>
> —PRESIDENT JOHN ADAMS

> I suggest a nationwide reading of the Holy Scriptures...for a renewed and strengthening contact with those eternal truths and majestic principles which have inspired such measure of true greatness as this nation has achieved.[11]
>
> —PRESIDENT FRANKLIN DELANO ROOSEVELT

The Bible is the best of books and I wish it were in the hands of everyone....Especially should the Bible be placed in the hands of the young. It is the best school book in the world....I would that all of our people were brought up under the influence of that Holy Book.[12]

—PRESIDENT ZACHARY TAYLOR

[The Bible] is the best gift God has given to men. All the good Saviour gave to the world was communicated through this book. But for it we could not know right from wrong.[13]

—PRESIDENT ABRAHAM LINCOLN

No book in the world deserves to be so unceasingly studied, and so profoundly meditated upon as the Bible.[14]

The first, and almost the only book, deserving such universal recommendation, is the Bible.[15]

—PRESIDENT JOHN QUINCY ADAMS

Significantly, in 1848 John Quincy Adams' writings on the Bible and its teachings were published to make his wise counsel available to all Americans. In that work Adams openly acknowledged:

I have myself, for many years, made it a practice to read through the Bible once every year....My custom is, to read four or five chapters every morning, immediately after rising from my bed. It employs about an hour of my time, and seems to me the most suitable manner of beginning the day.[16]

It was a common practice in previous generations for Christians to read the Bible from cover to cover each year, and this should also be our practice today. Sadly less than one out of every four of today's professing Christians say they have read through the entire Bible in the course of their lifetime, much less in a single year.[17] Until Christians regain their knowledge of the Bible, American government will never become sound, for it is merely a reflection of what the people know and believe. If they don't embrace biblical truths and principles, neither will their government.

Every Christian should therefore make the personal commitment, "Over the next twelve months, I will read the complete Bible." To do this does not require the one hour a day that President Adams dedicated to his own personal Bible study; it only requires reading an average of three chapters a day, which usually consumes less than half an hour. Many tools are available to help accomplish this, including the *One Year Bible*—a Bible divided into 365 daily readings. And there are also numerous apps you can download that will even read out loud a daily Bible passage to you.

If you are wondering which version of the Bible to read, a recommendation from John Quincy Adams may be helpful. When asked the one he preferred, he replied:

> You ask me *what* Bible I take as the standard of my faith?...Any Bible that I can read and understand.[18]

Once you have read the Bible from cover to cover, don't stop there; read it again. When Founding Father Elias Boudinot was fifty-five years old (and had thus read through the Bible numerous times) he openly acknowledged:

> For nearly half a century, have I anxiously and critically studied that invaluable treasure [the Bible]; and I still scarcely ever take it up, that I do not find something new— that I do not receive some valuable addition to my stock of knowledge; or perceive some instructive fact, never observed before.[19]

Every time you go through the Bible, you will find new things, which is why the term "unsearchable" (Rom. 11:33, NKJV) is used in describing God's Word. You can never get to the bottom of all the knowledge it contains, and each time you go through it, you will find new applications and insights.

And when you read the Bible, don't make the mistake of reading it merely as a devotional work. John Quincy Adams's wise recommendation is particularly useful here:

> I have always endeavored to read it [the Bible] with the same spirit...which I now recommend to you: that is, with the intention and desire that it may contribute to my advancement in wisdom and virtue.[20]

Always read the Bible looking for application—search out something that will change the way you think (i.e., your wisdom) or the way you behave (i.e., your virtue).

KNOW THE CONSTITUTION

Just as all Christians should read, study, and intimately know the content of the Bible, so too should they read, study, and intimately know the content of the Constitution. As with our government, the Constitution also cannot be properly understood or correctly applied according to its original intent apart from a knowledge of the Bible and its teachings. Notice how often national political leaders across the centuries reaffirmed the interconnectedness between the Bible and American government:

> [The Bible is] the rock on which our Republic rests.[21]
> —PRESIDENT ANDREW JACKSON

> The Bible is...indispensable to the safety and permanence of our institutions; a free government cannot exist without religion and morals, and there cannot be morals without religion, nor religion without the Bible.[22]
> —PRESIDENT ZACHARY TAYLOR

> In the formative days of the Republic the directing influence the Bible exercised upon the fathers of the Nation is conspicuously evident....We cannot read the history of our rise and development as a Nation, without reckoning with

the place the Bible has occupied in shaping the advances of the Republic.[23]

—PRESIDENT FRANKLIN DELANO ROOSEVELT

The fundamental basis of this Nation's law was given to Moses on the Mount. The fundamental basis of our Bill of Rights comes from the teachings which we get from Exodus and St. Matthew, from Isaiah and St. Paul. I don't think we emphasize that enough these days.[24]

—PRESIDENT HARRY TRUMAN

Of the many influences that have shaped the United States of America into a distinctive Nation and people, none may be said to be more fundamental and enduring than the Bible. Deep religious beliefs stemming from the Old and New Testaments of the Bible...laid the foundation for the spirit of nationhood that was to develop in later decades. The Bible and its teachings helped form the basis for the Founding Fathers' abiding belief in the inalienable rights of the individual, rights which they found implicit in the Bible's teachings of the inherent worth and dignity of each individual.[25]

—PRESIDENT RONALD REAGAN

America was born to exemplify that devotion to the elements of righteousness which are derived from the revelations of Holy Scripture.[26]

—PRESIDENT WOODROW WILSON

In these last 200 years we have guided the building of our Nation and our society by those principles and precepts brought to earth nearly 2,000 years ago on that first Christmas.[27]

—PRESIDENT LYNDON BAINES JOHNSON

American life, is builded and can alone survive upon... [the] fundamental philosophy announced by the Savior 19 centuries ago.[28]

—PRESIDENT HERBERT HOOVER

Suppose a nation in some distant region should take the Bible for their only law-book, and every member should regulate his conduct by the precepts there exhibited!...What a Utopia; what a Paradise would this region be![29]
—PRESIDENT JOHN ADAMS

A knowledge of the Bible and an application of its principles were key to American government becoming the most successful in the world. Sadly the more secular and biblically illiterate we and our leaders have become, the less properly have our institutions functioned, including those of law, government, economics, education, business, and others.

Founding Father John Jay has already offered clear advice about reading and studying the Bible; here is his parallel advice on the Constitution:

Every member of the State ought diligently to read and to study the constitution of his country, and teach the rising generation to be free. By knowing their rights, they will sooner perceive when they are violated, and be the better prepared to defend and assert them.[30]

Notice the six steps necessary for effective citizenship:

1. *Read* the Constitution.

2. *Study* constitutional rights.

3. *Teach* that our constitutional government produces freedom.

4. *Perceive/recognize* violations of constitutional rights.

5. *Defend* constitutional rights.

6. *Assert* constitutional rights.

A Sequence for Action

These six verbs provide a straightforward sequence for action. (By the way, these same six verbs apply equally to Bible reading and study.) Consider the order in which these six occur.

Read, study, and teach

Read the document, study its original intent, and teach it to others.

Reading the Constitution can be done in under half an hour. *Studying* its original intent (and thus gaining further insight and knowledge into its practical application today) can be accomplished by reading some of the excellent early commentaries—such as Justice Joseph Story's 1833 *Commentaries on the Constitution* or his 1854 *Familiar Exposition of the Constitution* or William Rawle's 1825 *A View of the Constitution of the United States*. These works have been republished and are available today. They can also be read online or freely downloaded as PDFs.

You should know that some modern constitutional commentaries are also sound, but many are not. Anytime a commentary differs with the simple, easy-to-understand, explicit language of the Constitution, reject the commentary and go with the simplicity of the original document itself (so too with commentaries on the Bible).

After reading and studying the Constitution, be sure to *teach* that knowledge to others—especially the young.

Perceive (recognize), defend, assert

Once there is a familiarity with the Constitution, it becomes much easier to *perceive* when something is constitutionally wrong or when its principles are being attacked. Whenever that occurs, stand up and *defend* it.

But as important as it is to defend the Constitution and our constitutional rights, it is even more important to *assert* them—that is, to go on the offense with them. The National War College in Washington DC teaches the brightest American military officers both the philosophy and the tactics necessary not just to engage in war but also to win that war. A course central to that training is "The Nine Principles of War." Significantly, offense is one of those key doctrines, but defense is not. In fact, defense is only considered a temporary condition during which assets are reorganized in order to go back onto offense. Going on offense, and then sustaining a strong offense, is the key to regaining sound government. As the Bible affirms in Proverbs 21:22, "A wise man *attacks* a city of warriors..." (GW, emphasis added)—that is, he goes on offense. So don't just *defend* constitutional rights; *assert* them.

The first two steps to restoring America's government are to read and know the Bible, and then the Constitution. The third step is found in the Book of Luke.

Jesus's disciples witnessed many miraculous displays of His divine power. Yet when they were approached by a man who asked help for his son, the disciples found themselves unable to do anything for him. At other times Jesus prodded the disciples to acts of spiritual maturity that were counterintuitive to their thinking— such as extending continual forgiveness to those who offended or injured them. Challenged by their own shortcomings in so many areas where Jesus had shown Himself strong, they understandably turned to Him and asked, "Lord, 'Increase our faith!'" (Luke 17:5, NIV). Jesus's response to them was interesting—and probably totally unexpected.

Rather than telling them to pray more, live more godly lives, or study the Scriptures for longer periods, He instead told them the story of a hardworking servant who plowed the fields and tended the sheep. After a long day of hard, grueling work, the servant came in from the field. But rather than sitting down to rest and eat, instead he was instructed to begin waiting on the master—to serve and feed him. And after the master had been served and fed, he didn't even bother to say thank you to the servant (v. 9). So not only did the servant have a difficult and exhausting day, but once he finished his outside work, he also found a long night of inside work; and to top it off, he was unappreciated for all he had done. Ending the story, Jesus then told His disciples, "So likewise you, when you have done all those things which you are commanded, say, 'We are unprofitable servants. We have done what was our duty to do'" (v. 10, NKJV).

Remember the initial question: "Lord, 'Increase our faith'"? Jesus's solution for their request was to talk to them about doing their duty—about learning to do what was right when they didn't feel like it, when no one noticed, and when no one appreciated what they did. Doing one's duty is a sign of spiritual maturity. This specific spiritual character trait was frequently stressed in previous generations:

> The man who is conscientiously doing his duty will ever be protected by that righteous and all powerful Being, and when he has finished his work he will receive an ample reward.[31]
>
> —SAMUEL ADAMS
> Signer of The Declaration

> All that the best men can do is, to persevere in doing their duty…and leave the consequences to Him who made it their duty; being neither elated by success, however great, nor discouraged by disappointments however frequent and mortifying.[32]

> We must go home to be happy, and that our home is not in this world. Here we have nothing to do but our duty, and by it to regulate our business and our pleasures.[33]
>
> —JOHN JAY
> Original Chief Justice of the US Supreme Court
> Coauthor of *The Federalist Papers*

> And having secured the approbation of our hearts, by a faithful and unwearied discharge of our duty…let us joyfully leave our concerns in the hands of Him who raiseth up and pulleth down the empires and kingdoms of the world as He pleases.[34]
>
> —JOHN HANCOCK
> Signer of The Declaration

> The sum of the whole is, that the blessing of God is only to
> be looked for by those who are not wanting in the discharge
> of their own duty.[35]
>
> —JOHN WITHERSPOON
> Signer of The Declaration

Christians must regain the concept of duty and would do well to adopt the phrase that characterized the efforts of John Quincy Adams: "Duty is ours; results are God's."[36]

What are the duties that a biblical Christian must perform in order to restore good government? There are four.

DUTY #1: PRAY

As with the directive to read the Bible, the duty to pray likewise seems to smack of patronizingly shallow religious platitudes. But not so—at least, not if done biblically rather than in the casual and haphazard manner with which prayer is often handled today.

There is no shortage of things to pray for, but it is especially wise to include those things for which the Bible explicitly tells us to pray. For example, Psalm 122:6 commands us to pray for the peace of Jerusalem; from John 17:20–23, we should pray for unity among believers; and in Matthew 9:37–38, Jesus explicitly tells us to pray for more workers to participate in God's harvest. But as already noted in chapter 3, 1 Timothy 2:1–2 also commands that we pray "first of all" for all people, *especially* for leaders and those in authority. God elevates nothing else to the level of "first of all" in our prayer lives—except the governmental arena. Thus, we have a God-mandated duty to pray "first" for our government.

Significantly, our heart will always be turned to whatever we faithfully pray for, whether the peace and prosperity of Israel, the unity of the Church, more workers in God's kingdom—or our own government. God thus commands us to pray for government, fully knowing that this will properly point our hearts and attention in that direction.

But while prayer is an important biblical directive, we cannot stop here. As John Hancock urged Christians in his generation:

I conjure [urge] you, by all that is dear, by all that is honorable, by all that is sacred, not only that ye pray, but that ye act.[37]

So beyond prayer, what are our other three duties?

DUTY #2: KNOW AND JUDGE

The Bible directs that we are to "examine everything carefully; hold fast to that which is good (1 Thess. 5:21, NAS). Numerous verses convey the same message: believers are to examine, evaluate, and judge what goes on around them.[38] This applies not merely to so-called "spiritual" things but to every aspect of life and culture—including the political realm. Affirming this principle, John Adams declared:

> We *Electors* have an important *constitutional* power placed in our hands: We have a check upon two branches of the legislature....It becomes necessary to every subject [citizen] then, to be in some degree a *statesman:* and to examine and judge for *himself*...the...political *principles* and *measures.* Let us examine them with a *sober...Christian* spirit.[39]

Christians have a duty to judge every "political principle and measure" (including those mentioned in this book) from a biblical point of view. (This is why all restoration begins with reading and knowing the Bible; you can't judge measures against the Bible if you don't know what the Bible says about those measures.)

Christians seem to have lost (or, perhaps more accurately, willfully abandoned) the concept of individual civic stewardship they once so strongly embraced—the concept that Christian leaders such as Founding Father Benjamin Rush clearly articulated:

> Every citizen of a republic...must watch for the state, as if its liberties depended upon his vigilance alone.[40]

DUTY #3: SPEAK UP AND SPEAK OUT

Once you have performed your duty to examine public measures against biblical standards, you then have a nonoptional duty to tell others what you have found—especially if you have discovered something that is antibiblical or will be harmful to individuals or the nation.

Ezekiel 3:16–21 makes clear that if we do not clearly warn others of what God has said is right and wrong and that if those others wander off the path, then we ourselves will be held personally accountable. Leviticus 5:1 similarly talks about the sin of silence, and Proverbs 24:11–12 likewise declares that if we see someone headed down a wrong path and remain silent, making the excuse that we didn't know anything was going on, then we will individually be held responsible. Such verses make clear that silence is not an option for a biblical Christian. In fact, consider the lesson of Aaron.

Most students of the Bible, even casual ones, know that Moses did not enter the land of milk and honey; but neither did Aaron, the high priest over Israel at the time. The reason is recorded in Numbers 20:9–12.

Israel was finally free from the bondage of slavery in Egypt, and the people were on their way to the Promised Land when they ran out of water. They murmured and complained against God for their hardship but eventually turned to Him for help. God first told Moses, "Speak to that rock over there, and it will pour out its water" (v. 8), and then instructed Moses and Aaron to gather the people together. As the two stood before the assembled crowd, Moses, frustrated at their continual whining, exploded, "Listen, you rebels!...Must we bring you water from this rock?" (v. 10).

But in that angry statement, Moses committed a profound sin. It was God who brought water out of the rock, not "we"—not Moses, not Moses and Aaron, and not Moses and God. It was God alone. But by declaring that "we" were bringing water out of the rock, Moses had elevated himself alongside God. For that egregious sin, God told Moses he would not be allowed to enter the Promised Land. He then told Aaron the same. But why? Aaron had said nothing sinful. That's true, but the problem was, *Aaron had said nothing at all*. Standing by Moses when Moses made his declaration, Aaron did not confront or correct the sin. For thus remaining silent, Aaron was denied entry into the Promised Land.

Biblical Christians have a duty to speak truth and to speak it clearly, sometimes to affirm and educate and sometimes to confront. American culture is dying because too many Christians and pastors in church pulpits refuse to boldly speak truth about the issues occurring around them. For example, Romans 1:32 unequivocally states that God does not approve of homosexuality and that He also does not approve of those who do approve of homosexuality. How many Christians have reminded those around them who have now embraced the belief that homosexuality is "moral" about this verse? And the same with those who now believe that sex outside of marriage, or divorce, or any of the other things listed at the beginning of chapter 7 are "moral"?

Standing up and speaking out may be difficult and may not be well received by others, especially if what you say contradicts something they might be doing or believing at the time. This is why it is a duty, for by definition it involves doing what is right even when it is uncomfortable to do so.

Duty #4: Take Action

Exodus 18:21 (HCSB) instructs:

> Select from all the people able men, God-fearing, trustworthy, and hating bribes. Place them over the people as commanders of thousands, hundreds, fifties, and tens.

This Bible verse was invoked by the Founding Fathers and often used in early sermons to provide biblical guidance for citizens in our republican form of government. In America selecting leaders of thousands, hundreds, fifties, and tens means choosing our federal, state, county, and local officials. The means of selecting these leaders is by voting—a nonoptional duty already covered in chapter 3. Founding Father Noah Webster (also called the "schoolmaster to America") discussed with public school students in his day both this Bible verse and the civic duty accompanying it:

> In selecting men for office, let principle be your guide.... It is alleged by men of loose principles or defective views of the subject, that religion and morality are not necessary or important qualifications for political stations. But the Scriptures teach a different doctrine. They direct that rulers should be men *who rule in the fear of God, able men, such as fear God, men of truth, hating covetousness* [Exodus 18:21].... It is to the neglect of this rule of conduct in our citizens, that we must ascribe the multiplied frauds, breaches of trust, peculations [white-collar larceny] and embezzlements of public property which astonish even ourselves; which tarnish the character of our country; which disgrace a republican government.[41]

Ignoring biblical qualifications for officeholders is what produces bad government.

Notice the four characteristics that are to be common to every elected official, whether a local dogcatcher or the president of the United States: (1) able and competent, (2) God-fearing, (3) trustworthy, and (4) hating bribes. Only one demands skill and experience; the other three address qualifications of character and morality.

In America today the second characteristic is of particular importance: "God-fearing." What does that mean—that someone acknowledges the existence of God and is therefore not an atheist? No. It means much more.

Proverbs 8:13 explains that "to fear the Lord is to hate evil" (NIV), and *evil* is defined as "any deviation...from the rules of conduct prescribed by God."[42] Therefore, *God-fearing* actually means someone who hates variances from God's standards of morality, or, in the words of Psalm 139:21, it is hating what God hates and loving what He loves. Thus, a God-fearing leader is one who recognizes and supports biblical morality—one who stands for what God approves and opposes what God opposes.

By this definition, many Christians certainly do not qualify as being God-fearing. They might believe in God and even have a professed love and respect for Him, but if they do not embrace His views of right and wrong, then they are not, biblically speaking, God-fearing. By the way, love for God is not judged by what we say to Him, how warm we feel inside, or even how vigorously we enter into worship at church. Rather, true love for God is measured by the standard that Jesus Himself erected in John 14:15: "If you love me, keep my commands" (NIV). Love for God is proven not by your words but by how well your life conforms to His Word.

So, to determine if a candidate meets the qualification of being God-fearing, a biblical citizen should ask, "What is your position on abortion? Homosexuality? Debt? Military? Welfare?" and other issues about which God has established clear moral standards. Sadly these are questions that most Christian voters don't consider at election time, largely because they themselves don't personally know God's stand on these issues. (Again, this is why restoring American government begins with each individual personally developing a biblical literacy.)

The importance of electing genuinely God-fearing leaders was stressed by the Founding Fathers (as well as in countless early sermons), and often their point could be made by simply citing a related Scripture—as when William Paterson, a signer of the Constitution and a justice on the US Supreme Court, told citizens, quoting Proverbs 29:2:

> When the righteous rule, the people rejoice; when the wicked rule, the people groan.[43]

Founding Father John Witherspoon (a signer of the Declaration of Independence and the president of Princeton University) likewise reminded Americans:

That he is the best friend to American liberty, who is most sincere and active in promoting true and undefiled religion, and who sets himself with the greatest firmness to bear down profanity and immorality of every kind. Whoever is an avowed enemy of God, I scruple not to call him an enemy to his country.[44]

Founding Father John Jay restated the same principle when he answered a question posed him by the Rev. Dr. Jedidiah Morse, one of America's leading theologians and educators. Morse inquired whether it was permissible for a godly person to vote for someone who did not support biblical positions, to which the chief justice replied:

[This] is a question which merits more consideration than it seems yet to have generally received, either from the clergy or the laity. It appears to me, that what the prophet said to Jehoshaphat about his attachment to Ahab, affords a salutary lesson.[45]

Jay's mention of the prophet is a reference to the account in 2 Chronicles 18–19, where wicked King Ahab approached righteous King Jehoshaphat and requested his help to fight an enemy. Righteous Jehoshaphat agreed and made an alliance with wicked Ahab, and together they set out to fight Ahab's enemy at Ramoth-Gilead. After the battle, as Jehoshaphat returned home, God sent him a prophet who rebuked him for making an alliance with the wicked. The prophet's specific words in that rebuke provided Jay's answer to the question of whether the godly could vote for the ungodly:

Jehu the seer [the prophet], the son of Hanani, went out to meet him and said to the king, "Should you help the wicked and love those who hate the LORD? Because of this, the wrath of the LORD is on you."
—2 CHRONICLES 19:2, NIV

Based on this clear declaration by the Lord's prophet, Jay therefore held that God would *not* bless those who voted for and placed unbiblical leaders (and thereby unbiblical policies) into office. He concluded:

> Providence has given to our people the choice of their rulers, and it is the duty, as well as the privilege and interest, of our Christian nation to select and prefer Christians for their rulers.[46]

For America's current situation, the intent of Jay's statement becomes more accurate by substituting the word *biblical* for the word *Christian*, for as has been clearly demonstrated, the majority of American Christendom today is not biblical in beliefs or actions. It is our duty to elect individuals to office who embrace and reflect biblical values, regardless of whether or not they call themselves Christians, which has now too often become a description with an ambiguous meaning.

As a final part of this fourth duty (the duty to take action), Judges 9:9–15 presents an applicable parable. In it, the trees of the forest seek the best and most productive from among them to be their ruler, first asking the olive tree, then the fig tree, and finally the grapevine. But in each case, the good trees make excuses for why they don't want to serve in office. With none of them willing to answer the call, the thornbush thus becomes their ruler. The lesson is simple: when the good refuse to make themselves available for public service, the people get bad leaders.

Too many good people today disqualify themselves for all the wrong reasons—*I don't have time, I'm not trained for this, I don't like politics*, etc. But it is interesting to see whom God has regularly chosen for leaders. As Benjamin Franklin noted:

> It is observable that God has often called men to places of dignity and honor, when they have been busy in the honest employment of their vocation. Saul was seeking his father's asses, and David keeping his father's sheep, when

called to the kingdom. The shepherds were feeding their flocks when they had their glorious revelation. God called the four Apostles from their fishery, and Matthew from the receipt of custom; Amos from among the herdsmen of Tekoah, Moses from keeping Jethro's sheep, Gideon from the threshing floor....God never encourages idleness and despises not persons in the meanest employments [i.e., simplest vocations].[47]

Simple, busy, hard-working, common individuals were chosen by God for public service rather than glamorous, credentialed, and pedigreed ones.

Significantly, the Founders held that if a good person was asked by others to serve them in a public office (as occurred on multiple occasions in Judges 9), then that individual was *not* at liberty to refuse the request. As explained by Declaration signer Benjamin Rush:

He [a citizen] must love private life, but he must decline no station, however public or responsible it may be, when called to it by the suffrages [votes] of his fellow citizens.[48]

Why was a citizen not allowed to decline a request to serve in office? Because as Rush explained, "'None...liveth to himself'" (Rom. 14:7, KJV), and our life "is not our own property; all its fruits of wisdom and experience belong to the public."[49] In his view God placed us here to serve others, and if others asked us to help them by entering public office, then we were not at liberty to place our own personal desires above the call to serve. Very simply it was selfishness to say no.

So, if you are looking at the ballot for school board, city council, mayor, state representative, or any other position and don't find a candidate who fulfills the qualifications of Exodus 18:21, then go recruit a good candidate for that position—or run for office yourself.

But what if there is not a good person on the ballot, and you don't have sufficient time (or the filing deadline has already passed) for you to recruit someone to run or for you to run?

First, understand that in such a situation, not voting is not an option. As established earlier, you have a duty to vote, and you will answer to God for the exercise of that duty—and for the failure to exercise that duty. Second, consider the response of those from history who faced similar situations, such as Abigail Adams, the outspoken Christian wife of Founding Father John Adams.

In the campaign of 1800, it appeared that a president might be elected who was not a strong God-fearing Christian (the leading candidates were Thomas Jefferson and Aaron Burr). Such an option actually mortified the patriotic-minded, and Abigail, who knew both candidates, lamented about what voters in that election were facing:

> Never were a people placed in more difficult circumstances than the virtuous part of our countrymen are at the present crisis. I have turned, and turned, and overturned in my mind at various times the merits and demerits of the two candidates. Long acquaintance, private friendship and the full belief that the private character of [Jefferson] is much purer than [Burr]...inclines me to [Jefferson]....If we ever saw a day of darkness [in America], I fear this is one. [50]

For her, the choices were definitely not optimal, but she chose the one she believed would do the least damage to the country.

If you find yourself in a similar situation, her example is worthy of emulation—and no, this is not a compromise of principle, for you are doing what you can to slow decay rather than to ignore and thus accelerate it. But that having been said, the day after the election is over, you should begin right then and there to start searching for someone to run in the next election cycle who does meet the qualifications of Exodus 18:21. Work to ensure that neither you nor any other Godly voter will ever again have to face that circumstance.

IN SUMMARY

The first step to restoring good government is for each citizen to read, study, and live the Bible. The second step is to read, study, and apply the Constitution. Then, from that foundation of biblical and constitutional knowledge arises the four duties of a biblical citizen: (1) to pray fervently and regularly for government; (2) to learn about various public-policy measures and judge them according to biblical standards; (3) to speak up and speak out about what you have learned, affirming that which is right and confronting and exposing that which is wrong; (4) to take action, which includes not only voting but also finding (or becoming) a good candidate to run for office. This is what is required to restore our government.

The responsibilities facing God-fearing citizens are somber, and the potential repercussions from our actions—or lack thereof—are both far-reaching and long-lasting. As Founding Father Samuel Huntington (a signer of the Declaration) accurately observed:

> While the great body of [citizens] are acquainted with the duties which they owe to their God, to themselves, and to men, they will remain free. But if ignorance and depravity should prevail, they will inevitably lead to slavery and ruin.[51]

The government of this nation can be blessed only to the extent that citizens become God-fearing and moral and then place God-fearing and moral individuals into office. What legacy will we leave the next generation? That is a decision we must make.

Chapter 10

RESTORING THE CHURCH

A MERICANS HAVE AN interesting view of the Christian Church. When most people hear the word *church*, they think of the "small *c*" version—an organization that puts on events and programs they can attend. A smaller proportion of people think of the "big *c*" version—the Church as the global body of followers of Christ. An infinitesimally small number of Americans think of *themselves as being the Church*. Addressing that deficiency is a good place to start as we consider how to restore health to the American Church.

Jesus did not die to create an institution or to found an organization. He died so that you might have life and have it abundantly while honoring Him by carrying out His work during your lifetime. In doing so, you are part of the Church—or *ekklesia*, the Greek term used in the Bible to indicate those who have been "called out." Called out of what? We are called away from identification with, and conformity and devotion to, the ways and purposes of the world. Called into what? We are called into a community of people who have been blessed by the grace of God through Jesus Christ, who identify with Him, and who are devoted and conformed to the ways and purposes of the Master.

The survey data presented throughout this book makes clear that the Church in America is being influenced by society more than it is influencing that society. As our nation decays from the inside out, the sole solution for that deterioration is for the Church to be the Church that Jesus intended, called, and prepared us to be.

The means to that outcome is not to sit back and point fingers at leaders who have dropped the ball or to criticize the un-Christian-like behavior of millions of churchgoing people. The solution starts with you. God is in the transformation business; nobody can renew a life like He can. The good news, literally, is that He wants to transform you, if you will allow Him to do so. And if you do not allow Him the freedom to do so, then you have no right to complain about the state of the nation or to expect it to improve. The trajectory of America today is a direct reflection of what happens when people push God out of the picture and take control of the world based on their own power and vision.

So if our nation is to be renewed, the process must start with you. God has challenged you to step up and collaborate with Him in the pursuit of truth and righteousness. Your decision of whether or not you will humble yourself and follow His lead will affect many lives: yours; friends, family, and acquaintances; and many people you do not know and may never meet.

The concept of the Church is a critical aspect of the renewal process. Remember this: God never called you to go to church. He has called you to *be* the Church. Time is running out to fulfill your calling.

How to Be the Church

You cannot change the world. In fact, you cannot even change one other person; only God can do that. But don't stress over that inability: transforming lives is God's job, and He does it to perfection. You will never become the ultimate human being you were conceived by God to be until you give Him full control of your life. Only God can supply exactly what you need to become who He created you to be.

Despite our occasional sense of omniscience and omnipotence—can you say *arrogance?*—we really are very limited. And yet you are invaluable to the kingdom of God. What can you do? You can turn your life over to His Holy Spirit and let Him transform you into the likeness of Christ. The more that you allow God to direct your life, the more of a difference you will make in other people's lives. And you will be given the chance to team with others who are also committed to being the hands and feet that God uses to alter our current reality.

Thousands of books are produced every year that provide guidance on how to live a more Christlike existence. In this chapter,we want to identify some practical steps to consider if you would like to integrate your faith into a life that moves America toward a more biblical environment. These ideas are neither exhaustive nor a definitive nonnegotiable agenda for your engagement in national reform. If nothing else this content may spark ideas and stoke your passion in relation to the role you can play in guiding America to make the cultural U-turn it so desperately needs.

Much of the challenge you face is about deepening and intensifying your relationship with God. But willingness to grow and taking advantage of the assistance that other like-minded people offer won't get you or the nation very far unless you have identified the irrevocable commitments you will make and the boundaries you will not transcend. In the end the world will not be affected by your efforts unless you put some "boots on the ground"—that is, put your faith in action. Let's spend the rest of the chapter describing what these three thrusts—your preparation, commitments, and action—might look like.

PERSONAL GROWTH

Becoming Christlike is a pretty tall order. He always made the right choices and said the wisest words. His timing was impeccable. He remained laser-focused on His primary life purpose, regardless of the temptations and challenges He faced. His heart was continually in the right place. He accomplished more in three years of ministry than any human being has ever achieved in a lifetime.

Yet you have been called to Christlikeness. The apostle Paul got right to the point in exhorting the people of Ephesus to mimic the Savior:

> Imitate God, therefore, in everything you do, because you
> are His dear children. Live a life filled with love, following
> the example of Christ.
> —Ephesians 5:1–2

After giving the Ephesians a detailed list of how to live so as to be a "pleasing aroma" to God (v. 2)—i.e., avoiding the likes of sexual immorality, greed, profanity, gossip, and idolatry, because such behavior has "no place among God's people" (v. 3)—Paul completed his straightforward command to Jesus's followers with these words:

> Carefully determine what pleases the Lord. Take no part in
> the worthless deeds of evil and darkness; instead, expose
> them.
> —Ephesians 5:10–11

Many of the great Christian thinkers and leaders throughout history have landed on the notion of imitating the life of Christ as the ultimate goal of life. Augustine described the imitation of Jesus as the most basic and meaningful purpose of human life. Francis of Assisi, the namesake of the current Catholic pope and a revered example of one whose life was devoted to Christlikeness, modeled his own life after that of Jesus in every dimension of his existence. Many Christian philosophers and disciplemakers, perhaps starting with the seminal work of Thomas à Kempis, have emphasized the importance of inner spiritual development that leads to more Christlike behavior. Ignatius of Loyola was so taken by the need to commit to Christlikeness that he developed his famous "spiritual exercises" to facilitate such a pursuit. Reformation icons Martin Luther and John Calvin prominently featured the concept of imitating the life of Christ in their teachings.

Isn't it interesting that Americans still embrace the notion of imitating people they respect, but rather than imitate Jesus, or even the likes of the apostle Paul, King David, or the prophet Daniel, we emulate entertainers and athletes who often do nothing beyond promoting themselves? We have to set our standard higher!

Based on the research we have reviewed regarding the lives of

American Christians, the state of the nation, and the potential of the Church, here are some components of personal growth you can certainly embrace and master.

PRIORITIES AND PURPOSE

The research shows that tens of millions of Americans are seeking a clear and compelling sense of purpose in life. This quest is every bit as common among Christians as non-Christians.[1] The statistics also point out that until people grasp that purpose, their life priorities are a mess—contradictory, unsatisfying, and incomplete. Fortunately your faith can help address these matters.

You were created by God for His purposes. What are they? In general terms your purpose is to experience life to the fullest by loving God and people, advancing the kingdom of God through your acts of love and responsibility. Investing yourself in the fulfillment of His purposes requires that you involve Him in your thoughts, hopes, conversations, and activities. As you do so, you will discover that He has called and prepared you for specific works, and He has provided opportunities for you to serve Him in ways that make a difference and provide fulfillment. To make the most of these opportunities, all it takes is following His guidance, obeying His commands and precepts, and using the gifts and resources He has entrusted to you.

Perhaps the appropriate starting place in this process is to get a clear sense of self. In our culture we refer to a person's identity. Many people struggle with the question of who they really are, perhaps because we start with ourselves rather than starting with God to understand His worldview and discern how we might fit into it. Understanding our true identity is easier than people make it; God has provided the answers you need to questions of identity and purpose. If you choose to live in Christ, embracing Him as your Savior and Master, you are given a new life and identity in Christ. That identity is comprised of an interrelated group of attributes. In His words to us He explains that you are:

- Adopted as a child of God (Eph. 1:5–6)

- Deeply loved by God, the Father (Rom. 1:7; Eph. 2:4; Col. 3:12)

- Living and serving under the authority of Jesus Christ (Eph. 1:10–11)

- An ambassador of God (2 Cor. 5:20)

- Joint heir to the kingdom of God (Rom. 8:17)

- Complete and whole (Col. 2:10)

- Possessing the mind of God (1 Cor. 2:16; Eph. 1:17–18)

- Free from condemnation by God (Rom. 8:1; Eph. 1:7)

- Set free from the power of sin over your life (Rom. 8:2; Col. 2:11)

- Guaranteed eternal glory (2 Tim. 2:10)

- Set apart—"holy"—to experience God and do His work (1 Cor. 1:2, 30; Eph. 1:4)

- Permanently connected to other followers of Christ, through Him (Gal. 3:28)

- Defined by a spirit endowed with power, love, and self-discipline but not fear (2 Tim. 1:7)

- A conqueror through His love and power (Rom. 8:37)

- Blessed with every spiritual blessing available from God (Eph. 1:3)

- A member of His Church—the cumulative followers of Christ (Eph. 5:29–30)

In the end you're not just another struggling Joe out on the streets, trying to get by. You're no longer one more well-intentioned person trying to figure out how to live a meaningful life or leave a desirable legacy. God tells you that you are His very own *masterpiece!* (See Ephesians 2:10.)

National research consistently underscores how off the mark people's self-identity really is. The studies show that people define themselves according to their education, profession, age, skills, talents, relationships, socioeconomic status, nationality, family, marriage, and hobbies. How silly that seems when you realize that the God who created the universe and everything in it has established your identity through your relationship with Him.

Please take some time to reread and reflect on these elements of your true identity—not the fragmented, incomplete, inadequate identity that the world tries to place upon you. Once you truly grasp the fullness of your genuine, God-given identity, your personal growth can soar to new heights, and your impact on the world will amaze even you.

More importantly, you will be capable of discerning your purpose and priorities like never before. You will better comprehend how your life purpose is about your relationship with God. You will gain a firmer grasp on what it means to love, obey, serve, and glorify Him. In other words, your daily focus will shift from how to satisfy yourself or appease the world in favor of devoting yourself to pleasing and honoring God.

With that purpose clearly in mind, you will also be capable of appropriately determining your priorities. Nobody else can tell you what God's priorities are for you. You are His cherished creation, one whom He bought for a steep price, prepared for important acts of service, and purposefully introduced into the present spiritual battle for such a time as this. In His wisdom and mercy He has assigned to you a special purpose that only you can fulfill—and which you will find incredibly rewarding—if you commit yourself to discerning and fulfilling it.[2]

SEEKING TRANSFORMATION

Jesus's final command to His followers was to make disciples of people. Perhaps we have intellectualized discipleship to its detriment. So often we perceive that process to be about the transmission of information. But as you know from your own experience, the people who have the most information are usually not the people who make the biggest difference. In like manner, possessing a storehouse of spiritual information does not automatically produce transformation. Knowing Bible content is valuable, but simply possessing knowledge about the content does not produce fruit unless that knowledge is applied.

The essence of discipleship is transformation: allowing God to have His way with us, in order to deliver us from a life devoted to worldliness into a life devoted to righteousness. Contrary to what many American Christians believe, transformation is more than accepting the forgiveness and salvation that God offers us through Christ. It is about handing over complete control of our lives to God, allowing Him to separate us from our love of idols (such as money, fame, power, or possessions, to name a few) and distractions (think about entertainment, sexuality, celebrity gossip, and consumerism, for starters), and showing people that we belong fully to Him by the consistent love we exhibit to God and people. As the apostle Paul noted, the things that get people all worked up and red in the face generally don't amount to a hill of beans: "What counts is whether we have been transformed into a new creation" (Gal. 6:15).

Research has shown that the major obstacle that keeps most Christians from becoming the person God made them to be is accepting brokenness. Numerous studies conducted by the Barna Group have revealed that while tens of millions of Americans have uttered the "salvation prayer," only a small fraction of those individuals have allowed God to break them of their addictions to sin, self, and society.[3] Most American Christians try to have it both ways, attempting to satisfy God by saying the right words while at the same time living a secular-minded life that the culture recognizes and rewards. We know intellectually that it is not possible to live with one foot in both worlds and satisfy God, but we fool ourselves into thinking that we can successfully walk the fine line between those two warring camps.

Make no mistake about it, God wants (and deserves) all of you. He will not settle for anything less; His terms are nonnegotiable. (See Exodus 20:5.) The prevailing notion among American Christians that you can be a transformed, mature follower of Christ without being fully broken, surrendered, and totally committed to God is one of the most insidious and widespread lies of this age.

There are a variety of stops on the path to wholeness. Confessing your sins and embracing Jesus as Savior is just one milestone on that journey to holiness. Being broken of our sins and selfishness, submitting our will to Him, surrendering control and our agenda in favor of His authority and guidance, loving Him unconditionally, and then allowing Him to love other people through us are all part of the adventure. But the research also shows that only one out of ten Americans ever gets more than halfway to these simple but profound behaviors.[4]

The Bible leaves no doubt about the necessity of embracing personal brokenness. We see it played out in the lives of biblical hero after biblical hero, from Moses and David to Paul and Peter. Even Jesus Himself was broken. He had to experience that devastation, not because of anything He did, but because of our sin. Not even the holy Son of God was spared the pain and suffering inherent in being separated from intimacy with God because of our offensive choices. As much as anything, the fact that our holy and righteous Savior had to endure brokenness in order to fulfill His destiny is an unmistakable sign to us of how important it is to abandon anything that stands in the way of our complete and sole reliance upon God for true life.

It is important to emphasize again that the biggest stumbling block to being fully transformed is the willingness to accept brokenness. Both the biblical narratives about brokenness and contemporary experiences show that God does not force us to accept brokenness. He always allows us to choose whether or not we will trust Him enough to endure the suffering, grieving, and recovery that accompanies being broken. The record unambiguously shows that your only choices are to allow God to use circumstances to shake you and break you or to resist His way and continue to endure the consequences. The data also reveals, however, that while He allows you to choose, He never gives up on you, so you can count on a lifetime of challenges designed to encourage you to accept brokenness and the healing and growth that He delivers in the aftermath.

As hard as it is to believe, brokenness is a gift from God that demonstrates His awesome and unyielding love. We typically examine the circumstances designed to guide us from a casual acquaintance to an intense and intimate lover of God and foolishly conclude that the crises He uses to facilitate brokenness are harmful to our well-being. In reality they are God's means of bringing us to our knees before Him, in full-on repentance, enabling us to see the truth of who we are, who He is, how we treat Him, how compassionate He is, how much we need Him, and how dramatically His means and ends differ from ours.

In our culture-driven confusion we focus on the deprivation, sacrifice, pain, suffering, hardship, and persecution that God injects into our experience as His route to grasping our attention and causing us to reconsider our ways. We mistakenly assume that once we believe nice things about God and invest a few personal resources into the development of our faith, the appropriate response by our Father should be continual affirmation, comfort, pleasure, rewards, and happiness. But that's only because we understand neither the nature of God nor the power of brokenness.

The bottom line is that we are called to become like Jesus: insatiably and pragmatically in love with God and people. Jesus suggested that true transformation is about letting God rewire the four areas of our minds, emotions, behavior, and spirit to get to that stage. Like the lukewarm believers in Laodicea (one of the seven churches evaluated by God in the second and third chapters of Revelation, infamous for being rejected because of their tepid faith), we typically allow God to alter one or maybe two of those four centers of control, but not all four. How can we invite Him to transform us in all four dimensions?

+ **Our minds.** To give God control of your mind, develop a worldview that is consistent with His principles and commands. Everyone has a worldview; it is simply the mental filter that helps us organize information to determine what we believe to be good and bad, right and wrong, significant and insignificant, appropriate and inappropriate. If you develop a perspective based on His principles and commands, the result is widely known as a "biblical worldview." Sadly only about one out of every ten born-again adults in the United States possess a biblical worldview.[5]

Filling your mind with this perspective enables you to make choices that are consistent with God's ways and that therefore honor Him. Developing a biblical worldview is a lifelong process that entails reading, studying, adopting, and memorizing biblical content. There are numerous books and guides that can help you in learning how to integrate appropriate insights into a way of thinking that equips you for the journey.[6]

+ **Our emotions.** Biblical information that is developed into a worldview will affect the way we feel about people, opportunities, resources, relationships, lifestyles, and spiritual matters. Examining your emotions in relation to your worldview will help you to align your mind and heart. For instance, one of the reasons few Christians lead a lifestyle characterized by worshipping God throughout the day is because their worldview does not champion the importance of worship, and their emotions consequently lack the requisite respect for and awe of who God is, what He has done for them, and why He deserves 24/7 worship. Most American Christians remain too wrapped up in themselves to have much love and gratitude left over for God. Carefully examine your emotional responses throughout the day, and determine how you can adjust them to reflect what you know to be right and true.

♦ **Our behavior.** A worldview is just an argument unless it is put into practice. Consequently, your behavior must reflect the principles that are reflected in a biblical worldview. Among the more telling behaviors affected in the transformation process are how you handle resources, how devoted you are to sharing your devotion to Jesus with people who are not followers of Christ, and how much time and energy you devote to serving others. While some would disagree, more than a decade of Barna Research studies has shown that an appropriate worldview produces practical Christianity. The reason is simple: beliefs produce action. In other words, we do what we believe to be right and true. Take an inventory of all of your actions in the past twenty-four hours. How well does your behavior correspond to the truths and principles conveyed in the Scriptures?

♦ **Our spirits.** When we commit to knowing, loving, serving, and obeying God, we tacitly grant His Holy Spirit permission to mold and shape us into the followers God designed us to be. Inviting Jesus to spare us from the full penalty of our sins is just the start. The more deeply we commit to following and imitating Him, the more completely the Holy Spirit takes control of our soul and guides us into an ever deeper and fulfilling relationship with God. Pray that God's Spirit will have full and unfettered control of your life, and try to be more sensitive to how His Spirit speaks to and influences you. Learn to discern the silent nudges of His Spirit. Become more attuned to the impact that reading certain verses or stories in the Bible has upon your mind and heart. See if you can reach a point of sensing that when you make a decision, God's Spirit is present, providing supernatural guidance to you.

MEANINGFUL COMMITMENTS

To reach your potential in Christ, consider the commitments you have made to people. Previously we described the importance of clarifying your identity in Christ and being sold out to that redefinition of who you are. With that altered self-image in mind, you may then invest in meaningful commitments to other people that naturally flow from that identity and its related purposes. It is through these commitments that the growth you have experienced and continue to pursue has the ability to bear fruit in the lives of others and through those relationships to change the culture. Let's consider three of the commitments that are important for the restoration of the Church and the redirection of our nation.

1. Community

The true Church of God is not simply a large number of isolated individuals whose bond is defined by assent to a particular slate of theological perspectives. Historically—and biblically—the Church has always been about the connection of believers to one another. Those faith-based relationships establish a new type of family, one based upon a common love for and devotion to Jesus Christ.

Unfortunately, in our fast-paced, self-absorbed world the Christian Church has become an assemblage of individuals who have limited ties to other believers. Christian relationships are often built on the basis of convenience, proximity, and absence of conflict more than upon a decision to accept, understand, support, and love everyone who is similarly sold out to Jesus. The result is a nationwide group of believers who are every bit as fragmented as any other social club or business association.

Given that the Bible does not call us to go to church but to *be* the church, we may wish to reflect on what we hope to invest in and take away from being associated with other Christians in a gathering such as a local congregation or other regular meetings of believers.

One value of our regular assembly is experiencing trustworthy teaching, God-centered worship, and opportunities for meaningful service. In a society that recognizes and promotes narcissism more than selfless sacrifice, having a safe and consistent environment in which people of like mind and purpose can renew that focus is an invaluable gift.

A second benefit of belonging to a group that meets regularly around its mutual love of Christ is the opportunity to receive tangible support through voluntary accountability to people we trust. The basis of that trust is the shared commitment to Christ and the principles set forth in God's Word. Accountability is not a concept that receives much attention or support in our nation these days. But one of the keys to a healthy community is the willingness of each participant to hear and accept positive, constructive feedback and, when necessary, to yield to the advice or discipline of the community. The Scriptures describe this responsibility to the submitted believer as looking out for a brother, warning him about deception and self-deceit, motivating him to engage in appropriate behavior, and caring for and building up the accountable brother.[7]

Leaning on research by the Barna Group regarding how transformation works, one of the underexploited opportunities that engagement with a group of Christians provides is taking advantage of coaches or mentors who are at a more advanced stage of the journey and are willing to guide us along the path of growth. The research described in *Maximum Faith*[8] regarding the transformational process emphasizes the value of connecting a believer with someone who is one or two stops further along the journey to wholeness. The research showed that participation in discipleship programs (e.g., Sunday school, small groups, Christian education classes), regular worship service attendance, and even personal Bible reading minimally correlate with spiritual maturation. The most effective strategy for growth was to connect one believer with another one who has made greater progress on the journey, allowing the more advanced believer to coach the less advanced believer toward greater spiritual maturity.

A relationship, however, is always a two-way street. You cannot grow if you simply take; you must give back to others as well. (In fact, when you share what you learn with someone else, it becomes a vital means of cementing that learning in your own mind and heart.) It is your responsibility to determine whose life you can invest in within the body of believers and to pursue the opportunity to do so. Based on the spiritual gifts and natural talents and skills you possess, you can find a role through which you add value to individual lives.

2. Family

The biblical model of spiritual growth largely centers on the efforts of the family. Throughout the Bible the assumption is that young people will be raised to know the truths and ways of God so that when they are adults, their task is less about figuring it all out as much as passing it on to their own children. Parents are to be the spiritual leaders of their families, providing the primary spiritual development and experience within the family context. Because the extended family lived and worked closely together in ancient times, the expectation was that grandparents and other relatives would be a support system for parents and their children. The community of faith with which the parents interacted would also provide a secondary line of support.

Americans have become heavily dependent upon religious schools and local churches to bear the primary, if not sole, responsibility for spiritually nurturing both children and adults. With the virtually undisputed acceptance of professional clergy operating in an institutional ministry environment (i.e., the "local church"), the burden of growing people spiritually has fallen primarily to those who are now paid to engage in such ministry. Parents, who are now busy earning a living, seeking to build a better life for their families, and trying to get some relaxation and refreshment in to their lives as well, believe they lack the time, training, and skills to satisfactorily do the job. This model is not promoted in the Bible, and it has proven to be relatively ineffective in our society today.

Various studies over the past two decades have persuasively shown that the most effective time to focus on a person's spiritual development is before a child reaches the teenage years. It is during this time that they are most receptive to learning about spiritual matters and most likely to retain the principles they are taught.

This truth is so clearly presented in the Bible[9] that previous generations openly acknowledged it, even though they lacked the sociological support for it that we have available today. For example, Founding Father Fisher Ames—a framer of the Bill of Rights—affirmed to his generation, "The reverence for the Sacred Book that is thus early impressed lasts long, and probably, if not impressed in infancy, never takes firm hold of the mind."[10] And Founding Father Benjamin Rush likewise avowed that "religious instruction [is] most useful, when imparted in early life" and that if the Bible is not diligently taught to children when they are young, then it "is seldom read in any subsequent period of life."[11] Children are not too young for such biblical instruction. In fact, Founding Father John Witherspoon, a signer of the Declaration, like others in that day, finished reading through the Bible for the first time when he was four years old.[12] (Yes, this also means that parents taught their children to read long before they went to school.)

American children are very sensitive to spiritual principles, typically embracing the same religious beliefs and behaviors as their parents have adopted. In fact, the research has discovered that the vast majority of religious beliefs and attitudes possessed by adults were initially adopted by those people when they were pre-teens.[13]

Over the past couple of decades, as Christian parents have become less involved in the spiritual development of their children in favor of letting the local church do the job, surveys have consistently shown that the youngest adults are entering their voting years with a more liberal perspective on politics and are more enthusiastic than usual about liberal candidates. Surveys also consistently demonstrate that the youngest voters are less biblically literate than were their predecessors and generally do not connect their spiritual views with their political beliefs.[14] The blame for the disconnection between faith, politics, and lifestyle falls squarely on the shoulders of Christian parents.

Today's culture wars persist primarily because we have done an inadequate job of training up our children in the way they should go. American children are the number one mission field for America to focus upon. It is not the job of churches, schools, the media, or political institutions to inculcate the moral and spiritual truths that our children should embrace. Christian parents must accept the responsibility to educate their children through instruction, discipline, and behavioral modeling to know, love, serve, and obey God with all of their hearts, souls, minds, and strength.

A Church that does not prioritize the spiritual development of its children is a Church that has resigned itself to both irrelevancy and rapid demise. For the sake of America's future, you and I must prioritize the proper spiritual nurture of children. As a parent, grandparent, or close relative to children in your family, how well are you doing at embracing the crucial role of spiritual leader in their lives and helping those children to grow in their relationships with Christ? As you examine the faith experience of those young people, how would you assess their present maturity and their growth curve in relation to worship, evangelism, worldview, stewardship, service, and openness to the full transformation process? How committed are you to intentionally and strategically aiding those children in their spiritual development? Unless you accept and champion the responsibility to help raise them to be godly citizens, America will continue down the path of spiritual deterioration that fosters national moral decay.

3. The disadvantaged and hurting

Unlike some religions or philosophical systems, Christianity is an other-centered faith. The essential attribute of a genuine Christian is love, which is to be shown in continual and practical ways toward God and other people. Interestingly, in national surveys that explore people's criticisms of the Christian faith, the dominant concerns are that Christians fail to do enough to help other people. A recent study by the Barna Group suggests that helping the poor, investing in the lives of children, supporting families, and offering effective recovery services for broken people are the most desired kinds of faith demonstrations that Americans are seeking from the Church. The study revealed that nobody listed a desire to see churches provide more worship services, Sunday school classes, small groups, stewardship campaigns, or potluck dinners, or for more believers to engage in evangelism.[15]

For the Church in America to be taken more seriously—and be looked upon more kindly—it must exude the love that Jesus has called us to embody. The Republican Party has been derisively described in recent years as the party that is against everything and for nothing. The Christian Church in the United States—especially that of the evangelical variety—is in danger of acquiring that same reputation if it is not careful. Most adults realize that the most vocal Christians are against same sex marriage, against abortion, against restrictive gun control, against Obamacare, against tax increases, and against stem-cell research. But recent public-opinion research highlights that most Americans—even many Christians—are hard-pressed to specify what the Christian Church supports.[16]

That failing would be less worrisome to people if they were more aware of the efforts Christians make to take care of "the least of these." To a very real degree, Christians and the ministries they support are very active in serving the disadvantaged segments of our population, but most of those efforts are invisible to the public. Where the president spends his vacation or what new tattoos movie stars have acquired is treated as information the public must know, but who is housing and feeding the homeless and what kind of resources are needed to continue that work is not.

For instance, churches already invest tens of millions of dollars on free services provided to the poor (e.g., food pantries, donated clothing, medical clinics, and homeless shelters). Similarly, some of the most successful counseling services in the country are those developed and offered by churches; Celebrate Recovery is an example of one widely recognized as a successful alcohol and drug recovery program that was birthed in the Church world and is offered on thousands of church campuses. Unfortunately, these types of efforts get little public attention.

However, the research indicates that fewer than one out of six Christian adults volunteer their time during any given week to serve people beyond assisting in the management of church services and systems.[17] When outsiders hear that Christianity is "all about loving God and loving people," they want to see a clear-cut and widespread demonstration of such love carried out by more than just a handful of zealots.

Such a broad-based exhibit of the love of Christ is something that should be obvious to anyone who is watching the Christian body. Such behavior softens the hearts of everyone involved: the believers who are nurturing the disadvantaged and the needy recipients who are touched by the compassion and kindness of God's servants. And it goes a long way toward eliminating the common criticism of Christians and churches as people who are "hypocrites," "judgmental," and "intolerant."

Not everyone is cut out to minister to a hardcore street person. Not every believer is prepared to interact effectively with an alcoholic or drug user. Some followers of Christ may not be capable of regularly visiting maximum security prisons to spend time with convicted killers and drug dealers. But there is no Christian in America who is incapable of finding a group of needy people whom they can serve in some manner. That service will go a long way toward not only reducing the need for a more intrusive government but also changing the hearts of those who serve, those who are served, and those who are observing the process with critical eyes. That impact will then open minds and hearts to more readily consider the things the Christian faith brings to bear on the social, political, and familial conditions of the nation.

THE LOCAL CHURCH

The recovery of American society will depend less upon the improvement of churches and more upon the commitment of individual followers of Christ to being the church. However, America's local churches can play a significant role in empowering and equipping Christians to be the church. In the same way that schools represent a valuable support system involved in the education of our children, so can local churches provide the kind of encouragement, relationships, experiences, and resources that will better enable followers of Christ to imitate the mind, heart, and actions of their master.

For churches to be more effective facilitators of kingdom living, providing better leadership as well as refining the emphasis of ministry activity would go a long way toward propelling the Church forward.

Leadership

Most people are not habitual leaders that is, individuals who have been called and gifted by God primarily to provide leadership in most of the situations in which they find themselves. However, everyone is in multiple environments every day in which they are the recipient of leadership and in which their own productivity and influence is dependent upon the quality of the leadership they receive.

The local church environment is no different. The chances are good that you are not a habitual leader, yet when you participate in the life of a local church, your personal spiritual development and your ministry to others is directly affected by the quality of the leadership provided by the church. In other words, you are a captive consumer of church leadership. As such, you have an extensive history as a follower who has been affected by leaders—and therefore, you are probably quite skilled at discerning a good leader from a well-intentioned but ineffective one. You are also probably well aware that many of our churches are not well led and that the absence of effective guidance has dampened the positive impact of churches on their communities.

While we have a tendency to blame various entities for this tragedy—such as the ineffective training and inappropriate credentialing of future church leaders by seminaries or the poor hiring choices by search committees or elder boards—a significant share of the blame must be placed upon us, the congregants, for accepting poor leadership in our churches. If things are going to change quickly—and they must, if the nation is going to pull the direly needed U-turn—then you and I must speak up for what our communities of faith need in order to move forward, and we must refuse to settle for anything less.

In the years to come, we must distinguish between teachers and leaders and refuse to give biblically sound teachers who are not also gifted leaders the responsibility of leading the congregation.[18] We need teachers who can help us understand what the Scriptures are calling us to be and how to become such people, but we must free those teachers from the bondage of trying to lead a congregation when God Himself has neither called nor gifted them to do so.

And by the way, the most effective leaders in our churches are probably congregants, not clergy. Turning them loose to use their gifts and skills in ministry may require some tinkering with our ministry models, but realize the models we currently use are not present in the Scriptures and therefore are not sacrosanct. Case studies of effective churches often reveal that those ministries build the structure around the gifted individuals who are available to move the people forward, rather than seeking gifted individuals to slot into a predetermined structure.

In the years ahead we must insist that those who lead us hold fast to a clear vision from God of what the congregation is called to do and to be. We cannot afford to pursue the vision of the pastor or other designated leader. The only vision that matters is God's. It is God's will that is going to be done, and thus we need His vision for how to get on board with where He wants to take a particular group of believers. Only those leaders who have that God-given vision firmly implanted in their mind and heart and who are dedicated to pursuing it deserve congregational support.

The greatest church leaders we will encounter are those who recognize that the most important spiritual leadership of all, as noted previously, must be delivered within our families and who do whatever is necessary to empower parents to get that job done. Fathers and mothers are obligated to raise their children in ways that usher them into God's presence and normalize His ways. This is not a job that can be delegated to the religious professionals or to the religious community, although those outsiders represent an important support system to the parents. The most important ministry each parent will ever have is that to his or her offspring. Imagine the impact of every Christian home committing to that responsibility and fulfilling their biblical calling as parents. When that happens, American society will become a vastly different place than it is today.

The bottom line, then, is for churches to put less emphasis on programs, staff, and buildings in favor of equipping the saints for ministry and for cultural impact. The apostle Paul made this point when he wrote that the job of pastors and teachers is simple: "Their responsibility is to equip God's people to do His work and build up the Church, the body of Christ" (Eph. 4:12).

Ministry emphasis and measurement

If you were to spend much time at pastors' conferences these days, one of the buzzwords you'd frequently encounter is *engagement*. The concept of getting Christians "engaged" in faith and ministry is alluring and makes sense—except that, as often as not, the object of such engagement is institutional advancement. We must be careful that people engage primarily with God and one another for the purpose of facilitating transformation. Anything less shortchanges the kingdom of God and disrespects the sacrifice of Christ.

Another caution is for us to abandon our obsession with bigness. We have had more than a quarter century of chasing the megachurch dream. Are we any better off because we have more then two thousand congregations of two thousand or more congregants spread around the country? Has the cause of Christ infiltrated the culture in new and groundbreaking ways because of these large gatherings?

Does American culture have greater respect and appreciation for the cause of Christ because of the big churches that dot the landscape?

The God of Abraham is a God of quality more than quantity. Yes, He wants to reach and win the hearts of all people, but He will never compromise His values—truth, love, grace, justice, and the rest—for the sake of numbers. In fact, the Scriptures show us how He punished David for his obsession with numbers. (See 2 Samuel 24.)

Bigness in itself is not the problem; human pride in leading or building such girth is the sin. God is neither impressed with nor in need of numbers. God has never needed—or used—a majority to accomplish His will.

The evidence is plentiful. He enabled Elisha and his servant to defeat the entire Syrian army because of their faith and obedience (2 Kings 6). God sent home 93 percent of Gideon's army in his victorious battle against the overwhelming number of Midianite soldiers (Judg. 7). When Moses was told to invade the Promised Land, Israel was dramatically outnumbered by the seven nations standing in his path—and it didn't matter (Deut. 7:1–12). Jonah, the reluctant prophet who had neither an entourage nor a weekly television program, successfully brought revival to more than one hundred twenty thousand spiritually lost people in Nineveh (Jon. 4).

In like manner, Christ's modern-day followers must focus on truth and obedience rather than the glamour and material advantage of massive numbers. The kingdom of God is better off with one hundred sold-out followers of Christ than one hundred million fair-weather fans. Frankly, in America today we are closer to the latter than the former. We can change that, but as with everything else, it must start with you.

One way that we can prepare for the U-turn is by changing our metrics. Perhaps we can wean ourselves off the big-numbers obsession by ceasing to count attendance, dollars, or numbers of programs; the quantity of staff on board; or square footage. If Jesus didn't die for it, we shouldn't be preoccupied with it. Instead, we might develop new metrics around what Jesus called us to examine: the fruit of our lives. The more fruit we produce for the advancement of His purposes, the more effective our ministry is and the healthier the Church becomes—regardless of how many people fill the seats or how many dollars fill the offering plate.

Jesus drove home the importance of bearing fruit when He taught His disciples, "When you produce much fruit, you are my true disciples. This brings great glory to my Father" (John 15:8). If each of us were to respond to our callings and gifts and pursue the vision and related opportunities God has uniquely provided to each of us, His work would be done in spectacular ways. His miraculous power and irrefutable authority would be even more evident to everyone than it is now.

To pursue this course of action would constitute a major shift in thinking for most believers. Would that be true for you too? Rather than worrying about your attendance record or your year-to-date offering total, how would your life change if your definition of a successful life and ministry hinged on practicing love, joy, peace, patience, kindness, goodness, gentleness, faithfulness, and self-control? (See Galatians 5:22–23.) How would the world be affected if your daily objectives revolved around embodying righteous character and internally offering continual praise to God? (See Philippians 1:11.)

In the end, armed with a profound identity in Christ, transformed from a self-made person accepting an undeserved gift of salvation into a humbled servant who lives to love and is driven by a desire to bear fruit for His kingdom every day, the Church will engage the culture in ways that hasten its transformation too. We will be used as His instruments in that process, prepared to sacrifice everything in order to do His will. When the nation sees that kind of faith, attitude, and commitment, it will be ripe for restoration.

PARTING WORDS

IN THE OPENING pages of this book, we noted that King Solomon astutely observed that nothing is new under the sun. What does that look like in the United States? Succinctly stated:

- ◆ The early settlers and Founding Fathers sought God and largely followed His ways.

- ◆ God blessed America.

- ◆ We reveled in His blessings.

- ◆ Then we took His blessings for granted.

- ◆ Eventually we took credit for His blessings.

- ◆ We then turned our back on His principles in favor of what seemed right in our own eyes.

- ◆ God allowed the consequences of our choices to affect our lives.

- ◆ Now we are in desperate need of a U-turn to return to His grace and guidance.

In many ways the United States has followed the path of Israel all too closely. They too were blessed by the hand of God. They too blew through seasons of gratitude, arrogance, and struggle. They too reached that terrifying point where they needed to make a U-turn or suffer long-term. They decided not to make the U-turn. But we still can.

A popular paraphrase of the Bible called *The Message* describes the apostle Paul's response to his own people (the Jews) and their disregard for the God who was seeking to save them:

> Israel, who seemed so interested in reading and talking about what God was doing, missed it. How could they miss it? Because instead of trusting God, *they* took over. They were absorbed in what they themselves were doing. They were so absorbed in their "God projects" that they didn't notice God right in front of them, like a huge rock in the middle of the road. And so they stumbled into him and went sprawling.
>
> —Romans 9:31–32

In the middle of its third century as a nation blessed by God, America is at a crossroads. We must choose—very, very soon—who we will be for the coming decades: a nation of grateful and humbled people who grasp the miracle that God has been performing on our shores and who choose to honor and obey Him; or a nation that continues its emergence as a self-indulgent, arrogant, self-reliant people who increasingly reject God's existence, His love, and His principles. It is a very distinct pair of options. Isn't the right way to go obvious?

Keep in mind: no nation that has resisted doing it God's way has ever prevailed. Objectively speaking, there is no reason to believe that we will be the first. God always prevails. Always.

Do not get caught up in the focus on what "the nation" must do. The heart of the matter is what *you* must do. Every one of us must slow down, take time to examine ourselves, and figure out what commitments we personally must make to pull our weight in the national turnaround.

It is so much easier to point the finger at society and wait for it to change. But that's not how cultural transformation works. It takes place one life at a time, and the first life that must change is yours. If you refuse to take that step, it is highly likely that others will join you in boycotting what is right. That's how we got in this mess in the first place—nothing big, no fanfare, not a global conspiracy, just a series of wrong turns, bad choices, errant decisions, and selfish leanings in life after life after life. Add it all up and you get what we have in America today.

Make your U-turn. Now!

And when you begin down the new path, realize that you can add value to your excellent choice by influencing those on whom you have influence. No, you're not the president or chief justice of the Supreme Court or the CEO of a major global corporation. But you are a child of God who has the responsibility and the capacity to impact the thinking and behavior of other people. Think about the family members, friends, work associates, neighbors, fellow volunteers in community organizations, and church members who interact with you, not to mention your social media contacts. What you say and do matters. These relationships represent a chance for you to impact and expand the restoration process. For the glory of God and the sake of America, exploit those opportunities by exerting godly influence. And do it soon.

This isn't rocket science. In fact, it's not science at all. It's art—the art of making good choices, the art of thinking and living biblically, the art of spending your life on the purposes of God. If you reflect and pray about the opportunities that lie before you, you will know exactly what to do.

Make a U-turn. Now!

NOTES

INTRODUCTION

1. Gallup poll conducted June 5–8, 2014, as quoted by PollingReport .com, "Direction of the Country," http://pollingreport.com/right.htm (accessed August 1, 2014).

2. Barna Group, "Frames Wave 2," national survey among 1,404 adults eighteen or older, June 2013; Barna Group, "Three Trends on Faith, Work, and Calling," February 11, 2014, https://www.barna.org/barna -update/culture/649-three-major-faith-and-culture-trends-for-2014# .U9vOfIBdWie (accessed August 1, 2014).

3. NBC News/*Wall Street Journal* poll conducted October 25–28, 2013, as quoted by PollingReport.com, "Direction of the Country."

4. NBC News/*Wall Street Journal* poll conducted June 11–15, 2014, as quoted by PollingReport.com, "Direction of the Country."

5. NBC News/*Wall Street Journal* poll conducted April 23–27, 2014, as quoted by PollingReport.com, "Life," http://pollingreport.com/life.htm (accessed August 1, 2014).

6. Frank Newport, "Most Americans Say Religion Is Losing Influence in US," Gallup Politics, May 29, 2013, http://www.gallup.com/poll/162803/ americans-say-religion-losing-influence.aspx (accessed August 1, 2014).

7. Rebecca Riffkin, "New Record Highs in Moral Acceptability," Gallup Politics, May 30, 2014, http://www.gallup.com/poll/170789/new-record -highs-moral-acceptability.aspx (accessed August 1, 2014).

8. Barna Group, "OmniPoll F-12," a national survey among 1,008 adults eighteen or older, November 2012; Barna Group, "Americans Con- cerned About Religious Freedom," January 18, 2013, https://www .barna.org/barna-update/5-barna-update/601-most-americans-are -concerned-about-restrictions-in-religious-freedom#.U9vPYIBdWic (accessed August 1, 2014).

9. Barna Group, "OmniPoll 1-13 PH," a national survey among 1,005 adults eighteen or older, January 2013. See also Barna Group and American Bible Society, "The State of the Bible: 2014," http://www

.americanbible.org/uploads/content/state-of-the-bible-data-analysis-american-bible-society-2014.pdf (accessed August 1, 2014).

10. CBS News/*New York Times* poll conducted April 24–28, 2013, as quoted by PollingReport.com, "Congress," http://pollingreport.com/congress.htm (accessed August 1, 2014).

11. Barna Group, "OmniPoll F-12."

12. CNN/ORC poll conducted March 15–17, 2013, as quoted by PollingReport.com, "Politics," http://pollingreport.com/politics.htm (accessed August 1, 2014).

13. Barna Group, "OmniPoll F-12."

14. Gallup poll conducted June 20–24, 2013, as quoted by PollingReport.com, "Life."

15. Barna Group, "Frames Wave 3," a national survey among 1,000 adults eighteen or olders, August 2013.

16. Ibid.

17. CBS News poll conducted February 12–16, 2014, as quoted by PollingReport.com, "Politics."

18. Barna Group, "OmniPoll F-12." See also Barna Group, "The Role of Faith in the 2012 Election."

19. Barna Group, "Frames Wave 3."

20. Ibid.

21. Barna Group, "OmniPoll 1-13 OL," national survey of 1,078 adults eighteen or older, January 2013.

22. AP-GfK poll conducted August 16–20, 2012, as quoted by PollingReport.com, "Life."

CHAPTER 1
A NEW AMERICAN DREAM

1. Benjamin Franklin had a list of thirteen virtues that were representative of that era, and especially so in the sense that these thirteen values were synthesized and expressed by someone who is acknowledged to be one of the least religious among the Founders. In Franklin's words those virtues were: Temperance: Eat not to dullness; drink not to elevation. Silence: Speak not but what may benefit others or yourself; avoid trifling conversation. Order: Let all your things have their places; let each part of your business have its time. Resolution: Resolve to perform what you ought; perform without fail what you resolve. Frugality: Make no expense but to do good to others or yourself; i.e., waste nothing. Industry: Lose no time; be always employed in something useful; cut off all unnecessary actions. Sincerity: Use no hurtful deceit;

think innocently and justly; and, if you speak, speak accordingly. Justice: Wrong none by doing injuries, or omitting the benefits that are your duty. Moderation: Avoid extremes; forbear resenting injuries so much as you think they deserve. Cleanliness: Tolerate no uncleanliness in body, clothes, or habitation. Tranquility: Be not disturbed at trifles, or at accidents common or unavoidable. Chastity: Rarely use venery but for health or offspring, never to dullness, weakness, or the injury of your own or another's peace or reputation. Humility: Imitate Jesus and Socrates. See Benjamin Franklin, *The Autobiography of Benjamin Franklin* (New York: Houghton, Mifflin and Company, 1888), 102–104.

2. This list is based on an evaluation of various research studies conducted in the past five years regarding peoples' driving values. The studies have been conducted by the Barna Group, the Gallup Organization, Harris Interactive, Higher Education Research Institute (UCLA), Kaiser Family Foundation, NORC, Peter D. Hart Research Associates, Pew Research Center, and the Survey Research Center (University of Michigan).

3. Barna Group, "OmniPoll 1-13," national survey among 1,005 adults, January 2013.

4. Ibid.

5. Ibid.

Chapter 2
New Beliefs for a New Era

1. Pew Research Religion and Public Life Project, "The Global Religious Landscape," December 18, 2012, http://www.pewforum.org/2012/12/18/global-religious-landscape-exec/ (accessed August 2, 2014); Pew Research Center for the People and the Press, "Muslim Americans: No Signs of Growth in Alienation or Support for Extremism," section 2, August 30, 2011, http://www.people-press.org/2011/08/30/section-2-religious-beliefs-and-practices/ (accessed August 2, 2014).

2. Jason Koebler, "Study: Americans Less Religious Than Ever Before," US *News and World Report*, March 13, 2013, http://www.usnews.com/news/articles/2013/03/13/study-americans-less-religious-than-ever-before (accessed August 2, 2014). See also Elise Hu, "America's Less Religious: Study Puts Some Blame on the Internet," NPR's All Tech Considered, April 21, 2014, http://www.npr.org/blogs/alltechconsidered/2014/04/21/303375159/americas-less-religious-study-puts-some-blame-on-the-internet (accessed August 2, 2014); Jon Terbush, "Why Are Millennials Less Religious? It's Not Just Because of Gay Marriage," The Week, February 27, 2014, http://theweek.com/article/index/257009/why-are-millennials-less-religious-its-not-just-because-of-gay-marriage

(accessed August 2, 2014); Jim Hinch, "What Happened to Religion in America? The I's Have It," FaithStreet.com, March 20, 2014, http://www .faithstreet.com/onfaith/2014/03/20/what-happened-to-religion-in -america-the-is-have-it/31366 (accessed August 2, 2014).

3. Barna Group, "OmniPoll 1-14, OL-PH" national survey among 2,036 adults eighteen or older, January 2014.

4. See Barry A. Kosmin and Ariela Keysar, "American Religious Identification Survey," Trinity College, September 2013, http://www.trincoll .edu/Academics/centers/isssc/Documents/ARIS_2013_College%20 Students_Sept_25_final_draft.pdf (accessed August 2, 2014); Focus on the Family Findings, "Millennial Faith Participation and Retention," August 2013, http://media.focusonthefamily.com/fotf/pdf/about-us/ focus-findings/millenial-faith-retention.pdf (accessed August 2, 2014); Kevin Eagan et al., "The American Freshman: National Norms Fall 2013," Higher Education Research Institute at UCLA, http://www.heri .ucla.edu/monographs/TheAmericanFreshman2013.pdf (accessed August 2, 2014); Barna Group and American Bible Society, "The State of the Bible: 2013"; Lydia Saad, "In US, Rise in Religious 'Nones' Slows in 2012," Gallup Politics, January 10, 2013, http://www.gallup.com/ poll/159785/rise-religious-nones-slows-2012.aspx (accessed August 2, 2014); and Bruce Drake, "Six New Findings About Millennials," Pew Research Center, March 7, 2014, http://www.pewresearch.org/fact -tank/2014/03/07/6-new-findings-about-millennials/ (accessed August 2, 2014).

5. Barna Group, "OmniPoll 1-14 OL-PH."

6. Barna Group, "Frames Wave 2."

7. Frank Newport, "Most Americans Say Religion Is Losing Influence in US."

8. Peter Moore, "Religion Doesn't Lead to Happiness, Say Young People," YouGov, March 25, 2014, https://today.yougov.com/news/2014/03/25/ religion-doesnt-lead-happiness/ (accessed August 2, 2014), with polling data available at http://cdn.yougov.com/cumulus_uploads/document/ h8znggahel/tabs_OPI_happiness_20140317.pdf (accessed August 2, 2014).

9. Frank Newport, "Majority Still Says Religion Can Answer Today's Problems," Gallup Politics, June 27, 2014, http://www.gallup.com/ poll/171998/majority-says-religion-answer-today-problems.aspx (accessed August 2, 2014).

10. Peter Moore, "Religion Doesn't Lead to Happiness."

11. Frank Newport, "Most Americans Believe in God," Gallup Politics, June 3, 2011, http://www.gallup.com/video/147893/Believe-God.aspx (accessed August 2, 2014); Gallup.org, "Religion," http://www.gallup

.com/poll/1690/Religion.aspx (accessed August 14, 2014); George Barna, *What Americans Believe* (Ventura, CA: Regal Books, 1991); Barna Group, "OmniPoll 1-14 OL-PH," a national survey among 2,036 adults eighteen or older, January 2014.

12. Pew Research Center for the People and the Press, "Partisan Polarization Surges in Bush, Obama Years," section 6, June 4, 2012, http://www.people-press.org/2012/06/04/section-6-religion-and-social-values/ (accessed August 2, 2014).

13. Barna Group, "OmniPoll 1-14 OL-PH."

14. Barna Research Group, "OmniPoll 1-92," a national survey of 1,005 adults eighteen or older, January 1992.

15. Barna Group, "OmniPoll 1-14 OL-PH."

16. Ibid.

17. Ibid.

18. GfK Public Affairs and Corporate Communications, "The AP-GfK Poll," March 2014, http://ap-gfkpoll.com/main/wp-content/uploads/2014/04/AP-GfK-March-2014-Poll-Topline-Final_SCIENCE.pdf (accessed August 2, 2014).

19. HarrisInteractive.com, "Americans' Belief in God, Miracles, and Heaven Declines," December 16, 2013, http://www.harrisinteractive.com/NewsRoom/HarrisPolls/tabid/447/ctl/ReadCustom%20Default/mid/1508/ArticleId/1353/Default.aspx (accessed August 2, 2014).

20. Ibid.

21. Wave III Baylor Religion Survey, "The Values and Beliefs of the American Public," September 2011, http://www.baylor.edu/content/services/document.php/153501.pdf (accessed August 2, 2014).

22. Public Policy Polling, "Americans' Perception of Congress Improves, but Still Poor," July 21, 2011, http://www.publicpolicypolling.com/main/2011/07/americans-perception-of-congress-improves-but-still-poor.html (accessed August 2, 2014).

23. Ibid.

24. Ibid.

25. Rasmussen Reports, "69 Percent Believe Jesus Christ Rose from the Dead," April 18, 2014, http://www.rasmussenreports.com/public_content/lifestyle/holidays/april_2014/69_believe_jesus_christ_rose_from_the_dead (accessed August 2, 2014).

26. Harris Interactive, "Americans' Belief in God, Miracles, and Heaven Declines."

27. Ibid.

28. Barna Reseach Group, "OmniPoll 1-94," survey of more than 1,000 adults, January 1994; see also Kenneth L. Woodward, "Rethinking the Resurrection," Newsweek.com, April 7, 1996, http://www.newsweek .com/rethinking-resurrection-176618 (accessed August 14, 2014).

29. Harris Interactive, "Americans' Belief in God, Miracles, and Heaven Declines"; see also Kenneth L. Woodward, "Rethinking the Resurrection," *Newsweek*, April 7, 1996, http://www.newsweek.com/rethinking -resurrection-176618 (accessed August 14, 2014).

30. Barna Research Group, "OmniPoll 1-94."

31. Harris Interactive, "Americans' Belief in God, Miracles, and Heaven Declines."

32. Barna Research Group, "OmniPoll 1-94."

33. Barna Group, "OmniPoll 1-04," survey of more than 1,000 adults, conducted January 2004.

34. Barna Group, "OmniPoll 1-14 OL-PH."

35. Ibid.

36. Barna Group, "OmniPoll 1-04."

37. Barna Group, "OmniPoll 1-14 PH," among 1,012 adults, conducted January 2014.

38. This figure is a result of Barna Group national research studies, each based on more than 1,000 interviews with adults eighteen or older, conducted in May 2008, January 2013, and January 2014.

39. Barna Group and American Bible Society, "The State of the Bible: 2014."

40. Ibid.

41. Ibid.

42. Ibid.

43. Barna Group and American Bible Society, "The State of the Bible, 2013," http://www.americanbible.org/uploads/content/State%20of%20 the%20Bible%20Report%202013.pdf (accessed August 2, 2014).

44. Ibid.

45. Barna Group, "OmniPoll 1-13 OL," a national survey of 1,078 adults, conducted January 2013.

46. Barna Group, "OmniPoll 1-14 OL-PH."

47. GfK Public Affairs and Corporate Communications, "The AP-GfK Poll."

48. See YouGov, Omnibus Poll conducted July 8–9, 2013, http://cdn .yougov.com/cumulus_uploads/document/d39q50o8bw/tabs_ evolution_0708092013.pdf (accessed August 2, 2014); Pew Research

Religion and Public Life Project, "Public's Views on Human Evolution," December 30, 2013, http://www.pewforum.org/2013/12/30/ (accessed August 2, 2014); GfK Public Affairs and Corporate Communications, "The AP-GfK Poll"; and Harris Interactive, "Americans' Belief in God, Miracles, and Heaven Declines."

49. YouGov, Omnibus Poll, July 8–9, 2013; Harris Interactive, "Americans' Belief in God, Miracles, and Heaven Declines."

50. Pew Research Religion and Public Life Project, "Public's Views on Human Evolution."

51. Harris Interactive, "Americans' Belief in God, Miracles, and Heaven Declines."

52. Yeoun Soo Kim-Godwin, "Prayer in Clinical Practice: What Does the Evidence Support," *Journal of Christian Nursing*, 30, no. 4 (October–December 2013): 208–215.

53. Data taken from Barna Group, "OmniPoll 1-14" and "OmniPoll 1-94," as well as surveys conducted by the Gallup Organization in 1983, 1993, and 2013.

54. Wave III Baylor Religion Survey, "The Values and Beliefs of the American Public."

55. Ibid.

56. Gallup Organization, "Religion," national survey among 1,000 adults, conducted May 2011, http://www.gallup.com/poll/1690/Religion.aspx#2 (accessed August 14, 2014).

57. Pew Research Center for the People and the Press, "Partisan Polarization Surges in Busy, Obama Years," section 6.

58. Ibid.; Gallup Organization, national survey of adults.

59. George Gallup, *Religion in America* (Princeton, NJ: Princeton Religious Research Center, 1996).

60. Barna Group, "OmniPoll 1-14 OL-PH."

61. Ibid.

62. Barna Group, "OmniPoll 1-06," national survey of 1,005 adults eighteen or older, January 2006.

63. Barna Group, "OmniPoll 1-14 OL-PH."

64. George Barna, *The Seven Faith Tribes: Who They Are, What They Believe, and Why They Matter* (Carol Stream, IL: Tyndale, 2009).

65. Ibid., 79.

66. Harris Interactive, "Americans' Belief in God, Miracles, and Heaven Declines."

67. Barna Group, "Frames Wave 2" and "OmniPoll 1-14." See also Riffkin, "New Record Highs in Moral Acceptability."

68. Ibid. The authors also received unpublished data from a 2013 Gallup study that was used in determining these percentages.

69. Barna Group, "OmniPoll May-08," national survey of 1,003 adults eighteen or older, May 2008.

70. Ibid.

71. Ibid.

72. Pew Research Center for the People and the Press, "Partisan Polarization Surges in Bush, Obama Years," section 6; see also Pew Research Center, "Worldwide Many See Belief in God as Essential to Morality," March 13, 2014, http://www.pewglobal.org/2014/03/13/worldwide-many-see-belief-in-god-as-essential-to-morality/ (accessed August 14, 2014),

73. Barna Group, "OmniPoll 1-14"; see also Pew Research Center, "Worldwide Many See Belief in God as Essential to Morality."

74. Kosmin and Keysar, "American Religious Identification Survey." The authors identified the sample size for each group then recalculated the source data to provide a national average.

75. American Religious Freedom, "Survey Fact Sheet: Americans' Views on Religious Freedom," December 2, 2011, http://www.religiousfreedom.org/research/detail/survey-fact-sheet-americans-views-on-religious-freedom (accessed August 14, 2014).

76. See, for example, Jonathan Mayhew, *A Discourse on Rev. XV. 3d. 4th, Occasioned by the Earthquakes in November 1755* (Boston: Edes and Gill, 1755); Jonathan Mayhew, *A Sermon Occasioned by the Great Fire in Boston, New England, Thursday, March 20, 1760* (Boston: Edes and Gill, 1760); Joseph Buckminster, *A Discourse Occasioned by the Late Desolating Fire, Delivered in the First Church in Portsmouth, the Lord's Day Succeeding That Melancholy Event* (Portsmouth, NH: Oracle Press, 1803); Jonathan Plummer, *Great and Dreadful Fire at Newburyport—Fire, Fire, Fire! An Ode and a Sermon Concerning a Tremendous Fire at Newburyport, Which Commenced on the Evening of the Thirty-First of May 1811* (Newburyport, MA: printed for the author, 1811); Alexander Archibald, *A Discourse Occasioned by the Burning of the Theatre in the City of Richmond, Virginia, on the 26th of December 1811, by Which Awful Calamity a Large Number of Valuable Lives Were Lost* (Philadelphia: John Welwood Scott, 1812); Samuel Macclintock, *The Choice: A Discourse Occasioned by the Present Severe Drought, the Mortal Fever Which Prevails in Portsmouth in This Near Vicinity and in Many of our Capitol Sea Port Towns, and the Threatening Prospects of a Calamitous War With a Powerful*

Nation (Boston: Thomas Adams, 1798); and Jonathan Plummer, *The Newbury Port Hurricane: An Elegiac Ode and a Funeral Sermon on the Death of Mr. John Bernard, Drowned by a Most Tremendous Hurricane or Tornado* (Newburyport, MA: printed for the author, 1808).

77. See, for example, Nathaniel Fisher, *A Sermon Delivered at Salem, January 14, 1796, Occasioned by the Execution of Henry Blackburn on That Day for the Murder of George Wilkinson* (Boston: S. Hall, 1796); James Dana, *The Intent of Capital Punishment: A Discourse Delivered in the City of New Haven, October 20, 1790, Being the Day of the Execution of Joseph Mountain for a Rape* (New Haven, CT: T. and S. Green, 1790); and Ezra Ripley, *Love to Our Neighbor Explained and Urged in a Sermon Delivered at Concord, Massachusetts, December 26, 1799, Being the Day on Which Samuel Smith Was Executed for Burglary* (Boston: Samuel Hall, 1800).

78. See, for example, Joseph Lathrop, *A Sermon Containing Reflections on the Solar Eclipse, Which Appeared on June 16, 1806* (Springfield, MA: Henry Brewer, 1806); Samuel Danforth, *An Astronomical Description of the Late Comet, or Blazing Star, as It Appeared in New England on the 9th, 10th, 11th, and in the Beginning of the 12th Month 1664, Together With a Brief Theological Explanation Thereof* (Cambridge: n.p., 1665); and C. A. Bartol, *The New Planet, or an Analogy Between the Perturbations of Matter and Spirit: A Sermon* (Boston: Leonard C. Bowles, 1847).

79. See, for example, Ashbel Green, *Obedience to the Laws of God, the Sure and Indispensable Defence of Nations: A Discourse Delivered in the Second Presbyterian Church in the City of Philadelphia, May 9, 1798, Being the Day Appointed by the President of the United States to Be Observed as a Season for Solemn Humiliation, Fasting, and Prayer* (Philadelphia: John Omrod, 1798); John Lathrop, *A Discourse Preached, December 15, 1774, Being the Day Recommended by the Provincial Congress to Be Observed in Thanksgiving to God for the Blessing Enjoyed and Humiliation on Account of Public Calamities* (Boston: D. Kneeland, 1774); Isaac Braman, *Union With France a Greater Evil Than Union with Britain: A Sermon Preached in Rowley, West Parish, at the Annual Fast, April 5, 1810* (Haverhill, MA: William B. Allen, 1810); Timothy Dwight, *The Duty of Americans at the Present Crisis, Illustrated in a Discourse, Preached on the Fourth of July 1798...at the Request of the Citizens of New Haven* (New Haven, CT: Thomas and Samuel Green, 1798); Jedidiah Morse, *A Sermon Exhibiting the Present Dangers and Consequent Duties of the Citizens of the United States of America* (Charlestown, MA: Samuel Etheridge, 1799); and Anonymous, *A Sermon on the Present Situation of the*

Affairs of America and Great Britain (Philadelphia: T. Bradford and P. Hall, 1782).

80. See, for example, Edward Dorr, *The Duty of Civil Rulers to Be Nursing Fathers to the Church of Christ* (Hartford, CT: Thomas Green, 1765); Stephen Johnson, *Integrity and Piety the Best Principles of a Good Administration of Government, Illustrated in a Sermon Preached Before the General Assembly of the Colony of Connecticut at Hartford* (New London, CT: Timothy Green, 1770); Chauncey Wittlesey, *The Importance of Religion in the Civil Ruler Considered* (New Haven, CT: Thomas and Samuel Green, 1778); Henry van Dyke, *The People Responsible for the Character of Their Rulers: A Sermon Delivered by the Rev. Henry van Dyke, DD, Before the Society of Sons of the Revolution in the State of New York, February 24, 1895* (New York: Society of the Sons of the Revolution, 1895); Alexander Proudfit, *Our Danger and Duty: Two Sermons, Delivered on Wednesday, the 30th Day of November 1808, Being a Day Appointed by the Presbytery of Washington for the Exercises of Fasting, Humiliation, and Prayer on Account of the Alarming Aspect of Divine Providence to Our Country* (Salem, MA: Dodd and Rumsey, 1808); Timothy Dwight, *The True Means of Establishing Public Happiness: A Sermon Delivered on the 7th of July 1795, Before the Connecticut Society of Cincinnati and Published at Their Request* (New Haven, CT: T. and S. Green, 1795); Joseph Buckminster, *The Duty of Republican Citizens in the Choice of Their Rulers: The Substance of Two Discourses Delivered in the First Church of Christ in Portsmouth, February 28, 1796* (Portsmouth, NH: Charles Peirce, 1796); Francis Wayland Jr., *The Duties of an American Citizen: Two Discourses Delivered in the First Baptist Meeting House in Boston on Thursday, April 7, 1825, the Day of Public Fast* (Boston: James Loring, 1825); Joseph Lathrop, *The Happiness of a Free Government and the Means of Preserving It, Illustrated in a Sermon Delivered in West Springfield on July 4, 1794, in Commemoration of American Independence* (Springfield, MA: James R. Hutchins, 1794); and David Oliphant, *The Happy Nation: A Sermon Preached at Beverly, November 24, 1825, Being the Day Appointed by the Executive Authority of the Commonwealth for the Annual Thanksgiving* (Salem, MA: Warwick Palfray, 1825).

81. Joseph Lathrop, *The Infirmities and Comforts of Old Age: A Sermon to Aged People* (Springfield, MA: Henry Brewer, 1805); Joseph Lathrop, *Old Age Improved: A Sermon Delivered to the People of the First Parish in West Springfield by Joseph Lathrop, DD, Their Pastor, October 31, 1811, the Day Which Completed the 80th Year of His Age* (Springfield, MA: T. Dickman, 1811).

82. See, for example, J. M. Homer, *The Modern Emigrant, or Lover of Liberty: Being a Discourse Delivered in the City of New York* (New York: W. Mitchell, 1832).

83. See, for example, Thomas Smith Grimke, *Oration on the Advantages to Be Derived From the Introduction of the Bible and of Sacred Literature as Essential Parts of All Education, in a Literary Point of View Merely, From the Primary School to the University* (New Haven, CT: Hezekiah Howe, 1830); J. W. Wellman, *The Organic Development of Christianity in the Direction of Education and Learning* (Boston: T. R. Marvin and Son, 1860); Cotton Mather, *Corderius Americanus: A Discourse on the Good Education of Children...Delivered at the Funeral of Ezekiel Cheever, Principal of the Latin School in Boston, Who Died August 1708 in the Ninety-Fourth Year of His Age, With an Elegy and an Epitaph* (Boston: Dutton and Wentworth, 1828); Leonard Bacon, *Christianity and Learning* (New Haven, CT: B. L. Hamlen, 1848); and George W. Blagden, *The Influence of the Gospel Upon the Intellectual Powers: A Sermon Preached in the Central Church, Philadelphia, May 25, 1835* (Philadelphia: American Sunday School Union, 1835).

84. See, for example, C. A. Bartol, *The Relation of the Medical Profession to the Ministry: A Discourse Preached in the West Church on Occasion of the Death of Dr. George C. Shattuck* (Boston: John Wilson and Son, 1854).

85. Charles Chauncy, *A Discourse on the Good News From a Far Country, Delivered July 24, a Day of Thanksgiving to Almighty God Throughout the Province of the Massachusetts Bay in New England, on Occasion of the Repeal of the Stamp Act* (Boston: Kneeland and Adams, 1766); and John Joachim Zubly, *The Stamp Act Repealed: A Sermon Preached in the Meeting at Savannah in Georgia* (Charleston, SC: Peter Timothy, 1766).

86. John Adams, *The Works of John Adams*, vol. 4, ed. Charles Francis Adams (Boston: Charles C. Little and James Brown, 1851), 56.

87. John Wingate Thornton, *The Pulpit of the American Revolution: Or the Political Sermons of the Period of 1776* (Boston: Gould and Lincoln, 1860), xxii–xxiii.

88. See, for example, *The Trial of Samuel Tulley and John Dalton, on an Indictment for Piracy and Murder, Committed January 21, 1812, Before the Circuit Court of the United States at Boston, 28th October 1812, Containing the Evidence at Large, a Sketch of the Arguments of Counsel, and the Charge of the Hon. Judge Story on Pronouncing Sentence of Death* (Boston: Joshua Belcher, 1814) 22–26; and *New York Times*, "The Slave Trade: Sentence of Capt. Gordon of the Slaver Erie," December 2, 1861, http://query.nytimes.com/gst/abstract.html?res= 9804EFDD113FEE34BC4A53DFB467838A679FDE (accessed August 2,

2014). See also Thomas C. McCarthy, "Why Was the Tombs the Execution Site for the Only American Ever Hanged as a Slave Trader?," New York Correction History Society, February 2003, http://www .correctionhistory.org/html/chronicl/tombs/gordon/whytombs1.htm (accessed August 2, 2014); William B. Reed, *Life and Correspondence of Joseph Reed*, vol. 2 (Philadelphia: Lindsay and Blakiston, 1847), 36–37; Jacob Rush, *Charges and Extracts of Charges on Moral and Religious Subjects* (Philadelphia: Geo Forman, 1804), 144–147; and *The Globe*, "Sentence of Horn, the Murderer," December 6, 1843.

89. During a speech given March 23, 1775, he quoted phrases from Deuteronomy 32:4; 2 Chronicles 32:8; Joshua 24:15; Psalm 75:7; Ecclesiastes 9:11; Jeremiah 6:14; 8:11; 50:22; Daniel 4:17; Matthew 20:6; and 2 Thessalonians 1:6. See William Wirt, *Sketches of the Life and Character of Patrick Henry* (Philadelphia: James Webster, 1817), 123.

90. In his speech to the Constitutional Convention on June 28, 1787, Benjamin Franklin quoted phrases from Genesis 11:1–9; Deuteronomy 28:37; 2 Chronicles 7:20; 1 Kings 9:7; Job 12:25; Psalm 44:14; 75:7; 127:1; Daniel 4:17; Matthew 10:29; Luke 12:6; and James 1:5, 17. See James Madison, *The Papers of James Madison*, vol. 2, ed. Henry D. Gilpin (Washington DC: Langtree and O'Sullivan, 1840), 984–985.

91. In a letter dated July 25, 1785, George Washington used phrases from Genesis 1:28; Exodus 3:8; 12:25; Deuteronomy 24:14; Isaiah 40:3; Matthew 11:28; 22:38. See George Washington, *The Writings of George Washington*, vol. 28, ed. John C. Fitzpatrick (Washington DC: Government Printing Office, 1940), 206–207. See also Peter A. Lillback, *George Washington's Sacred Fire* (Bryn Mawr, PA: Providence Forum Press, 2006), 323.

92. In a letter to the Hebrew congregation of Newport, Rhode Island, dated August 18, 1790, George Washington quoted phrases from Deuteronomy 12:10; 1 Kings 4:25; Psalm 119:105; Proverbs 4:18; Ecclesiastes 3:11; Isaiah 35:10; Micah 4:4; Acts 13:26; 2 Corinthians 1:3; and Ephesians 4:1. See George Washington, *The Papers of George Washington*, vol. 6, ed. W. W. Abbot (Charlottesville, VA: University Press of Virginia, 1996), 286. See also Lillback, *George Washington's Sacred Fire*, 321–322.

93. Donald S. Lutz, "The Relative Influence of European Writers on Late Eighteenth Century American Political Thought," *American Political Science Review* 78, no. 1 (March 1894): 191–193. See also Donald S. Lutz, *The Origins of American Constitutionalism* (Baton Rouge: Louisiana State University Press, 1988), 141–142.

94. *Journals of the Continental Congress 1774–1789*, vol. 4 (Washington DC: Government Printing Office, 1906), 209.

95. William DeLoss Love, *The Fast and Thanksgiving Days of New England* (Boston: Houghton, Mifflin and Company, 1895), 464–514. By way of further example, yet by no means an exhaustive list, consider also the following: John Hancock called for a day of fasting, humiliation, and prayer on April 15, 1775; Jonathan Trumbull, governor of Connecticut, called for a day of fasting and prayer on March 9, 1774; the Massachusetts Council issued a call for a day of public humiliation, fasting, and prayer on April 5, 1777; John Langdon, the governor of New Hampshire, called for a day of fasting on February 21, 1786; Samuel Adams, governor of Massachusetts, issued a proclamation for a day of fasting, humiliation, and prayer on February 28, 1795; and John Adams, while president of the United States, called for a day of humiliation, fasting, and prayer on March 23, 1798.

96. Adams, *The Works of John Adams*.

97. *The Constitution of the Commonwealth of Pennsylvania* (Philadelphia: Daniel Humphreys, 1786), 15.

98. Constitution of the state of Pennsylvania, in *The Constitutions of the Several Independent States of America* (Philadelphia: published by order of Congress, 1782), 80. For other examples, see the constitution of the state of Vermont, in *The Federal and State Constitutions, Colonial Charters, and Other Organic Laws of the States, Territories, and Colonies Now Heretofore Forming the United States of America*, vol. 6, ed. Francis Newton Thorpe (Washington DC: Government Printing Office, 1909), 3743; the constitution of the state of South Carolina, in *The Constitutions of the Several Independent States of America*, 135; and the constitution of the state of Tennessee, in *The Constitutions of the Sixteen States* (Boston: Manning and Loring, 1797), 274.

99. See, for example, *Updegraph v. Commonwealth*, 11 Serg. & Rawle 394 (Pa. 1824).

100. James Kent, *Memoirs and Letters of James Kent*, ed. William Kent (Boston: Little, Brown, and Company, 1898), 123.

101. James Madison, *Papers of James Madison*, vol. 3, ed. Henry Gilpin (Washington DC: Langtree and O'Sullivan, 1840), 1391. See also similar declarations by Founding Fathers, such as the declaration made by Samuel Adams to John Scollay on April 30, 1776, as quoted in Paul H. Smith, ed., *Letters of Delegates to Congress*, vol. 3 (Washington DC: Library of Congress, 1978), 603; the inaugural address of President Washington on April 30, 1789, as quoted in *American State Papers: Documents, Legislative and Executive, of the Congress of the United States*, vol. 1 (Washington DC: Gales and Seaton, 1833), 10; and Benjamin Franklin speaking at the Constitution Conventional on June 28, 1787, as quoted in Madison, *Papers of James Madison*, vol. 2, 985.

See also Benjamin Rush, *An Address to the Inhabitants of the British Settlements in America Upon Slave-Keeping* (Boston: John Boyles, 1773), 30; Thomas Jefferson, *Notes on the State of Virginia* (Philadelphia: Mathew Carey, 1794), 237; and Luther Martin and Thomas Cockey Deye, *The Genuine Information Delivered to the Legislature of the State of Maryland Relative to the Proceedings of the General Convention Lately Held at Philadelphia* (Philadelphia: Eleazor Oswald, 1788), printed in Jonathan Elliot, ed., *The Debates in the Several State Conventions of the Adoption of the Federal Constitution*, vol. 1 (Washington DC: 1836), 374.

102. Peter Force, *American Archives*, Fourth Series (Washington DC: M. St. Claire Clark and Peter Force under the authority of Congress, 1846), 1277–78. See also Evans #16854, issued by Massachusetts Bay Council on June 27, 1780; a proclamation issued by Josiah Bartlett of New Hampshire on October 5, 1793, and printed on page 1 of *The Oracle of the Day*, October 26, 1793; a proclamation issued by Samuel Adams of Massachusetts on February 19, 1794 and printed on page 3 of the *Eastern Herald*; and Evans #14275, issued by Matthew Thornton of the Continental Congress on June 6, 1775.

103. See, for example, the 1824 race of Daniel Webster for the US House, when 4,990 out of 5,000 citizens cast ballots in that uncontested election, as reported in Frederic Austin Ogg, *Daniel Webster* (Philadelphia: George W. Jacobs and Company, 1914), 135.

104. Samuel Adams, *The Writings of Samuel Adams*, vol. 4, ed. Harry Alonzo Cushing (New York: G. P. Putnam's Sons, 1908), 253; see also 256.

105. Benjamin Rush, *Essays: Literary, Moral, and Philosophical* (Philadelphia: Thomas and Samuel F. Bradford, 1798), 11.

106. Benjamin Rush, *Letters of Benjamin Rush*, vol. 1, ed. L. H. Butterfield (Princeton, NJ: Princeton University Press, 1951), 478.

107. Martha Washington, draft of a letter written in the hand of Tobias Lear to President John Adams on December 31, 1799, as quoted in Helen Bryan, *Martha Washington: Lady of Liberty* (New York: John Wiley and Sons, 2002), 374.

108. John Quincy Adams, *Letters of John Quincy Adams to His Son on the Bible and Its Teachings* (Auburn, New York: Derby, Miller, and Co., 1848), 34.

109. See The Heritage Foundation, "2014 Index of Economic Freedom: Country Rankings," http://www.heritage.org/index/ranking (accessed on March 4, 2014), where America for the first time is shown to have fallen out of the top ten.

110. Scott Cohn and Robert Ferris, "Study: Government Corruption Rampant Worldwide," December 8, 2013, http://www.usatoday.com/story/money/business/2013/12/08/cnbc-government-corruption/3872767/ (accessed August 2, 2014).

111. National Center for Education Statistics, "PIAAC 2012 Results," http://nces.ed.gov/surveys/piaac/results/summary.aspx (accessed August 2, 2014).

112. Pew Research Global Attitudes Project, "Global Views on Morality," http://www.pewglobal.org/2014/04/15/global-morality/country/united-states/ (accessed August 2, 2014).

CHAPTER 3
OUR RESPONSIBILITY AS CITIZENS

1. United States Census Bureau, "Table 2: Reported Voting and Registration, by Race, Hispanic Origin, Sex, and Age, for the United States: November 2012," http://www.census.gov/hhes/www/socdemo/voting/publications/p20/2012/tables.html (accessed August 2, 2014).

2. Federal Election Commission, "Federal Elections 2012: Election Results for the US President, the US Senate, and the US House of Representatives," July 2013, http://www.fec.gov/pubrec/fe2012/federalelections2012.pdf (accessed August 2, 2014).

3. United States Election Project, "2010 General Election Turnout Rates," http://elections.gmu.edu/Turnout_2010G.html (accessed August 2, 2014). With 67.1 percent of adults registered to vote, and an average of 39 percent voter turnout in non-presidential elections, only about 26 percent of of adults actually votes in non-presidential elections.

4. Jeffrey M. Jones, "Congress Job Approval Starts 2014 at 13%," Gallup Politics, January 14, 2014, http://www.gallup.com/poll/166838/congress-job-approval-starts-2014.aspx (accessed August 2, 2014).

5. Steven Hill, *Fixing Elections: The Failure of America's Winner Take All Politics* (New York: Routledge, 2002), vii.

6. Joel Stein, "Who's in Charge Here?," *Time*, May 13, 2013, 58.

7. FoxNews.com, "As America Votes, America Also Wonders, 'Who's Running'?," November 6, 2012, http://www.foxnews.com/tech/2012/11/06/as-america-votes-america-also-wonders-who-running (accessed August 2, 2014).

8. *The New York Times*, "The 2012 Money Race: Compare the Candidates," http://elections.nytimes.com/2012/campaign-finance) (accessed August 2, 2014).

9. See, for example, InfoWars.com, "Only One-Third of Americans Can Name Three Branches of Government," March 8, 2009, http://www

.infowars.com/only-one-third-of-americans-can-name-three-branches-of-government/ (accessed August 2, 2014); Lion Calandra, "Why Do Americans Get the Constitution So Wrong?," *Christian Science Monitor*, September 17, 2010, http://www.csmonitor.com/Commentary/Opinion/2010/0917/Why-do-Americans-get-the-Constitution-so-wrong (accessed August 2, 2014); and Brit Hume, "Zogby Poll: Most Americans Can Name Three Stooges, But Not Three Branches of Gov't," FoxNews.com, August 15, 2006, http://www.foxnews.com/story/0,2933,208577,00.html#ixzz2E1kq5uZS (accessed August 2, 2014).

10. AEI Program on American Citizenship, "Americans Failing Citizenship Test Again," April 30, 2012, http://www.citizenship-aei.org/2012/04/americans-failing-citizenship-test-again/ (accessed August 2, 2014).

11. *Newsweek*, "Take the Quiz: What We Don't Know," March 20, 2011, http://www.newsweek.com/2011/03/20/take-the-quiz-what-we-don-t-know.html (accessed August 2, 2014).

12. AEI Program on American Citizenship, "Americans Failing Citizenship Test Again"; *Newsweek*, "Take the Quiz: What We Don't Know."

13. AEI Program on American Citizenship, "Americans Failing Citizenship Test Again."

14. Andrew Romano, "How Ignorant Are Americans?" *Newsweek*, March 20, 2011, http://www.newsweek.com/how-ignorant-are-americans-66053 (accessed August 2, 2014).

15. Francie Grace, "Simpsons Outpace US Constitution," CBSNews.com, March 1, 2006, http://www.cbsnews.com/news/simpsons-outpace-us-constitution/ (accessed August 2, 2014).

16. Ibid.

17. Information Clearing House, "Shocking Poll: Majority of Americans Cannot Name a Single Department in the President's Cabinet," November 4, 2003, http://www.informationclearinghouse.info/article5158.htm (accessed August 2, 2014).

18. FindLaw.com, "Two-Thirds of Americans Can't Name Any US Supreme Court Justices, Says New FindLaw.com Survey," August 20, 2012, http://company.findlaw.com/press-center/2012/two-thirds-of-americans-can-t-name-any-u-s-supreme-court-justice.html (accessed August 2, 2014).

19. *Newsweek*, "Take the Quiz: What We Don't Know," *Newsweek.com*.

20. Benjamin Rush, *Letters*, 83.

21. Henry van Dyke, *People Responsible for Character*.

22. Remarks made at a public reception by the ladies of Richmond, Virginia, on October 5, 1840, as recorded in Daniel Webster, *The Works of*

Daniel Webster, vol. 2, ed. Edward Everett (Boston: Little, Brown, and Company, 1853), 108.

23. Rush, *Essays*, 8–12.

24. Adams, *Writings of Samuel Adams*, vol. 4, 252, emphasis added.

25. See, for example, John Adams, *The Works of John Adams*, vol. 10, ed. Charles Francis Adams (Boston: Little, Brown and Company, 1854), 311; John Adams, *The Works of John Adams*, vol. 1, ed. Charles Francis Adams (Boston: Little, Brown and Company, 1856), 53–54; John Adams, *Works*, vol. 4, 82–83; Benjamin Franklin, *The Papers of Benjamin Franklin*, vol. 17, ed. William B. Willcox (New Haven, CT: Yale University Press, 1973), 6; Benjamin Franklin, *The Papers of Benjamin Franklin*, vol. 4, ed. Leonard W. Labaree (New Haven, CT: Yale University Press, 1961), 107; Thomas Jefferson, *The Works of Thomas Jefferson*, vol. 6, ed. Paul Leicester Ford (New York: G. P. Putnam's Sons, 1905), 63; Thomas Jefferson, *The Works of Thomas Jefferson*, vol. 10, ed. Paul Leicester Ford (New York: G. P. Putnam's Sons, 1905), 416; Thomas Jefferson, *The Works of Thomas Jefferson*, vol. 12, ed. Paul Leicester Ford (New York: G. P. Putnam's Sons, 1905), 307; Benjamin Rush, *The Selected Writings of Benjamin Rush*, ed. Dagobert D. Runes (New York: The Philosophical Library, 1947), 78; Benjamin Rush, *Medical Inquiries and Observations*, vol. 1 (Philadelphia: T. and G. Palmer, 1805), 402; Benjamin Rush, *Medical Inquiries and Observations*, vol. 2 (Philadelphia: J. Conrad and Co., 1805), 19; John Quincy Adams, *The Jubilee of the Constitution* (New York: Samuel Colman, 1839), 40–41; and James Wilson, *The Works of the Honourable James Wilson*, vol. 1, ed. Bird Wilson (Philadelphia: Lorenzo Press, 1804), 67–68.

26. *United States Oracle of the Day*, Portsmouth, NH (May 24, 1800). See also Maeva Marcus, ed., *The Documentary History of the Supreme Court*, vol. 3 (New York: Columbia University Press, 1988), 436.

27. See, for example, Samuel Hooker, *Righteousness Rained From Heaven, or a Serious and Seasonable Discourse Exciting All to an Earnest Enquiry After and Continued Waiting for the Effusions of the Spirit Unto a Communication and Increase of Righteousness That Faith, Holiness, and Obedience May Yet Abound Among Us and the Wilderness Become a Fruitful Field, as It Was Delivered in a Sermon Preached at Hartford on Connecticut in New England, May 10, 1677, Being the Day of Election There* (Cambridge, MA: Samuel Green, 1677), 9; Jeremiah Wise, *A Funeral Sermon Preached Upon the Death of the Honorable Charles Frost, Esq., One of His Majesty's Council for the Province of the Massachusetts Bay in NE* (Boston: D. Henchman, 1725), 15; Timothy Edward, *All the Living Must Surely Die and Go to Judgment: A Sermon Preached Before the General Assembly of the Colony of Connecticut at Hartford on the Day of Election There, on*

May 11, 1732 (New London, CT: T. Green, 1732), 42–43; Nathaniel Chauncey, *The Faithful Ruler Described and Excited, in a Sermon Preached Before the General Assembly of the Colony of Connecticut at Hartford, May 9, 1734, the Day for the Election of the Honourable the Governor, the Deputy Governor, and the Worshipful Assistant There* (New London, CT: T. Green, 1734), 32; Archibald Cummings, *The Character of a Righteous Ruler: A Sermon Upon the Death of the Honorable Patrick Gordon, Esq., Lieutenant Governor of the Province of Pennsylvania & c.* (Philadelphia: Andrew Bradford, 1736), 14; Isaac Stiles, *A Looking Glass for Changelings: A Seasonable Caveat Against Meddling With Them That Are Given to Change, in a Sermon Preached at the Free Men's Meeting at New Haven, April 11, 1743* (New London, CT: n.p., 1743), 24; Ebenezer Gay, *The Character and Work of a Good Ruler and the Duty of an Obliged People: A Sermon Preached Before His Excellency William Shirley, Esq., the Honourable His Majesty's Council, and House of Representatives of the Province of the Massachusetts Bay in New England, May 29, 1745* (Boston: Daniel Gooking, 1745), 5; Samuel Cooke, *A Sermon Preached at Cambridge in the Audience of His Honor Thomas Hutchinson, Esq., Lieutenant Governor and Commander in Chief, the Honorable His Majesty's Council, and the Honorable House of Representatives of the Province of the Massachusetts Bay in New England, May 30, 1770, Being the Anniversary for the Election of His Majesty's Council for the Said Province* (Boston: Edes and Gill, 1770), 11; Benjamin Trumbull, *A Discourse Delivered at the Anniversary Meeting of the Freeman of the Town of New Haven, April 12, 1773* (New Haven, CT: n.p., 1773), 38; Gad Hitchcock, *A Sermon Preached Before His Excellency Thomas Gage, Esq., Governor, the Honorable His Majesty's Council, and the Honorable House of Representatives of the Province of the Massachusetts Bay in New England, May 25, 1774* (Boston: Edes and Gill, 1774), 11; Gershom C. Lyman, *A Sermon Preached at Manchester Before His Excellency Thomas Chittenden, Esq., Governor, His Honor Paul Spooner, Esq., Lieutenant Governor, the Honorable Council, and the Honorable House of Representatives of the State of Vermont on the Day of the Anniversary Election, October 10, 1782* (Windsor, VT: Hough and Spooner, 1784), 16; Josiah Whitney, *The Essential Requisites to Form the Good Ruler's Character, Illustrated and Urged: A Sermon Preached in the Audience of His Excellency Samuel Huntington, Esq. LLD, Governor and Commander in Chief; His Honor Oliver Wolcott, Esq., Lieutenant Governor; and the Honorable the Counselors and House of Representatives of the State of Connecticut at Hartford on the Day of the Anniversary Election, May 8, 1788* (Hartford, CT: Elisha Babcock, 1788), 19; William Morison, *A Sermon Delivered at Dover, State of New Hampshire, Before the Honorable General Court at the Annual*

Election, June 7, 1792 (Exeter, NH: Henry Ranlet, 1792), 41; Timothy
Stone, *A Sermon Preached Before His Excellency Samuel Huntington,
Esq. LLD, Governor, and the Honorable the General Assembly of the
State of Connecticut, Convened at Hartford on the Day of the Anni-
versary Election, May 10, 1792* (Hartford, CT: Hudson and Goodwin,
1792), 17; William Dyer, *Christ's Famous Titles and a Believer's Golden
Chain, Handled in Diverse Sermons, Together With His Cabinet of
Jewels* (n.p.: Stewart and Cochran, 1793), 21; Samuel West, *A Sermon
Delivered Upon the Late National Thanksgiving, February 19, 1795*
(Boston: Samuel Etheridge, 1795), 13; Joseph Buckminster, *Duty of
Republican Citizens*; Stephen Peabody, *A Sermon Delivered at Concord
Before the Honorable General Court of the State of New Hampshire
at the Annual Election Holden on the First Wednesday in June 1797*
(Concord, NH: George Hough, 1797), 12; Isaac Lewis, *The Political
Advantages of Godliness: A Sermon Preached Before His Excellency
the Governor and the Honorable Legislature of the State of Connecticut, Convened at Hartford on the Anniversary Election, May 11,
1797* (Hartford, CT: Hudson and Goodwin, 1797), 15; Abiel Holmes,
*A Sermon Preached at Cambridge, the Lord's Day After the Interment
of His Excellency Increase Sumner, Esq., Governor of the Commonwealth of Massachusetts, Who Died June 7, 1799* (Boston: Manning
and Loring, 1799), 10–11; David M'Clure, *A Discourse Commemora-
tive of the Death of General George Washington, First President of
the United States of America, Who Departed This Life December 14,
1799* (East Windsor, CT: Luther Pratt, 1800), 7; Noah Worcester, *An
Election Sermon Delivered at Concord, June 4, 1800, in Presence of
His Excellency the Governor John Taylor Gilman, Esq., the Honorable Council and Senate and Gentlemen of the House of Representatives* (Concord, NH: Elijah Russell, 1800), 1; Aaron Bancroft, *A Sermon
Preached Before His Excellency Caleb Strong, Esq., Governor, the Hon-
orable the Council, Senate, and House of Representatives of the Com-
monwealth of Massachusetts, May 27, 1801, Being the Day of General
Election* (Boston: Young and Minns, 1801), 18–19; Joseph Woodman,
*A Sermon Preached at Concord, June 3, 1802, on the Annual Election
of the Governor, Council, Senate, and House of Representatives of the
State of New Hampshire* (Concord, MA: George Hough, 1802), 8; and
Leonard Worcester, *A Sermon Preached at Peacham, April 28, 1802,
Being a Day of Public Fasting and Prayer in the State of Vermont* (n.p.,
1802), 29.

28. See, for example, William Gordon, *A Sermon Preached Before the
Honorable House of Representatives on the Day Intended for the
Choice of Counselors* (Watertown: Benjamin Edes, 1775); Allyn
Mather, *The Character of a Well-Accomplished Ruler Described: A
Discourse Delivered at the Freeman's Meeting in New Haven, April 8,*

1776 (New Haven, CT: Thomas and Samuel Green, 1776), 14–15; Josiah Whitney, *Essential Requisites*, 34–35; William F. Rowland, *A Sermon Delivered in Presence of His Excellency John Taylor Gilman, Esq., Governor, the Honorable the Council, Senate, and House of the Representatives of the State of New Hampshire Convened at Exeter on the Day of the Anniversary Election, June 2, 1796* (Exeter, MA: Henry Ranlet, 1796), 26; Joseph Buckminster, *Duty of Republican Citizens*, 12–13; John Marsh, *A Sermon Preached Before His Honor Oliver Wolcott, Esq. LLD, Lieutenant Governor and Commander in Chief, and the Honorable the General Assembly of the State of Connecticut, Convened at Hartford on the Day of the Anniversary Election, May 12, 1796* (Hartford, CT: Hudson and Goodwin, 1796), 30; John Mitchell Mason, *The Voice of Warning to Christians on the Ensuing Election of a President of the United States* (New York: G. F. Hopkins, 1800); Mellish Irving Motte, *The Christian Patriot* (Cambridge: Folsom, Wells, and Truston, 1840); Willard Spaulding, *The Pulpit and the State* (Salem: Charles Beckford, 1863); and Henry van Dyke, *People Responsible for Character.*

29. Motte, The *Christian Patriot.*

30. Spaulding, *Pulpit and the State*, 15–16.

31. Matthias Burnett, *An Election Sermon Preached at Hartford on the Day of the Anniversary Election, May 12, 1803* (Hartford: Hudson and Goodwin, 1803), 27–28.

32. Charles G. Finney, "Hindrances to Revivals," in *Lectures on Revivals of Religion* (New York: Leavitt, Lord, and Co., 1835), 274–275.

33. Pew Research Center for the People and the Press, "Public Knowledge of Current Affairs Little Changed by News and Information Revolutions," April 15, 2007, http://www.people-press.org/2007/04/15/public -knowledge-of-current-affairs-little-changed-by-news-and-information -revolutions/ (accessed August 3, 2014).

34. Alexander Burns, "How Much Do Voters Know?," Politico, March 13, 2012, http://www.politico.com/news/stories/0312/73947 .html#ixzz33cYAKA3D (accessed August 3, 2014).

35. Martin Wisckol, "Study: Voters' Ill-Informed Decision Making," *Orange County Register*, December 26, 2012; http://www.ocregister .com/totalbuzz/strong-469582-voters-allocator.html (accessed August 3, 2014). See also Martin Wisckol, "'Facts' Colored by Partisanship," *Orange County Register*, June 19, 2013, http://www.ocregister.com/ totalbuzz/political-513514-study-know.html (accessed August 3, 2014).

36. Kevin Charles Redmon, "American Voters: Plenty of Opinions but Without a Clue," *Pacific Standard*, November 5, 2012, http://www .psmag.com/navigation/politics-and-law/plenty-of-opinions-but

-without-a-clue-49086 (accessed August 3, 2014); Pew Research Center, "Public Knowledge of Current Affairs"; Larry M. Bartels, "The Irrational Electorate," *Wilson Quarterly* (Autumn 2008), as quoted at http://www.princeton.edu/~bartels/how_stupid.pdf (accessed August 3, 2014).

37. Jonathan Bender and John Bullock, "Lethal Incompetence: Voters, Officials, and Systems," *Critical Review* 20 (March): 1–24, as quoted by Redmon, "American Voters."

38. Ibid.

39. Ibid.

40. James A. Garfield, "A Century of Congress," in *The Works of James Abram Garfield*, vol. 2, ed. Burke A. Hinsdale (Boston: James R. Osgood and Company, 1883), 486, 489.

41. Noah Webster, *History of the United States* (New Haven, CT: Durrie and Peck, 1832), 336–337.

42. Noah Webster, *Letters to a Young Gentleman Commencing His Education, to Which Is Subjoined a Short History of the United States* (New Haven, CT: S. Converse, 1823), 18–19.

43. Samuel Adams, *The Writings of Samuel Adams*, vol. 3, ed. Harry Alonzo Cushing (New York: G. P. Putnam's Sons, 1907), 236–237.

44. Gouverneur Morris, "An Inaugural Discourse Delivered Before the New York Historical Society by the Honorable Gouverneur Morris (President), 4th September, 1816," in *Collections of the New York Historical Society for the Year 1821*, vol. 3 (New York: E. Bliss and E. White, 1821), 32, 34.

45. John Witherspoon, *The Works of the Rev. John Witherspoon*, vol. 3 (Philadelphia: William W. Woodward, 1802), 82.

46. John Witherspoon, *The Works of the Rev. John Witherspoon*, vol. 4 (Philadelphia: William W. Woodward, 1802), 350.

47. Matthias Burnet, *An Election Sermon Preached at Hartford on the Day of the Anniversary Election, May 12, 1803* (Hartford, CT: Hudson and Goodwin, 1803), 26–27.

CHAPTER 4
THE SEARCH FOR GOOD GOVERNMENT

1. Adams, *Letters to His Son*, 23.

2. Adams, *Works*, vol. 4, 106.

3. US Constitution, article 4, section 4, as quoted at http://constitution center.org/constitution/full-text (accessed July 30, 2014).

4. Alexander Hamilton, John Jay, and James Madison, *The Federalist on the New Constitution* (Philadelphia: Benjamin Warner, 1818), 53.

5. John Adams, *The Works of John Adams*, vol. 6, ed. Charles Francis Adams (Boston: Charles C. Little and James Brown, 1850), 484.

6. Fisher Ames, *Works of Fisher Ames, Compiled by a Number of His Friends, to Which Are Prefixed Notices of His Life and Character* (Boston: T. B. Wait and Co., 1809), 24.

7. John Adams, *The Papers of John Adams*, vol. 1, ed. Robert J. Taylor, Mary-Jo Kline, and Gregg L. Lint (Cambridge: Belknap Press, 1977), 83.

8. Shannon Bream, "Regulation Nation: Gov't Regs Estimated to Pound Private Sector With $1.8T in Costs," FoxNews.com, December 6, 2013, http://www.foxnews.com/politics/2013/12/06/regulation-nation-govt -regs-estimated-to-cost-18t (accessed August 3, 2014).

9. Penny Starr, "Under Obama, 11,327 Pages of Federal Regulations Added," CNSNews.com, September 10, 2012, http://cnsnews.com/news/ article/under-obama-11327-pages-federal-regulations-added#sthash .TRHEldYE.dpuf (accessed August 3, 2014).

10. Christopher Santarelli, "Overreach? 81,000 Rules Issued by Feds Since 1993," The Blaze, May 29, 2013, http://www.theblaze.com/ stories/2013/05/29/overreach-81000-rules-issued-by-feds-in-2012 (accessed August 3, 2014).

11. Bream, "Regulation Nation."

12. Santarelli, "Overreach?"

13. Samuel Adams, *The Writings of Samuel Adams*, vol. 2, ed. Harry Alonzo Cushing (New York: G. P. Putnam's Sons, 1906), 317, emphasis in original.

14. See, for example, Jim McElhatton, "Nice Work if You Can Get It: Federal Workers Keep Jobs Despite Misconduct," *Washington Times*, May 13, 2014, http://www.washingtontimes.com/news/2014/may/13/federal -workers-hold-on-to-jobs-despite-blatant-mi/?page=all#pagebreak (accessed August 3, 2014); Angie Drobnic Holan, "Firing Federal Workers Is Difficult," Politifact.com, September 5, 2007, http://www .politifact.com/truth-o-meter/article/2007/sep/05/mcain-federal/ (accessed August 3, 2014); and John Fund, "Hard to Fire," National Review Online, June 17, 2013, https://www.nationalreview.com/nrd/ articles/349675/hard-fire (accessed August 3, 2014).

15. Cristina Marcos, "House Votes 390-33 to Speed Up VA Firings," The Hill, May 21, 2014, http://thehill.com/blogs/floor-action/house/206845 -house-passes-bill-to-speed-up-va-firings (accessed August 3, 2014); see also Pete Kasperowicz, "The Senate Just Blocked Legislation to Speed Up VA Firings," The Blaze, May 22, 2014, http://www.theblaze

.com/stories/2014/05/22/the-senate-just-blocked-legislation-to-speed
-up-va-firings/ (accessed August 2, 2014).

16. Fox News Insider, "Shocking Report: IRS Handed Out Nearly $100
Million in Bonuses Since 2009," May 16, 2013, http://foxnewsinsider
.com/2013/05/16/report-nearly-100-million-bonuses-handed-out-irs
-2009 (accessed August 3, 2014).

17. Michelle Tuccitto Sullo, "Convicted Connecticut Workers Still Get
Pensions Despite Forfeiture Law," *New Haven Register*, May 21, 2012,
http://www.governing.com/news/state/mct-convicted-connecticut
-workers-still-get-pensions-despite-forfeiture-law.html (accessed
August 3, 2014).

18. Catalina Camia, "Ex-Conn. Gov Who Served Jail Time to Get Pen-
sion," *USA Today*, April 30, 2012, http://content.usatoday.com/
communities/onpolitics/post/2012/04/john-rowland-governor-pension
-convicted-/1#.UrybZPbFZGQ (accessed August 3, 2014).

19. Sullo, "Convicted Connecticut Workers."

20. Ibid.

21. Ibid.

22. Ben Chapman, "Troubled City Teachers Still Bouncing Around the
Supposedly Shutdown 'Rubber Rooms' as City Wastes $22 Million a
Year," *New York Daily News*, October 16, 2012, http://www.nydaily
news.com/new-york/education/city-schools-rubber-rooms-bounce
-back-article-1.1184406#ixzz340SG7evj (accessed August 3, 2014).

23. See, for example, Hamilton, Jay, and Madison, *The Federalist*, 420;
John Dickinson, *The Political Writings of John Dickinson*, vol. 1
(Wilmington, DE: Bonsal and Niles, 1801), 229; Thomas Jefferson,
Memoir, Correspondence, and Miscellanies, vol. 4, ed. Thomas Jef-
ferson Randolph (Charlottesville, VA: F. Carr and Co., 1829), 27, 317–
318; *The Debates and Proceedings in the Congress of the United States*,
seventh Congress, first session (Washington DC: Gales and Seaton,
1851), 140–141; *The Debates and Proceedings in the Congress of the
United States*, seventh Congress, second session (Washington DC:
Gales and Seaton, 1851), 645, where Congress voted not to print the
actual articles of impeachment against Pickering; *The Debates and
Proceedings in the Congress of the United States*, eighth Congress, first
session (Washington DC: Gales and Seaton, 1852), 272, 298, 1237–
1240; Jonathan Elliot, ed., *The Debates in the Several State Conventions on the Adoption of the Federal Constitution as Recommended by
the General Convention at Philadelphia in 1787*, vol. 4 (Washington:
Printed for the Editor, 1836), 32; *Register of Debates in Congress Comprising the Leading Debates and Incidents of the First Session of the
Twenty-First Congress*, vol. 4 (Washington DC: Gales and Seaton,

1830), 383, 411–413; *Congressional Record Containing the Proceedings and Debates of the Fifty-Eighth Congress, Third Session*, vol. 39 (Washington DC: Government Printing Office, 1905), 1281–1283; *Congressional Record: Proceedings and Debates of the First Session of the Sixty-Ninth Congress*, vol. 67, part 6 (Washington DC: Government Printing Office, 1926), 6585–6589; John Randolph Tucker, *The Constitution of the United States: A Critical Discussion of Its Genesis, Development, and Interpretation*, vol. 1 (Littleton, CO: Fred B. Rothman and Co., 1981), 421–422; Floyd M. Riddick, *Procedure and Guidelines for Impeachment Trials in the United States Senate* (Washington DC: US Government Printing Office, 1974), 11n, 12n, etc.; *The Debates and Proceedings in the Congress of the United States*, vol. 1 (Washington DC: Gales and Seaton, 1834), 568; Thomas Jefferson, *The Writings of Thomas Jefferson*, vol. 7, ed. H. A. Washington (Washington, D. C.: Taylor and Maury, 1854), 178, 216; James Madison, *Letters and Other Writings of James Madison*, vol. 1 (Philadelphia: J. B. Lippincott and Co., 1865), 194; Max Farrand, ed., *The Records of the Federal Convention of 1787*, vol. 1 (New Haven: Yale University Press, 1911), 108; and James Madison, *The Papers of James Madison…and His Records of Debates in the Federal Convention*, vol. 2 (Mobile, AL: Allston Mygatt, 1842), 1166. See additionally the United States Constitution clauses of impeachment at article 1, section 2, clause 5; article 1, section 3, clauses 6–7; article 2, section 2, clause 1; article 2, section 4, clause 1; article 3, section 1, clause 1; and article 3, section 2, clause 3.

24. See, for example, Michael Lipkin, "Ark. Gay Marriage Ban Unconstitutional, State Judge Rules," Law360.com, May 9, 2014, http://www .law360.com/articles/536761/ark-gay-marriage-ban-unconstitutional -state-judge-rules (accessed August 3, 2014). See also *Guinn v. Legislature of the State*, 119 Nev. 277 (2003).

25. See, for example, *Whitewood v. Wolf*, No. 1:13-cv-1861, 2014 U.S. Dist. LEXIS 68771, at *50-1 (M. D. Pa. May 20, 2014); *Bostic v. Rainey*, 970 F. Supp. 2d 456, 483-484 (E. D. Va. 2014); and transcript of excerpt of proceedings for *Doe v. Santa Fe Indep. Sch. Dist.* (1995) (No. G-95-176), with subsequent procedural history at *Doe v. Santa Fe Indep. Sch. Dist.* 168 F.3d 806 (5th Cir. 1999); *Santa Fe Indep. Sch. Dist. v. Doe*, 530 U.S. 290 (2000).

26. See, for example, Hamilton, Jay, and Madison, *The Federalist*, 412; Joseph Story, *Commentaries on the Constitution of the United States*, vol. 3 (Boston: Hilliard, Gray, and Company, 1833), 377.

27. Wikipedia, "List of US executive branch czars," http://en.wikipedia .org/wiki/List_of_U.S._executive_branch_czars (accessed on August 3, 2014).

28. See, for example, refusing to execute WELFARE REFORM LAWS: Joe
    Newby, "Obama Bypasses Congress, Rewrites Welfare Reform Law
    With Policy Directive," Examiner.com, July 13, 2012, http://www
    .examiner.com/article/obama-bypasses-congress-rewrites-welfare
    -reform-law-with-policy-directive (accessed August 3, 2014); and
    Richard Wolf, "Republicans Cry Foul Over Obama Welfare Revisions,"
    USA Today, July 13, 2012, http://content.usatoday.com/communities/
    theoval/post/2012/07/republicans-cry-foul-over-obama-welfare
    -revisions/1#.UsNDqPbFZGQ (accessed August 3, 2014); FEDERAL
    IMMIGRATION LAWS: Matthew Boyle, "Big Sis: Obama Admin Can
    Pick Which Laws to Enforce," Breitbart.com, April 24, 2013, http://
    www.breitbart.com/Big-Government/2013/04/24/Big-Sis-declares
    -Obama-has-power-to-pick-which-laws-to-enforce-as-immigration
    -bill-would-grant-admin-more-authority (accessed August 3, 2014);
    and Michael C. Bender, "Deportations Drop as Obama Pushes for New
    Immigration Law," Bloomberg.com, December 17, 2013, http://www
    .bloomberg.com/news/2013-12-17/deportations-drop-as-obama-pushes
    -for-new-immigration-law.html?cmpid=yhoo (accessed August 3, 2014);
    CONSCIENCE PROTECTION LAWS: Leigh Jones, "Selective Enforcement,"
    World, January 4, 2013, http://www.worldmag.com/2013/01/selective_
    enforcement (accessed August 3, 2014); FEDERAL HEALTH CARE LAWS:
    Charles Krauthammer, "An Outbreak of Lawlessness," National Review
    Online, November 28, 2013, http://www.nationalreview.com/article/
    365101/outbreak-lawlessness-charles-krauthammer/page/0/1?splash
    (accessed August 3, 2014); Shannon Bream, "Obama's End-Runs
    Around Congress Spark Bipartisan Criticism," FoxNews.com,
    December 5, 2013, http://www.foxnews.com/politics/2013/12/05/
    obama-end-run-around-congress-sparks-bipartisan-criticism/
    (accessed August 3, 2014); Mario Murillo Ministries, "Employer Man-
    date? Never Mind Obama Decides Not to Enforce the Heart of His
    Health Care Law," July 5, 2013, http://mariomurilloministries
    .wordpress.com/2013/07/05/employer-mandate-never-mind-obama
    -decides-not-to-enforce-the-heart-of-his-health-care-law/ (accessed
    August 3, 2014); and *Wall Street Journal*, "Employer Mandate? Never
    Mind," July 4, 2013, http://online.wsj.com/news/articles/SB1000142412
    7887323899704578583493972896364 (accessed August 3, 2014); EDU-
    CATION LAWS: Lindsey M. Burke, "Rewriting No Child With Waivers
    and Conditions," *Washington Times*, September 28, 2011, http://www
    .washingtontimes.com/news/2011/sep/28/burke-rewriting-no-child
    -with-waivers-and-conditio/ (accessed August 3, 2014); MILITARY
    DEFENSE LAWS: Devin Dwyer and Luis Martinez, "U.S. Tomahawk
    Cruise Missiles Hit Targets in Libya," ABCNews.com, March 19, 2011,
    http://abcnews.go.com/International/libya-international-military
    -coalition-launch-assault-gadhafi-forces/story?id=13174246#

.T35yGdl0SZR (accessed August 3, 2014); Nick Carey, "Rebels Dismiss Election Offer, NATO Pounds Tripoli," Reuters, June 16, 2011, http://www.reuters.com/article/2011/06/16/us-libya-idUSTRE7270JP20110616 (accessed August 3, 2014); Jennifer Steinhauer, "House Rebukes Obama for Continuing Libyan Mission Without Its Consent," *The New York Times*, June 3, 2011, http://www.nytimes.com/2011/06/04/world/africa/04policy.html?_r=1 (accessed August 3, 2014); David A. Fahrenthold, "House Rebukes Obama on Libya Mission, but Does Not Demand Withdrawal," *The Washington Post*, June 3, 2011, http://www.washingtonpost.com/politics/house-rebukes-obama-on-libya-mission-but-does-not-demand-withdrawal/2011/06/03/AGdrK8HH_story.html (accessed August 3, 2014); David A. Fahrenthold, "House Passes Another Libya Rebuke of Obama," *The Washington Post*, June 13, 2011, http://www.washingtonpost.com/blogs/2chambers/post/house-passes-another-libya-rebuke-of-obama/2011/06/13/AGj0YtTH_blog.html (accessed August 3, 2014); and many others, including Scotty Starnes, "Nine Republican State Attorney Generals Point Out Illegal Obama Administration Violations," *Scotty Starnes's Blog* (blog), March 6, 2012, http://scottystarnes.wordpress.com/2012/03/06/nine-republican-state-attorney-generals-point-out-illegal-obama-administration-violations/ (accessed August 3, 2014); Right Side News, "Attorneys General Join Forces to Call Into Account Illegal Obama Administration Violations," March 7, 2012, http://www.rightsidenews.com/2012030723042/us/homeland-security/attorneys-general-join-forces-to-call-into-account-illegal-obama-administration-violations.html (accessed August 3, 2014); *The Wall Street Journal*, "The Beltway Choom Gang," September 5, 2013, http://online.wsj.com/news/articles/SB10001424127887323324904579044771286022400 (accessed August 3, 2014); Marc Ambinder, "Obama Won't Go to Court Over Defense of Marriage Act," *National Journal*, February 23, 2011, http://www.nationaljournal.com/obama-won-t-go-to-court-over-defense-of-marriage-act-20110223 (accessed August 3, 2014); M. Northrop Buechner, "Obama's Disdain for the Constitution Means We Risk Losing Our Republic," Forbes.com, November 19, 2013, http://www.forbes.com/sites/realspin/2013/11/19/obamas-disdain-for-the-constitution-means-we-risk-losing-our-republic/ (accessed August 3, 2014); and Dave Boyer, "Obama 'Won't Be Waiting on Congress,' Plans More Executive Orders to Advance Agenda," *Washington Times*, January 14, 2014, http://www.washingtontimes.com/news/2014/jan/14/aide-obama-plans-more-executive-orders-advance-age/ (accessed August 3, 2014). One report by Senator Ted Cruz specifically enumerates seventy-six different laws the president has either blatantly broken or brazenly ignored; see Ted Cruz, "The Legal Limit: The Obama Administration's Attempts to Expand Federal Power," no. 4, as published by the Daily Caller, "Ted Cruz: Legal Limit Report 4," http://www.scribd.com/doc/222704929/Ted-Cruz-Legal-Limit-Report-4 (accessed August 3, 2014).

29. President Obama has done this in diverse areas, including law enforcement operations (such as orders on "Fast and Furious"), abortion policies, religious liberty and conscience-protection policies, environmental policies, gun control and regulation policies, welfare and social policies, and other major issues. See, for example, Greg Abbott, "Federal Court Slams Obama's EPA for Violating Texas State Rights," Examiner.com, August 21, 2012, http://www.examiner.com/article/federal-court-slams-obama-s-epa-for-violating-texas-state-rights (accessed August 3, 2014); Valerie Volcovici, "Court Strikes Down EPA Rule on Coal Pollution," Reuters, August 21, 2012, http://www.reuters.com/article/2012/08/21/us-usa-epa-ruling-idUSBRE87K0NQ20120821 (accessed August 3, 2014); Terence P. Jeffrey, "Obama Doesn't Rule Out Bypassing Congress and Using EPA Regulations to Cap Carbon Emissions," CNSNews.com, November 4, 2010, http://cnsnews.com/news/article/obama-doesn-t-rule-out-bypassing-congress-and-using-epa-regulations-cap-carbon (accessed August 3, 2014); Adele Hampton, "Newt Gingrich Attacks Obama Over Executive Order, Comparing It to Watergate," The Hill, June 21, 2012, http://thehill.com/video/administration/234051-newt-gingrich-attacks-obama-over-executive-order-compares-to-watergate#ixzz2J2AoQjei (accessed August 3, 2014); Scott Neuman, "Facing Stiffened Opposition, Obama Goes It Alone," NPR, October 31, 2011, http://www.npr.org/2011/10/31/141879854/facing-stiffened-opposition-obama-goes-it-alone (accessed August 3, 2014); CNN Wire Staff, "Obama Signs Executive Order on Abortion Funding Limits," CNN Politics, March 24, 2010, http://www.cnn.com/2010/POLITICS/03/24/obama.abortion/index.html; and Joe Herring, "The Executive Order Controversy," American Thinker, March 20, 2012, http://www.americanthinker.com/2012/03/the_executive_order_controversy.html#ixzz2J263wzVY (accessed August 3, 2014).

30. See, for example, Office of Compliance, "Recommendations for Improvements to the Congressional Accountability Act," State of the Congressional Workplace Series, December 2012, http://www.compliance.gov/wp-content/uploads/2012/12/102B-Report_web.pdf (accessed August 3, 2014); Associated Press, "Congress Exempt From Several Federal Laws," *Seattle Times*, February 3, 2012, http://seattletimes.com/html/politics/2017409775_apuscongressunderlaw.html (accessed August 3, 2014); Kai Jackson, "Poll: Exempt From Laws?," UpperMichigansSource.com, February 13, 2014, (accessed August 3, 2014); and Theodoric Meyer, "Do as We Say, Congress Says,

Then Does What It Wants," ProPublica, January 31, 2013, http://www
.propublica.org/article/do-as-we-say-congress-says-then-does-what-it
-wants (accessed August 3, 2014).

31. GovTrack.us, "H.R. 1343 (107th): Local Law Enforcement Hate Crimes
Prevention Act of 2001," https://www.govtrack.us/congress/bills/107/
hr1343 (accessed August 3, 2014); GovTrack.us, "H.R. 4204 (108th):
Local Law Enforcement Hate Crimes Prevention Act of 2004," https://
www.govtrack.us/congress/bills/108/hr4204 (accessed August 3, 2014);
GovTrack.us, "H.R. 2662 (109th): Local Law Enforcement Hate Crimes
Prevention Act of 2005," https://www.govtrack.us/congress/bills/109/
hr2662 (accessed August 3, 2014); GovTrack.us, "H.R. 1592 (110th):
Local Law Enforcement Hate Crimes Prevention Act of 2007," https://
www.govtrack.us/congress/bills/110/hr1592 (accessed August 3, 2014);
and GovTrack.us, "H.R. 1913 (111th): Local Law Enforcement Hate
Crimes Prevention Act of 2009," https://www.govtrack.us/congress/
bills/111/hr1913 (accessed August 3, 2014).

32. GovTrack.us, "H.R. 2647 (111th): National Defense Authorization Act
for Fiscal Year 2010," https://www.govtrack.us/congress/bills/111/
hr2647 (accessed August 3, 2014); the related bill can be found in section 4703–4713, entitled "Matthew Shepard and James Byrd Jr. Hate
Crimes Prevention Act."

33. Marlin Stutzman and Michael Needham, "The 'Farm' Bill Is No Such
Thing," *Wall Street Journal*, August 1, 2012, http://online.wsj.com/
news/articles/SB100008723963900443687504577562900872562794
(accessed August 3, 2014); and Brad Plumer, "The Senate Farm Bill, in
One Graph," *Washington Post*, June 14, 2012, http://www.washington
post.com/blogs/wonkblog/post/the-senate-farm-bill-in-one-graph/
2012/06/14/gJQAdAx4cV_blog.html (accessed August 3, 2014).

34. Adams, *Works*, vol. 4, 404.

35. Compare table 330 in 1980-04 at http://www2.census.gov/prod2/
statcomp/documents/1980.zip with table 338 at http://www.census.gov/
compendia/statab/2012/tables/12s0337.pdf.

36. Joseph Story, *Commentaries on the Constitution of the United States*,
vol. 1 (Boston: Little, Brown, and Company, 1873), 528.

37. The Heritage Foundation, "Country Rankings."

38. Cohn and Ferris, "Government Corruption Rampant Worldwide";
Transparency International, "Corruption Perceptions Index 2013,"
http://cpi.transparency.org/cpi2013/results/ (accessed August 3, 2014).

39. National Center for Education Statistics, "PIAAC 2012 Results."

40. Associated Press, "US Education Spending Tops Global List, Study
Shows," CBSNews.com, June 25, 2013, http://www.cbsnews.com/news/

us-education-spending-tops-global-list-study-shows/ (accessed August 3, 2014); and NationMaster, "USD: Countries Compared," 2008, http://www.nationmaster.com/country-info/stats/Education/Spending/USD (accessed August 3, 2014).

41. See, for example, Rasmussen Reports, "Voters Strongly Defend Their Basic Freedoms but See Government as a Threat," November 19, 2013, http://www.rasmussenreports.com/public_content/politics/general_politics/november_2013/voters_strongly_defend_their_basic_freedoms_but_see_government_as_a_threat (accessed August 3, 2014); Rasmussen Reports, "56% View Feds as Threat to Individual Rights," June 5, 2013, http://www.rasmussenreports.com/public_content/politics/general_politics/june_2013/56_view_feds_as_threat_to_individual_rights (accessed August 3, 2014); Paul Steinhauser, "CNN Poll: Majority Says Government a Threat to Citizens' Rights," CNN Politics, February 26, 2010, http://politicalticker.blogs.cnn.com/2010/02/26/cnn-poll-majority-says-government-a-threat-to-citizens-rights/?fbid=t4h1xBvP3pp (accessed August 3, 2014); and Pew Research Center for the People and the Press, "Majority Says the Federal Government Threatens Their Personal Rights," January 31, 2013, http://www.people-press.org/2013/01/31/majority-says-the-federal-government-threatens-their-personal-rights/ (accessed August 3, 2014).

42. Pew Research Center, "Views of Government: Key Data Points," October 22, 2013, http://www.pewresearch.org/key-data-points/views-of-government-key-data-points/ (accessed August 3, 2014).

43. 5News Web Staff, "Congressional Approval Drops to 5%," 5NewsOnline.com, May 21, 2014, http://5newsonline.com/2014/05/21/congressional-approval-drops-to-5/ (accessed August 3, 2014).

44. Public Religion Research poll conducted May 15–19, 2013, as quoted by PollingReport.com, "Supreme Court/Judiciary," http://www.pollingreport.com/court.htm (accessed August 3, 2014); CBS News/*New York Times* poll conducted May 31–June 3, 2012, as quoted by PollingReport.com, "Supreme Court/Judiciary"; and Kaiser Family Foundation Health Tracking poll conducted January 12–17, 2012, as quoted by PollingReport.com, "Supreme Court/Judiciary."

45. Pew Research Center for the People and the Press, "Supreme Court's Favorable Rating Still at Historic Low," March 25, 2013, http://www.people-press.org/2013/03/25/supreme-courts-favorable-rating-still-at-historic-low/ (accessed August 3, 2014).

46. Barna Group, "OmniPoll 1-13," national survey among 1,005 adults, January 2013.

CHAPTER 5
THE FADING INFLUENCE OF INSTITUTIONS

1. Robert D. Kaplan, "Elections Don't Matter, Institutions Do," Forbes. com, January 15, 2014, http://www.forbes.com/sites/stratfor/2014/01/15/ elections-dont-matter-institutions-do/ (accessed August 3, 2014).

2. Interestingly, as another subtle indicator of America's steady creep away from our constitutionally mandated republican form of government, de Tocqueville's work is now called *Democracy in America*, whereas in previous generations, its title was *The Republic of the United States of America and Its Political Institutions, Reviewed and Examined*.

3. Alexis de Tocqueville, *Democracy in America* (New York: Penguin Classics, 2003); also, Alexis de Tocqueville, *American Institutions and Their Influence* (Ann Arbor, MI; Univ. of Michigan Library, 2006).

4. Data drawn from Gallup. "Confidence in Institutions," June 1–4, 2013, http://www.gallup.com/poll/1597/confidence-institutions.aspx (accessed August 3, 2014).

5. Edelman, "2012 Edelman Trust Barometer: Global Results," http:// www.edelman.com/insights/intellectual-property/2012-edelman-trust -barometer/the-state-of-trust/key-findings/ (accessed August 3, 2014).

6. Kevin Robillard, "Poll: Distrust of Media Sets Record." Politico, September 21, 2012, http://www.politico.com/news/stories/0912/81504. html#ixzz33inG00CO (accessed August 3, 2014); see also Lymari Morales, "U.S. Distrust in Media Hits New High," Gallup Politics, September 21, 2012, http://www.gallup.com/poll/157589/distrust-media -hits-new-high.aspx?utm_source=alert&utm_medium=email&utm_ campaign=syndication&utm_content=morelink&utm_term=All%20 Gallup%20Headlines (accessed August 3, 2014).

7. HechingerEd, "New Poll: Public Trusts Teachers, Likes Technology and School Choice," August 17, 2011, http://hechingered.org/content/new -poll-public-trusts-teachers-likes-technology-and-school-choice_4126/ (accessed August 3, 2014).

8. Dan R. Dick, "In God We Trust, in Church We Don't," *United Method- eviations* (blog), May 29, 2009, http://doroteos2.com/2009/05/29/in -god-we-trust-in-church-we-dont/ (accessed August 3, 2014).

9. Edelman, "2012 Edelman Trust Barometer."

10. Art Swift, "Honesty and Ethics Rating of Clergy Slides to New Low," Gallup Politics, December 16, 2013; http://www.gallup.com/ poll/166298/honesty-ethics-rating-clergy-slides-new-low.aspx (accessed August 3, 2014).

11. Harvard University Institute of Politics, "Levels of Trust Continue to Slide Across [the] Board, All Institutions Below 50%," http://www.iop .harvard.edu/trust-institutions-and-political-process (accessed August 3, 2014).

CHAPTER 6
AMERICA'S FAMILY MAKEOVER

1. Population Reference Bureau, "Do Parents Spend Enough Time With Their Children?," January 2007, http://www.prb.org/Publications/ Articles/2007/DoParentsSpendEnoughTimeWithTheirChildren.aspx/ (accessed August 4, 2014); see also *USA Today*, "Family Time Eroding in US as Internet Use Soars," as quoted by ABCNews.com, http:// abcnews.go.com/Technology/story?id=7848914 (accessed August 4, 2014).]]

2. Economic Policy Foundation, "American Workplace: Labor Day 1997 Report," as quoted by PBS.org, "Working Family Values Factoids," http://www.pbs.org/livelyhood/workingfamily/familytrends.html (accessed August 4, 2014).

3. Rose M. Kreider and Diana B. Elliott, "Historical Changes in Stay-at-Home Mothers: 1969 to 2009," Fertility and Family Statistics branch of the US Census Bureau, paper presented at the American Sociological Association 2010 annual meetings, Atlanta, GA, http://www.census .gov/population/www/socdemo/ASA2010_Kreider_Elliott.pdf (accessed August 4, 2014).

4. United States Census Bureau, "Table FG2: Married Couple Family Groups, by Family Income, and Labor Force Status of Both Spouses: 2013" and "Table A1: Marital Status of People 15 Years and Over, by Age, Sex, Personal Earnings, Race, and Hispanic Origin: 2013," http:// www.census.gov/hhes/families/data/cps2013.html (accessed August 4, 2014).

5. Sharon Jayson, "A Time-Use Study Finds Converging Roles for Moms and Dads," *USA Today*, March 14, 2013, http://www.usatoday.com/ story/news/nation/2013/03/14/men-women-work-time/1983271/ (accessed August 4, 2014).

6. Kim Parker and Wendy Wang, "Modern Parenthood," Pew Research Social and Demographic Trends, March 14, 2013, http://www .pewsocialtrends.org/2013/03/14/modern-parenthood-roles-of-moms -and-dads-converge-as-they-balance-work-and-family/ (accessed August 4, 2014).

7. Ibid.

8. Wikipedia, "History of the Family," http://en.wikipedia.org/wiki/History_of_the_family (accessed August 4, 2014).

9. Ibid.

10. *Merriam-Webster's Collegiate Dictionary*, 11th ed., s.v. "secularism."

11. Frank Newport, "In US, Four in Ten Report Attending Church in Last Week," Gallup Politics, December 24, 2013, http://www.gallup.com/poll/166613/four-report-attending-church-last-week.aspx (accessed August 4, 2014).

12. Ibid.

13. Frank Newport, "Most Americans Say Religion Is Losing Influence in US."

14. Pew Research Religion and Public Life Project, "'Nones' on the Rise," October 9, 2012, http://www.pewforum.org/2012/10/09/nones-on-the-rise/ (accessed August 4, 2014).

15. Ibid.

16. National Longitudinal Survey of Adolescent Health, 1995, as quoted by Patrick F. Fagan, "Family and Faith: The Roots of Prosperity, Stability, and Freedom," The Heritage Foundation, March 21, 2001, http://www.heritage.org/Research/Family/WM1.cfm (accessed August 4, 2014).

17. Institute for American Values, "The Marriage Movement: A Statement of Principles," January 2000, http://americanvalues.org/catalog/pdfs/marriagemovement.pdf (accessed August 4, 2014).

18. Cynthia Harper and Sara S. McLanahan, "Father Absence and Youth Incarceration," *Journal of Research on Adolescence* 14, no. 3 (2004), 369–397, available at http://www.gwu.edu/~pad/202/father.pdf (accessed August 4, 2014).

19. Statistic from *Los Angeles Times*, September, 19, 1988, as cited in Daniel Amneus, *The Garbage Generation* (Alhambra, CA: Primrose Press, 1990), 179, as quoted in DivorceReform.org, "Children of Divorce: Crime Statistics," http://www.divorcereform.org/crime.html (accessed August 4, 2014).

20. Todd Michael Franke, "Adolescent Violent Behavior: An Analysis Across and Within Racial/Ethnic Groups," *Journal of Multicultural Social Work* 8 (2000): 47–70, as quoted in iMAPP Policy Brief, "Can Married Parents Prevent Crime? Recent Research on Family Structure and Delinquency 2000–2005," September 21, 2005, http://www.marriagedebate.com/pdf/imapp.crimefamstructure.pdf (accessed August 4, 2014).

21. Les B. Whitbeck et al., "Predictors of Gang Involvement Among American Indian Adolescents," *Journal of Gang Research* 10 (2002): 11–26, as quoted in iMAPP, "Can Married Parents Prevent Crime?"

22. Wade C. Mackey and Nancy S. Coney, "The Enigma of Father Presence in Relationship to Sons' Violence and Daughters' Mating Strategies: Empiricism in Search of a Theory," *Journal of Men's Studies* 8 (2000): 349–373, as quoted in iMAPP, "Can Married Parents Prevent Crime?"

23. Ramsey Clark, *Crime in America: Observations on Its Nature, Causes, Prevention, and Control* (New York: Simon and Schuster, 1970), 140.

24. Robert M. O'Brien and Jean Stockard, "The Cohort-Size Sample-Size Conundrum: An Empirical Analysis and Assessment Using Homicide Arrest Data From 1960 to 1999," *Journal of Quantitative Criminology* 19 (2003): 1–32, as quoted in iMAPP, "Can Married Parents Prevent Crime?"

25. Patrick F. Fagan, Andrew J. Kidd, and Henry Potrykus, "Marriage and Economic Well-Being: The Economy of the Family Rises or Falls with Marriage," Marriage and Religion Research Institute, May 4, 2011, http://downloads.frc.org/EF/EF11E70.pdf (accessed August 4, 2014).

26. United States Census Bureau, 2012 Family Income, "Married-Couple Families, All Races" and "Female Householder, Husband Absent, All Races," http://www.census.gov/hhes/www/cpstables/032013/faminc/finc03_000.htm (accessed August 4, 2014).

27. DivorceRoom.com, "No Fault Divorce Statistics," http://www.divorceroom.com/no-fault-divorce/no-fault-divorce-statistics.html (accessed August 4, 2014); DivorceStatistics.info, "No Fault Divorce Statistics and More," http://www.divorcestatistics.info/no-fault-divorce-statistics-and-more.html (accessed on August 4, 2014).

28. Ted Gest, "Divorce: How the Game Is Played Now," *US News and World Report*, November 21, 1983, 39–42.

29. W. Bradford Wilcox, "The Evolution of Divorce," *National Affairs* 1 (Fall 2009), available at http://nationalaffairs.com/publications/detail/the-evolution-of-divorce (accessed August 4, 2014). See also Benjamin Scafidi, "A Report to the Nation: The Taxpayer Costs of Divorce and Unwed Childbearing; First-Ever Estimates for the Nation and All Fifty States," Georgia Family Institute, 2008, 7, 19; Patrick F. Fagan and Robert Rector, "The Effects of Divorce on America," The Heritage Foundation, June 5, 2000 http://www.heritage.org/research/reports/2000/06/the-effects-of-divorce-on-america (accessed August 4, 2014); W. Bradford Wilcox et al., "Why Marriage Matters, Second Edition: Twenty-Six Conclusions From the Social Sciences," Institute for American Values, 2005, http://americanvalues.org/catalog/pdfs/why_marriage_matters2.pdf (accessed August 4, 2014); and Institute for American Values, "The Marriage Movement"; and Bridget Maher, "Patching Up the American Family," WorldAndI.com, January 2003.

30. Institute for American Values, "The Marriage Movement."

31. Elizabeth Marquardt, *Between Two Worlds: The Inner Lives of Children and Divorce* (New York: Crown Publishers, 2005), 189, as quoted in Chuck Donovan, "Marriage, Parentage, and the Constitution of the Family," The Heritage Foundation, January 27, 2010, http://www.heritage.org/research/reports/2010/01/marriage-parentage-and-the-constitution-of-the-family#_ftn14 (accessed August 4, 2014).

32. Wilcox, "The Evolution of Divorce."

33. Ibid.

34. Institute for American Values, "The Marriage Movement"; Steven Nelson, "Census Bureau Links Poverty With Out-of-Wedlock Births," *US News and World Report*, May 6, 2013 http://www.usnews.com/news/newsgram/articles/2013/05/06/census-bureau-links-poverty-with-out-of-wedlock-births (accessed August 4, 2014); and FamilyFacts.org, "Marriage and Poverty," http://www.familyfacts.org/briefs/8/marriage-and-poverty (accessed August 4, 2014).

35. United States Census Bureau, "Income, Poverty, and Health Insurance Coverage in the United States: 2012," September 17, 2013, http://www.census.gov/newsroom/releases/archives/income_wealth/cb13-165.html (accessed August 4, 2014). See also Gordon Berlin, "The Effects of Marriage and Divorce on Families and Children: Presented Before the Science, Technology, and Space Subcommittee of the Committee on Commerce, Science, and Transportation, United States Senate," May 2004, http://www.mdrc.org/publication/effects-marriage-and-divorce-families-and-children (accessed August 4, 2014).

36. Linda Mintle, "A Child-Focused Divorce? Nice Idea, Wrong Solution," CBN.com, September 8, 2011, http://blogs.cbn.com/familymatters/archive/2011/09/08/a-child-focused-divorce-nice-idea-wrong-solution.aspx (accessed August 4, 2014), reviewing the book by Judith S. Wallerstein, Julia M. Lewis, and Sandra Blakeslee, *The Unexpected Legacy of Divorce: A Twenty-Five-Year Landmark Study* (New York: Hyperion, 2000).

37. Wilcox, "The Evolution of Divorce."

38. Elizabeth Marquardt, "The Children Left Behind," *Los Angeles Times*, November 15, 2005, http://articles.latimes.com/2005/nov/15/opinion/oe-marquardt15 (accessed August 4, 2014).

39. Cathy Meyer, "No-Fault Divorce Laws: The Impact of No-Fault Divorce on Our Children," *Divorced Women Online*, March 22, 2011 http://divorcedwomenonline.com/2011/03/22/no-fault-divorce-laws-the-impact-of-no-fault-divorce-on-our-children/ (accessed August 4, 2014).

40. eDivorcePapers.com, "No Fault Divorce Statistics," http://www
    .edivorcepapers.com/divorce-statistics/no-fault-divorce-statistics.html
    (accessed August 4, 2014).

41. Randall Hekman, as quoted by Michael J. McManus, "From the Detroit
    News: Another View," Retrouvaille.org, http://www.retrouvaille.org/
    pages.php?page=16 (accessed August 4, 2014).

42. Wilcox, "The Evolution of Divorce."

43. US Census Bureau, "America's Families and Living Arrangements:
    2000," as quoted by Unmarried Equality, "Statistics," http://www
    .unmarried.org/statistics/ (accessed August 4, 2014).

44. Wilcox, "The Evolution of Divorce."

45. Anna Challet, "'It's Chaos When They Return Home'—Children and
    Parents Speak About Re-Entry," New America Media, November 5,
    2013, http://newamericamedia.org/2013/11/its-chaos-when-they-return
    -home----children-and-parents-speak-about-reentry.php (accessed
    August 4, 2014).

46. Ibid.

47. R. D. Lee, X. Fang, and F. Luo, "The Impact of Parental Incarceration
    on the Phyiscal and Mental Health of Young Adults," *Pediatrics* 131
    (2013): e1188–e1195, as quoted by G. Roger Jarjoura et al., "Mentoring
    Children of Incarcerated Parents: A Synthesis of Research and Input
    From the Listening Session Held by the Office of Juvenile Justice
    and Delinquency Prevention and the White House Domestic Policy
    Council and Office of Public Engagement," http://www.ojjdp.gov/about/
    MentoringCOIP2013.pdf (accessed August 4, 2014).

48. J. M. Eddy and J. Poehlmann, eds., *Children of Incarcerated Parents: A
    Handbook for Researchers and Practitioners* (Washington DC: Urban
    Institute Press, 2010), as quoted in G. Roger Jarjoura, "Mentoring Chil-
    dren of Incarcerated Parents."

49. Ibid.

50. Center for Research on Child Well-Being, *Fragile Families Research
    Brief, Parental Incarceration and Child Wellbeing in Fragile Fami-
    lies* (Princeton, NJ: Princeton University, 2008), as quoted in Steve
    Christian, "Children of Incarcerated Parents," National Conference
    of State Legislatures, March 2009, http://www.ncsl.org/documents/
    cyf/childrenofincarceratedparents.pdf (accessed August 4, 2014); and
    Susan Phillips et al., "Disentangling the Risks: Parent Criminal Justice
    Involvement and Children's Exposure to Family Risks," *Criminology
    and Public Policy* 5, no. 4 (November 2006): 677–702, as quoted in
    Steve Christian, "Children of Incarcerated Parents."

51. Center for Research on Child Well-Being, *Fragile Families*, as quoted in Steve Christian, "Children of Incarcerated Parents."

52. Z. K. Snyder, T. A. Carlo, and M. M. Coats Mullins, "Parenting From Prison: An Examination of a Children's Visitation Program at a Women's Correctional Facility," *Marriage and Family Review* 32 (2001): 33–61, as quoted in Emily Sanders and Rachel Dunifon, "Children of Incarcerated Parents," Cornell University College of Human Ecology, 2011, http://www.human.cornell.edu/pam/outreach/parenting/research/loader.cfm?csModule=security/getfile&PageID =84011 (accessed August 4, 2014).

53. National Crime Prevention Council, "The Need," http://www.ncpc.org/cms/cms-upload/ncpc/File/mentor_need.pdf (accessed August 4, 2014). See also US Department of Health and Human Services, statement by Joan E. Ohl, Commissioner Administration on Children, Youth, and Families, on the reauthorization of three programs before the Finance Committee of the US Senate, May 10, 2006, http://www.hhs.gov/asl/testify/t060510.html (accessed August 4, 2014).

54. Bureau of Justice Statistics, "Three in Four Former Prisoners in Thirty States Arrested Within Five Years of Release," April 22, 2014, http://www.bjs.gov/content/pub/press/rprts05p0510pr.cfm (accessed August 4, 2014).

55. Baylor University Institute for Studies of Religion, "Can a Faith-Based Prison Reduce Recidivism?," April 13, 2012, http://www.baylorisr .org/2012/04/%E2%80%9Ccan-a-faith-based-prison-reduce -recidivism%E2%80%9D/ (accessed August 4, 2014).

56. Burton W. Folsom, "Teen Challenge: Kicking Two Bad Habits," Mackinac Center for Public Policy, August 5, 1996, http://www.mackinac .org/article.asp?ID=56 (accessed August 4, 2014).

57. Statement of Dave Batty, executive director of Teen Challenge Inc., before the Subcommittee on Human Resources of the House Committee on Ways and Means at a hearing on the impact of substance abuse on families receiving welfare, October 28, 1997, http://waysandmeans.house.gov/legacy/humres/105cong/10-28-97/1028batt .htm (accessed August 4, 2014).

58. *Oxford Advanced Learner's Dictionary* (n.p., n.d.), s.v. "nuclear family."

59. The Witherspoon Institute, "Marriage and the Public Good: Ten Principles," August 2008, http://protectmarriage.com/wp-content/uploads/2012/11/WI_Marriage.pdf (accessed August 4, 2014).

60. Ibid.

61. Ibid.

62. Barack Obama, as quoted in Robert Rector, "Reducing Poverty by Revitalizing Marriage in Low-Income Communities: A Memo to President-Elect Obama," The Heritage Foundation, January 13, 2009, http://www.heritage.org/Research/Family/sr0045.cfm (accessed August 4, 2014); Chuck Donovan, "Marriage, Parentage, and the Constitution of the Family."

63. Mark R. Rank and Thomas A. Hirschl, "The Economic Risk of Childhood in America: Estimating the Probability of Poverty Across the Formative Years," *Journal of Marriage and Family* 61, no. 4 (November 1999): 1058–1067, as quoted in FamilyFacts.org, "Marriage and Poverty."

64. Wilcox, "The Evolution of Divorce."

65. Ibid.

66. Patrick Fagan et al., "The Positive Effects of Marriage: A Book of Charts," The Heritage Foundation, April 2002, http://thf_media.s3 .amazonaws.com/2002/pdf/positive_effects_of_marriage.pdf?ac=1 (accessed August 4, 2014).

67. Wilcox, "The Evolution of Divorce."

68. John Bouvier, *Bouvier's Law Dictionary and Concise Encyclopedia*, vol. 2, ed. Francis Rawle (St. Paul, MN: West Publishing Company, 1914), 1186–1188.

69. *The American Heritage Dictionary*, 4th ed. (Boston: Houghton Mifflin Company, 2006), s.v. "family."

70. "According to David Cheal (1993), the 1980s and 1990s have brought a shift from defining the family as the modern family to defining it as the postmodern family. The family is no longer a fixed form; it is now more free form. The term family has been replaced by families and has become the embodiment of whatever the individual perceives to be family." As quoted in Brenda and Gordon Munro, *International Encyclopedia of Marriage and Family* (Farmington Hill, MI: The Gale Group Inc., 2003), Encyclopedia.com, http://www.encyclopedia.com/ doc/1G2-3406900145.html (accessed August 28, 2014).

71. Tara Parker-Pope, "Surprisingly, Family Time Has Grown," *New York Times*, April 5, 2010, http://well.blogs.nytimes.com/2010/04/05/ surprisingly-family-time-has-grown/comment-page-3/ (accessed August 4, 2014).

72. Mark Mather, "Fact Sheet: The Decline in US Fertility," Population Reference Bureau, http://www.prb.org/Publications/Datasheets/2012/ world-population-data-sheet-fact-sheet-us-population.aspx (accessed August 4, 2014); and Terence P. Jeffrey, "CDC: US Fertility Rate Hits Record Low for Second Straight Year; 40.7% of Babies Born to

Unmarried Women," CNSNews.com, January 8, 2014, http://www
.cnsnews.com/news/article/terence-p-jeffrey/cdc-us-fertility-rate-hits
-record-low-2nd-straight-year-407-babies (accessed August 4, 2014).

73. Lee Kuan Yew, "Warning Bell for Developed Countries: Declining
Birth Rates," Forbes.com, October 16, 2012, http://www.forbes.com/
sites/currentevents/2012/10/16/warning-bell-for-developed-countries
-declining-birth-rates/ (accessed August 4, 2014).

74. Dustin Siggins, "US Ferility Rate Hits All-Time Low," LifeSiteNews
.com, July 1, 2014, http://www.lifesitenews.com/news/us-fertility-rate
-hits-all-time-low (accessed August 4, 2014).

75. Jonathan Last, as quoted in *USA Today*, "As US Birth Rate Drops,
Concern for the Future Mounts," February 13, 2013, http://www
.usatoday.com/story/news/nation/2013/02/12/us-births-decline/
1880231/ (accessed August 4, 2014).

76. Pew Research Religion and Public Life Project, "'Nones' on the Rise."

77. Ibid.

78. Barna Group, "Barna Survey Examines Changes in Worldview Among
Christians Over the Past Thirteen Years," March 6, 2009, http://www
.barna.org/barna-update/article/21-transformation/252-barna-survey
-examines-changes-in-worldview-among-christians-over-the-past
-13-years (accessed August 4, 2014).

79. Ken Ham and Britt Beemer with Todd Hillard, *Already Gone: Why
Your Kids Will Quit Church and What You Can Do to Stop It* (Green
Forest, AR: Master Books, 2010), 23–25, 30.

80. George Barna, as quoted in Christine Wicker, "Dumbfounded by
Divorce: Survey Inspires Debate Over Why Faith Isn't a Bigger Factor
in Marriage," *Dallas Morning News*, 2000, http://www.adherents.com/
largecom/baptist_divorce.html (accessed August 4, 2014).

81. Barna Group, "New Research Explores the Changing Shape of Temptation," January 4, 2013, https://www.barna.org/barna-update/
culture/600-new-years-resolutions-temptations-and-americas-favorite
-sins#.U1gMMMfY8s9 (accessed August 4, 2014).

82. Ibid.

83. Andrew Cherlin, Elizabeth Talbert, and Suzumi Yasutake, "Changing
Fertility Regimes and the Transition to Adulthood: Evidence From a
Recent Cohort," a paper presented to the Population Association of
America, as quoted in Jill Rosen, "Most Millennial Moms Who Skip
College Also Skip Marriage, Data Shows," *Hub* (blog), June 16, 2014,
http://hub.jhu.edu/2014/06/16/millennials-marriage-children#http://
hub.jhu.edu/2014/06/16/millennials-marriage-children (accessed
August 4, 2014).

84. US Census Bureau, "America's Families and Living Arrangements: 2000," as quoted in Unmarried Equality, "Statistics."

85. Jonathan Vespa, Jamie M. Lewis, and Rose M. Kreider, "America's Families and Living Arrangements: 2012," US Census Bureau, August 2013, http://www.census.gov/prod/2013pubs/p20-570.pdf (accessed August 4, 2014).

CHAPTER 7
LAWS AND POLICIES THAT DEFINE THE NEW AMERICA

1. See, for example, Frank Newport, "In US, 77% Identify as Christian," Gallup Politics, December 24, 2012, http://www.gallup.com/poll/159548/identify-christian.aspx (accessed August 4, 2014); Frank Newport, "This Easter, Smaller Percentage of Americans Are Christian," Gallup, April 10, 2009, http://www.gallup.com/poll/117409/Easter-Smaller-Percentage-Americans-Christian.aspx (accessed August 4, 2014); and Frank Newport, "Mississippi and Alabama Most Protestant States in US," Gallup Well-Being, February 5, 2014, http://www.gallup.com/poll/167120/mississippi-alabama-protestant-states.aspx#1 (accessed August 4, 2014).

2. Barna Group, "Frames Wave 2" and "OmniPoll 1-14." See also Riffkin, "New Record Highs in Moral Acceptability." The authors also received unpublished data from a 2013 Gallup study that was used in determining these percentages.

3. Riffkin, "New Record Highs in Moral Acceptability."

4. Ibid.

5. Ibid.

6. Ibid.

7. George Washington, *Address of George Washington, President of the United States... Preparatory to His Declination* (Baltimore: George and Henry S. Keatinge, 1796), 22–23.

8. Zachary Taylor, "The President and the Bible," *New York Semi-Weekly Tribune*, 4, no. 11, May 9, 1849.

9. Theodore Roosevelt, *A Square Deal* (Allendale, NJ: The Allendale Press, 1906), 203–204.

10. Zephaniah Swift, *The Correspondent* (Windham, CT: John Byrne, 1793), 119.

11. John McLean, letter dated November 4, 1852, in *Testimony of Distinguished Laymen to the Value of the Sacred Scriptures, Particularly in their Bearing on Civil and Social Life* (Astor Place, NY: American Bible Society, 1853), 52.

12. *Vidal v. Girard's Executors*, 43 US 127, 200 (1844), as quoted at http://supreme.justia.com/cases/federal/us/43/127/case.html (accessed August 4, 2014).

13. American Medical Association, introduction to the *Code of Medical Ethics Adopted by the Medical Association at Philadelphia in May 1847 and by the New York Academy of Medicine in October 1847* (New York: H. Ludwig and Co., 1848).

14. Noah Webster, *An American Dictionary of the English Language*, (New York: S. Converse, 1828), s.v. "moral."

15. See, for example, *The Free Dictionary Online*, s.v. "moral," http://www.thefreedictionary.com/moral (accessed August 4, 2014); and Dictionary.com, s.v. "moral," http://dictionary.reference.com/browse/moral (accessed August 4, 2014).

16. For examples of the Bible's view of homosexual behavior, see Leviticus 20:13; Romans 1:18, 26–28; 1 Corinthians 6:9–10; 1 Timothy 1:9–10; Jude 1:6–7.

17. US Food and Drug Administration, "Blood Donations From Men Who Have Sex With Other Men Questions and Answers," http://www.fda.gov/BiologicsBloodVaccines/BloodBloodProducts/QuestionsaboutBlood/ucm108186.htm (accessed August 4, 2014). See also AABB, "Blood Donation FAQs," http://www.aabb.org/tm/donation/Pages/donatefaqs.aspx (accessed August 4, 2014).

18. UCSF Medical Center, "MSM and Blood Donations," http://www.ucsfhealth.org/education/msm_and_blood_donations/ (accessed August 4, 2014). See also Christian News Wire, "Gay Activist Would Risk Lives to Push Political Agenda," March 20, http://www.christiannewswire.com/news/694626045.html (accessed August 4, 2014); Centers for Disease Control and Prevention, "HIV Among Gay and Bisexual Men: Fact Sheet," http://www.cdc.gov/hiv/risk/gender/msm/facts/index.html (accessed August 4, 2014).

19. Frank Newport, "LGBT Americans Continue to Skew Democratic and Liberal," Gallup Politics, July 30, 2014, http://www.gallup.com/poll/174230/lgbt-americans-continue-skew-democratic-liberal.aspx (accessed August 21, 2014).

20. Centers for Disease Control and Prevention, "Gay and Bisexual Men's Health: Sexually Transmitted Diseases," http://www.cdc.gov/msmhealth/STD.htm (accessed August 4, 2014).

21. Lawrence K. Altman, "New Homosexual Disorder Worries Officials," *The New York Times*, May 11, 1982, http://www.nytimes.com/1982/05/11/science/new-homosexual-disorder-worries-health-officials.html (accessed August 4, 2014); AVERT, "The History of AIDS Up to 1986," http://www.avert.org/history-aids-1986.htm (accessed August 4, 2014).

22. Centers for Disease Control and Prevention, "HIV in the United States: At a Glance," http://www.cdc.gov/hiv/statistics/basics/ataglance .html (accessed August 4, 2014). See also Centers for Disease Control and Prevention, "HIV Among Gay and Bisexual Men," March 2014, http://www.cdc.gov/nchhstp/newsroom/docs/CDC-MSM-508.pdf (accessed August 4, 2014).

23. See, for example, Todd Heywood, "Listen: HIV Is Still a Gay Disease," HIVPlusMag.com, February 19, 2014, http://www.hivplusmag.com/ opinion/guest-voices/2014/02/19/listen-hiv-still-gay-disease?page=full (accessed August 4, 2014); John-Manuel Andriote, "AIDS: Still a Gay Disease in America," *Atlantic*, November 30, 2011, http://www .theatlantic.com/health/archive/2011/11/aids-still-a-gay-disease-in -america/249242/ (accessed August 4, 2014); Daniel O'Neill, "HIV Remains a Gay Disease," Washington Blade, September 23, 2010, http://www.washingtonblade.com/2010/09/23/hiv-remains-a-gay -disease/ (accessed August 4, 2014); Alice Park, "HIV Continues to Spread Among Gay Men, Studies Show," *Time*, July 20, 2012, http:// healthland.time.com/2012/07/20/hiv-continues-to-spread-among-gay -men-studies-show/ (accessed August 4, 2014); AIDS.gov, "US Statistics," http://aids.gov/hiv-aids-basics/hiv-aids-101/statistics/ (accessed August 4, 2014); and Matt Foreman, "State of the Movement Address," National Gay and Lesbian Task Force, February 8, 2008, http://www .thetaskforce.org/press/releases/prcc08_mfspeech_020808 (accessed August 4, 2014).

24. US Food and Drug Administration, "Blood Donations From Men Who Have Sex With Other Men." See also Centers for Disease Control and Prevention, "Gay and Bisexual Men's Health: HIV/AIDS," http://www .cdc.gov/msmhealth/HIV.htm (accessed August 4, 2014); and Centers for Disease Control and Prevention, "HIV/AIDS: HIV Incidence," http://www.cdc.gov/hiv/statistics/surveillance/incidence/index.html (accessed August 4, 2014).

25. The Henry J. Kaiser Family Foundation, "US Federal Funding for HIV/ AIDS: The President's FY 2014 Budget Request," May 23, 2013, http:// www.fairfoundation.org/$000a_HIV2014_Budget.pdf (accessed August 4, 2014).

26. Centers for Disease Control and Prevention, "HIV/AIDS: HIV Cost-Effectiveness," http://www.cdc.gov/hiv/prevention/ongoing/ costeffectiveness/index.html (accessed August 4, 2014).

27. AIDS.gov, "How We're Spending," http://www.aids.gov/federal -resources/funding-opportunities/how-were-spending/ (accessed August 4, 2014).

28. The Henry J. Kaiser Foundation, "Medicaid and HIV: A National Analysis," October 2011, http://kaiserfamilyfoundation.files.wordpress.com/2013/01/8218.pdf (accessed August 4, 2014).

29. As of 2014, those countries with homosexual marriage include the Netherlands, Belgium, Spain, Canada, South Africa, Norway, Sweden, Portugal, Iceland, Argentina, Denmark, France, Brazil, Uruguay, New Zealand, England and Wales, Scotland, and Luxembourg. Other nations have legalized gay marriage in certain jurisdictions or officially recognize civil unions, an equivalent of homosexual marriage. These nations include Mexico, Andorra, Australia, Colombia, Croatia, Czech Republic, Finland, Germany, Greenland, Hungary, Ireland, Lichtenstein, Malta, Slovenia, and Switzerland.

30. For general information, see TimothyJ. Dailey, "Comparing the Lifestyles of Homosexual Couples to Married Couples," Family Research Council, http://www.frc.org/get.cfm?i=IS04C02 (accessed August 4, 2014); John R. Diggs Jr., "The Health Risks of Gay Sex," http://www.catholiceducation.org/articles/homosexuality/ho0075.html (accessed August 4, 2014); and "Homosexuality Statistics," *Conservapedia*, http://www.conservapedia.com/Homosexuality_Statistics (accessed August 4, 2014).

31. Frank Newport, "LGBT Americans Continue to Skew Democratic and Liberal;," Gallup Politics, July 30, 2014, http://www.gallup.com/poll/174230/lgbt-americans-continue-skew-democratic-liberal.aspx (accessed August 21, 2014).

32. Wikipedia, "Demographics of Sexual Orientation," http://en.wikipedia.org/wiki/Demographics_of_sexual_orientation (accessed August 4, 2014).

33. See, for example, Vandaag.be, "Gay Marriages Decreasing and Increasing Separations," June 5, 2011, http://www.vandaag.be/binnenland/69729_homohuwelijken-in-dalende-lijn-en-steeds-meer-scheidingen.html (accessed August 4, 2014); Omroep Brabant, "Lesbians Divorce Much More Than Gay Men," January 24, 2012, http://www.omroepbrabant.nl/?anp/2401122491583/Lesbiennes+scheiden+veel+meer+dan+homos.aspx (accessed August 4, 2014); and Pink News, "Less Than 1% of Civil Partnerships End in 'Divorce,'" August 7, 2008, http://www.pinknews.co.uk/2008/08/07/less-than-1-of-civil-partnerships-ending-in-divorce/ (accessed August 4, 2014).

34. Statistics Iceland, "Marriages and Divorces," http://www.statice.is/?PageID=1176&src=https://rannsokn.hagstofa.is/pxen/Dialog/varval.asp?ma=MAN06301%26ti=Same+sex+marriages+and+divorces+1996-2011++%26path=../Database/mannfjoldi/Giftingar/%26lang=1%26units=Number (accessed August 25, 2014).

35. See, for example, Bradley Miller, "Same-Sex Marriage Ten Years On: Lessons From Canada," The Witherspoon Institute, November 5, 2012, http://www.thepublicdiscourse.com/2012/11/6758/ (accessed August 4, 2014); Statistics Iceland, "Same-Sex Marriages and Divorces 1996-2011," 2011 numbers; Maia de la Baume and Alissa J. Rubin, "France Joins Gay Couples by Thousands, Amid Gripes," *New York Times*, April 24, 2014, http://www.nytimes.com/2014/04/25/world/europe/thousands-of-same-sex-couples-have-married-in-france.html (accessed August 4, 2014); Statistics New Zealand, "Marriages, Civil Unions, and Divorces: Year Ended December 2013," May 5, 2014, http://www.stats.govt.nz/browse_for_stats/people_and_communities/marriages-civil-unions-and-divorces/MarriagesCivilUnionsandDivorces_HOT-PYeDec13.aspx (accessed August 4, 2014); Dean Kalahar, "The Annulment of Same-Sex Marriage," American Thinker, http://www.americanthinker.com/2013/03/the_annulment_of_same-sex_marriage.html (accessed August 4, 2014); and Wikipedia, "Same-Sex Marriage in Spain," http://en.wikipedia.org/wiki/Same-sex_marriage_in_Spain (accessed August 4, 2014).

36. Timothy J. Dailey, "The Slippery Slope of Same-Sex Marriage," Family Research Council, 2004, http://downloads.frc.org/EF/EF04C51.pdf (accessed August 4, 2014). See also Maria Xiridou et al., "The Contribution of Steady and Casual Partnerships to the Incidence of HIV Infection Among Homosexual Men in Amsterdam," *AIDS* 17, no. 7 (2003): 1,031. Helen Ross, Karen Gask, and Ann Berrington, "Civil Partnerships Five Years On," *Population Trends* 145 (Autumn 2011), http://www.ons.gov.uk/ons/rel/population-trends-rd/population-trends/no--145--autumn-2011/ard-pt145-civil-partnerships.pdf (accessed August 4, 2014); see also G. Andersson et al. (2006) "The Demographics of Same-Sex Marriages in Norway and Sweden," *Demography* 43 (2006): 79–98.

37. Dailey, "The Slippery Slope of Same-Sex 'Marriage.'"

38. Ibid. See also Maria Xiridou et al., "Steady and Casual Partnerships."

39. Stanley Kurtz, "The End of Marriage in Scandinavia," *Weekly Standard*, 9, issue 20, February 2, 2004, http://www.weeklystandard.com/Content/Public/Articles/000/000/003/660zypwj.asp (accessed August 4, 2014).

40. Office for National Statistics, "Marriages in England Wales (Provisional), 2011," June 26, 2013, http://www.ons.gov.uk/ons/dcp171778_315549.pdf (accessed August 4, 2014); *London Evening Standard*, "Marriage Rates Hit Lowest Rate Since Records Began

Almost 150 Years Ago," March 26, 2008, http://www.thisislondon.co
.uk/news/article-23465208-details/Marriage+rates+hit+lowest+rate
+since+records+began+almost+150+years+ago/article.do (accessed
August 4, 2014).

41. See, for example, Dennis Altman, Jeanette Winterson, Benjamin Law,
and Mesha Gessen, panel discussion at the Syndney Writers' Festival,
interviewed by Annette Shun Wah, "Why Get Married When You
Could Be Happy?," RN Life Matters, July 11, 2012 http://www.abc.net
.au/radionational/programs/lifematters/why-get-married/4058506
(accessed August 4, 2014); and Mike Opelka, "Lesbian Activist's Surprisingly Candid Speech: Gay Marriage Fight Is a 'Lie' to Destroy Marriage," The Blaze, April 29, 2013, http://www.theblaze.com/stories/
2013/04/29/lesbian-activists-surprisingly-candid-speech-gay-marriage
-fight-is-a-lie-to-destroy-marriage (accessed August 4, 2014).

42. Brad Harrub, Bert Thompson, and Dave Miller, "'This Is the Way God
Made Me': A Scientific Examination of Homsexuality and the 'Gay
Gene,'" The True Origin Archive, 2003, http://www.trueorigin.org/
gaygene01.asp (accessed August 4, 2014); IsThereAGayGene.com, "Scientific Evidence," http://www.isthereagaygene.com/scientific-evidence/
(accessed August 4, 2012); Bryan Fischer, "The Latest in Scientific
Research: There Is No Gay Gene," One News Now, June 17, 2014 http://
www.onenewsnow.com/perspectives/bryan-fischer/2014/06/17/the
-latest-in-scientific-research-there-is-no-gay-gene (accessed August 4,
2014); and Ian Sample, "Male Sexual Orientation Influenced by Genes,
Study Shows," The Guardian, February 13, 2014, http://www.the
guardian.com/science/2014/feb/14/genes-influence-male-sexual
-orientation-study (accessed August 4, 2014).

43. Lawrence v. Texas, 539 U.S. 558 (2003).

44. Goodridge v. Department of Public Health, 798 N.E.2d 941 (Mass.
2003).

45. See, for example, Elane Photography, LLC v. Willock, 309 P.3d 53
(N.M. 2013); Final Agency Order, Craig v. Masterpiece Cakeshop, Inc.
(Colo. Civ. Rights Comm'n, Colo., May 30, 2014) (Case No. CR 2013-
0008), http://www.adfmedia.org/files/MasterpieceFinalAgencyOrder
.pdf (accessed August 4, 2014); Order, Cervelli v. Aloha Bed & Break-
fast (1st Cir. Haw., Apr. 15, 2013) (Civil No. 11-1-3103-12 ECN), http://
www.lambdalegal.org/sites/default/files/2013-04-15_-_cervelli_order
.pdf (accessed August 4, 2014); and Initial Decision, Bernstein v. Ocean
Grove Camp Meeting Ass'n (Office of Admin. Law, N.J. Jan. 12, 2012)
(OAL Dkt. No. CRT 6145-09; Agency Dkt. No. PN34XB-03008), http://
www.aclu-nj.org/files/8713/2639/9826/CRT_6145-09_Bernstein_ID.pdf
(accessed August 4, 2014). See also Todd Starnes, "Oregon Ruling
Really Takes the Cake—Christian Bakery Guilty of Violating Civil

Rights of Lesbian Couple," FoxNews.com, January 21, 2014, http://www.foxnews.com/opinion/2014/01/21/christian-bakery-guilty-violating-civil-rights-lesbian-couple/ (accessed August 4, 2014); Annette Cary, "Arlene's Flowers in Richland Sued by Gay Couple," *Tri-City Herald*, April 18, 2013, http://www.tri-cityherald.com/2013/04/18/2361691/arlenes-flowers-in-richland-sued.html (accessed August 4, 2014).

46. See Mike Morris, "Council Passes Equal Rights Ordinance," *Houston Chronicle*, May 28, 2014, http://www.chron.com/news/politics/houston/article/Council-passes-equal-rights-ordinance-5510672.php (accessed August 4, 2014); Jerry Pierce, David Roach, "San Antonio LGBT Nondiscrimination Ordinance Passes 8-3, Criticized as 'Unprecedented,'" Baptist Press, September 6, 2013, http://www.bpnews.net/printerfriendly.asp?ID=41037 (accessed August 14, 2014); Associated Press, "San Antonio City Council Extends Anti-Bias Protections to Gays Over Conservative Protests," FoxNews.com, September 5, 2013 http://www.foxnews.com/us/2013/09/05/san-antonio-city-council-extends-anti-bias-protections-to-gays-over/ (accessed August 4, 2014); Laura Lawless Robertson, "City of Phoenix Prohibits Discrimination on the Basis of Sexual Orientation and Gender Identity," Employment Law Worldview, February 20, 2013 http://www.employmentlawworldview.com/city-of-phoenix-prohibits-discrimination-on-the-basis-of-sexual-orientation-and-gender-identity/; and *Transgender Law & Policy Institute*, "Non-Discrimination Laws that include gender identity and expression," http://www.transgenderlaw.org/ndlaws/index.htm (accessed August 28, 2014); and others.

47. See Job 31:15; Psalm 22:9–10; 139:13–16; Isaiah 44:2; Jeremiah 1:4–5; 49:5; Luke 1:15.

48. See Psalm 106:38; Isaiah 59:7; Jeremiah 22:3; Joel 3:19.

49. Pew Research Religion and Public Life Project, "*Roe v. Wade* at 40: Most Oppose Overturning Abortion Decision," January 16, 2013 http://www.pewforum.org/2013/01/16/roe-v-wade-at-40/ (accessed August 25, 2014).

50. Ibid.; Lydia Saad, "Americans Misjudge US Abortion Views," Gallup Politics, May 15, 2013, http://www.gallup.com/poll/162548/americans-misjudge-abortion-views.aspx (accessed August 4, 2014).

51. There are about one million abortions each year; see Rachel K. Jones and Jenna Jerman, "Abortion Incidence and Service Availability in the United States, 2011," *Perspectives on Sexual and Reproductive Health* 46, no. 1 (March 2014), http://www.guttmacher.org/pubs/journals/psrh.46e0414.pdf (accessed August 4, 2014). See also Guttmacher

Institute, "Fact Sheet: Induced Abortion in the United States," July 2014 http://www.guttmacher.org/pubs/fb_induced_abortion.html (accessed August 4, 2014).

52. Rachel K. Jones, Lawrence B. Finer, and Susheela Singh, "Characteristics of US Abortion Patients, 2008," Guttmacher Institute, May 2010, http://www.guttmacher.org/pubs/US-Abortion-Patients.pdf (accessed August 4, 2014).

53. "The Oath by Hippocrates," translated by Francis Adams, available at http://classics.mit.edu/Hippocrates/hippooath.html (accessed August 4, 2014).

54. Justin McCarthy, "Seven in Ten Americans Back Euthenasia," Gallup Politics, June 18, 2014, http://www.gallup.com/poll/171704/seven -americans-back-euthanasia.aspx (accessed August 4, 2014).

55. Noah Webster, *Dictionary*, s.v., "suicide."

56. See Judges 9:54; 1 Samuel 31:3–6; 2 Samuel 17:23; 1 Kings 16:18; Matthew 27:5.

57. William Blackstone, *Commentaries on the Laws of England*, vol. 4 (Oxford: Clarendon Press, 1769), 189.

58. James Wilson, *The Works of the Honourable James Wilson*, vol. 3, ed. Bird Wilson (Philadelphia: Lorenzo Press, 1804), 84–85.

59. See Nehemiah 4:11, 18; Esther 8:11; Luke 11:21.

60. Declaration of Independence, emphasis added, http://www.archives .gov/exhibits/charters/declaration_transcript.html (accessed August 4, 2014).

61. David Codrea, "Did New York Gun Owner Who Fired Warning Shots Save Lives?," Examiner.com, September 9, 2010, http://www.examiner .com/article/did-new-york-gun-owner-who-fired-warning-shots-save -lives (accessed August 4, 2014).

62. Daryl Burden, "Self Defense Punished in South Dakota," Women Against Gun Control, http://www.wagc.com/self-defense-punished-in -south-dakota/ (accessed August 4, 2014).

63. Dan Cannon, "Circle K Clerk Fired for Shooting at Armed Robber Who Was Holding a Gun to His Head," Guns Save Lives, November 17, 2013, http://gunssavelives.net/self-defense/video/video-circle-k -clerk-fired-for-shooting-at-armed-robber-who-was-holding-a-gun -to-his-head/ (accessed August 4, 2014); and MrConservative.com, "Circle K Clerk Fired for Using His Concealed Carry Gun to Thwart Armed Robbery," November 9, 2013, http://www.mrconservative.com/ 2013/11/27028-circle-k-clerk-fired-for-using-his-concealed-carry-gun -to-thwart-armed-robbery/ (accessed August 4, 2014).

64. Andrea Noble, "DC Man Who Shot Dogs Biting Boy Could Face Charges," *Washington Times*, January 23, 2013, http://www .washingtontimes.com/news/2013/jan/23/man-who-shot-dogs-biting -boy-could-face-charges/ (accessed August 4, 2014).

65. Dan Cannon, "Gas Station Clerk Pulls Gun on Knife Wielding Armed Robber—Is Then Promptly Fired," Guns Save Lives, October 15, 2013, http://gunssavelives.net/self-defense/gas-station-clerk-pulls-gun-on -knife-wielding-armed-robber-is-then-promptly-fired/ (accessed August 4, 2014); and 68truthseeker, "Watch: Store Clerk Pull Gun on Knife Wielding Robber, Then Gets Fired!," Before It's News, October 18, 2013, http://beforeitsnews.com/economy/2013/10/watch-store -clerk-pull-gun-on-knife-wielding-robber-then-gets-fired-2562552.html (accessed August 4, 2014).

66. Spokesman-Review, "Gonzaga Univ Students Punished for Self Defense," GOPUSA.com, November 11, 2013, http://www.gopusa.com/ news/2013/11/11/gonzaga-univ-students-punished-for-self-defense/ (accessed August 4, 2014).

67. See Deuteronomy 15:6; 28:12; Nehemiah 5:3–5; Proverbs 22:7; Romans 13:8.

68. See, for example, Adam Hersh, "Chart: States That Cut the Most Spending Have Lost the Most Jobs," Think Progress, June 27, 2011, http://thinkprogress.org/economy/2011/06/27/255010/chart-states -cut-most-spending-jobs/ (accessed August 4, 2014); Sylvain Leduc and Daniel Wilson, "Highway Grants: Roads to Prosperity?," as quoted in Economist's View, "'The Multiplier Is at Least Two,'" November 26, 2012, http://economistsview.typepad.com/economistsview/2012/11/the -multiplier-is-at-least-two.html (accessed August 4, 2014); *Democracy in America* (blog), "Tax Cuts Can in Fact Create Jobs," *The Economist*, February 24, 2010, http://www.economist.com/blogs/democracyin america/2010/02/stimulus_and_jobs_bills (accessed August 4, 2014); Paul Krugman, "The Conscience of a Liberal," *New York Times*, February 23, 2010, http://krugman.blogs.nytimes.com/2010/02/23/ brad-delongs-foolishness/?_php=true&_type=blogs&_php=true&_ type=blogs&_r=1& (accessed August 4, 2014); Brad DeLong, "Yep; Chicago's John Cochrane: Still Certifiable," *Brad DeLong's Grasping Reality* (blog), February 22, 2010, http://delong.typepad.com/sdj/ 2010/02/yep-chicagos-john-cochrane-still-certifiable.html (accessed August 4, 2014); and Stan Collender, "I Hate to Pile On to Brian Riedl, but He Deserves It," *Capital Gains and Games* (blog), February 19, 2010, http://www.capitalgainsandgames.com/blog/stan-collender/ 1505/i-hate-pile-brian-riedl-he-deserves-it (accessed August 4, 2014).

69. Tim Mullaney, "More Americans Debt-Free, but the Rest Owe More," *USA Today*, March 21, 2013, http://www.usatoday.com/story/money/

personalfinance/2013/03/21/census-household-debt-report/2007195/ (accessed August 4, 2014).

70. Bill Fay, "Americans in Debt," Debt.org, http://www.debt.org/faqs/americans-in-debt/ (accessed August 4, 2014).

71. Steve Lander, "The Average Household Mortgage Debt," *The Nest* (blog), http://budgeting.thenest.com/average-household-mortgage-debt-32568.html (accessed August 4, 2014).

72. Daniel Wesley, "A Lifetime of Debt: The Financial Journey of the Average American," Credit Loan, http://www.creditloan.com/infographics/a-lifetime-of-debt-the-financial-journey-of-the-average-american/ (accessed August 4, 2014).

73. Melinda Opperman, "The Average Student Loan Debt Continues to Climb," Credit.org, December 27, 2013 http://credit.org/blog/average-student-loan-debt/ (accessed August 4, 2014).

74. Bill Fay, "Americans in Debt."

75. Treasury Direct, "The Debt to the Penny and Who Holds It" http://www.treasurydirect.gov/NP/debt/current (accessed August 4, 2014).

76. "Debt-to-GDP Ratio," *Investopedia*, http://www.investopedia.com/terms/d/debtgdpratio.asp (accessed August 4, 2014).

77. USGovernmentDebt.us, "Government Debt Chart" http://www.usgovernmentdebt.us/spending_chart_1900_2016USp_15s2li011lcn_H0sH0lH0f (accessed August 4, 2014).

78. Ibid.

79. 2014 Federal Budget in Pictures, "Publicly Held Debt to Skyrocket," The Heritage Foundation, http://www.heritage.org/federalbudget/national-debt-skyrocket (accessed August 4, 2014).

80. Jefferson, *Writings*, vol. 7, 14, emphasis in original.

81. Ibid., 19.

82. Alexander Hamilton, *The Papers of Alexander Hamilton*, vol. 12, ed. Harold C. Syrett (New York: Columbia University Press, 1967), 364.

83. George Washington, *The Writings of George Washington*, vol. 12, ed. Jared Sparks (Boston: American Stationers Company, 1837), 53.

84. 2014 Budget in Pictures, "Each American's Share of the Public Debt Is Skyrocketing" The Heritage Foundation, http://www.heritage.org/federalbudget/national-debt-burden (accessed August 4, 2014).

85. Thomas Jefferson, *The Writings of Thomas Jefferson*, vol. 3, ed. Henry Augustine Washington (Washington DC: Taylor and Maury, 1854), 104–106. See also Thomas Jefferson, *The Writings of Thomas Jefferson*, vol. 6, ed. Henry Augustine Washington (Washington DC: Taylor and Maury, 1857), 136–137.

86. Jefferson, *Writings*, vol. 6, 608.

87. Washington, *Writings*, vol. 12, 227–228.

88. USGovernmentSpending.com, "US Entitlement Spending Growth," http://www.usgovernmentspending.com/entitlement_spending (accessed August 4, 2014).

89. Ibid.

90. Brad Plumer, "Who Receives Government Benefits, in Six Charts," *Washington Post*, September 18, 2012, http://www.washingtonpost .com/blogs/wonkblog/wp/2012/09/18/who-receives-benefits-from-the -federal-government-in-six-charts/ (accessed August 4, 2014); and Tami Luhby, "Government Assistance Expands," CNN Money, February 7, 2012 http://money.cnn.com/2012/02/07/news/economy/ government_assistance/index.htm (accessed August 4, 2014).

91. Luhby, "Government Assistance Expands."

92. Ibid.

93. Suzanne Mettler, "Reconstituting the Submerged State: The Challenges of Social Policy Reform in the Obama Era," *Perspectives on Politics* 8, no. 3 (September 2010), http://government.arts.cornell.edu/assets/ faculty/docs/mettler/submergedstat_mettler.pdf (accessed August 4, 2014).

94. Plumer, "Who Receives Government Benefits."

95. Elizabeth Harrington, "101M Get Food Aid From Federal Gov't; Outnumber Full-Time Private Sector Workers," CNSNews.com, July 8, 2013, http://cnsnews.com/news/article/101m-get-food-aid-federal-gov-t -outnumber-full-time-private-sector-workers (accessed August 4, 2014); for number of public school students, see National Center for Education Statistics, "Fast Facts: Back to School Statistics," 2013, http://nces.ed.gov/fastfacts/display.asp?id=372 (accessed August 4, 2014).

96. Jake Grovum, "Thousands More Students to Get Free Lunch Next Fall," *USA Today*, June 23, 2014, http://www.usatoday.com/story/ news/nation/2014/06/23/stateline-school-lunch-program/11260497/ (accessed August 4, 2014).

97. Harrington, "101M Get Food Aid."

98. Hannah Bleau, "Eleven Things You Didn't Know You Could Buy With Food Stamps," The Daily Caller, June 30, 2014, http://dailycaller.com/ 2014/06/30/11-things-you-didnt-know-you-could-buy-with-food -stamps/ (accessed August 4, 2014).

99. Mike Sunnucks, "Arizona Looks to Restrict Food Stamp Use at Liquor Stores, Casinos," *Phoenix Business Journal*, April 29, 2013, http://www .bizjournals.com/phoenix/news/2013/04/29/arizona-looks-to-restrict

-food-stamp.html (accessed August 4, 2014); CNN News Room, "Food Stamps for Strippers," July 5, 2010, http://newsroom.blogs.cnn.com/ 2010/07/05/food-stamps-for-strippers/ (accessed August 4, 2014); Jeremy Jojola, "Colorado Welfare Debit Cards Used at Casinos, Strip Clubs," *Denver Post*, February 28, 2012, http://www.denverpost.com/ commented/ci_20058326?source=commented-news (accessed August 4, 2014); Dan Tilkin, "Oregon Welfare Being Withdrawn at Strip Clubs, Casinos," KATU.com, May 2, 2012, http://www.katu.com/news/ local/Oregon-welfare-money-being-withdrawn-at-strip-clubs-casinos -149930975.html (accessed August 4, 2014); Daniel Greenfield, "Welfare Recipients Take EBT to Disney World and Vegas," *Frontpage Mag*, January 13, 2014, http://www.frontpagemag.com/2014/dgreenfield/ welfare-recipients-take-ebt-to-disney-world-and-vegas/ (accessed August 4, 2014); and CBS Sacramento, "Lotto Loophole Allows Ticket Purchases With EBT Cards," March 30, 2012, http://sacramento .cbslocal.com/2012/03/30/lotto-loophole-allows-ticket-purchases-with -ebt-cards/ (accessed August 4, 2014).

100. Bleau, "Eleven Things You Didn't Know."

101. TimesFreePress.com, "The Food Stamp Bonus," June 23, 2012, http:// www.timesfreepress.com/news/2012/jun/23/the-food-stamp-bonus/ (accessed August 4, 2014).

102. Philip Klein, "CRS Report: Number of Able-Bodied Adults on Food Stamps Doubled After Obama Suspended Work Requirement," *Washington Examiner*, September 19, 2012, http://washingtonexaminer.com /crs-report-number-of-able-bodied-adults-on-food-stamps-doubled -after-obama-suspended-work-requirement/article/2508430 (accessed August 28, 2014).

103. Mary Kate Cary, "The Shocking Truth on Entitlements," *US News and World Report*, December 19, 2012, http://www.usnews.com/opinion/ articles/2012/12/19/the-shocking-truth-on-entitlements (accessed August 4, 2014).

104. Ibid.

105. Ibid.

106. Ibid.

107. Alison Acosta Fraser, "Federal Spending by the Numbers: 2012," The Heritage Foundation, October 16, 2012, http://www.heritage.org/ research/reports/2012/10/federal-spending-by-the-numbers-2012 (accessed August 4, 2014).

108. Cary, "The Shocking Truth on Entitlements."

109. Karen Tumulty, "The Great Society at 50," *Washington Post*, May 17, 2014, http://www.washingtonpost.com/sf/national/2014/05/17/the -great-society-at-50/ (accessed August 4, 2014).

110. Ibid.

111. Ibid.

112. Gallup Editors, "Most Americans Practice Charitable Giving, Volun-teerism," Gallup Well-Being, December 13, 2013, http://www.gallup .com/poll/166250/americans-practice-charitable-giving-volunteerism .aspx#2 (accessed August 4, 2014).

113. Federal Safety Net, "Welfare Opinion: Public Opinion Polls on Wel-fare and Poverty," http://federalsafetynet.com/welfare-opinion.html (accessed August 4, 2014).

114. Lyndon B. Johnson, "Special Message to the Congress Proposing a Nationwide War on the Sources of Poverty," March 16, 1964, as quoted in The American Presidency Project, http://www.presidency.ucsb.edu/ ws/index.php?pid=26109&st=war+on+poverty&st1 (accessed August 4, 2014).

115. Ibid.

116. Eric Boehm, "In Many States, Welfare Can Pay Better Than an Honest Day's Work," Watchdog.org, August 21, 2013, http://watchdog.org/ 102295/in-many-states-welfare-can-pay-better-than-an-honest-days -work/ (accessed August 4, 2014).

117. Ibid.

118. Daniel Halper, "Over $60,000 in Welfare Spent Per Household in Pov-erty," The Weekly Standard, October 26, 2012, http://www .weeklystandard.com/blogs/over-60000-welfare-spentper-household -poverty_657889.html (accesssed August 4, 2014).

119. See Exodus 23:3, 6; Leviticus 19:15; Proverbs 29:14.

120. Passages addressing the responsibility of *individuals* to care for the poor include Leviticus 25:25, 35, 39; Deuteronomy 15:7–8, 10–11; 24:12; Job 29:12–16; Psalm 41:1; Proverbs 14:21; 19:17; 31:20; Isaiah 58:6–10; Matthew 19:21; 25:34–40; Mark 10:21; 14:7; Luke 14:13–14; 18:22; and Galatians 2:10, among others. Scriptures addressing the responsibility of the *congregation* to care for the poor include Levit-icus 27:8; Esther 9:22; Acts 4:34–35; and Romans 15:26–37.

121. Thomas Jefferson, *The Writings of Thomas Jefferson*, vol. 4, ed. Henry Augustine Washington (Washington DC: Taylor and Maury, 1854), 589–590.

122. George Washington, *The Writings of George Washington*, vol. 3, ed. Worthington Chauncey Ford (New York: G. P. Putnam's Sons, 1889), 236.

123. See Exodus 23:11; Leviticus 19:9–10; 23:22; Deuteronomy 24:19–21.

124. Benjamin Franklin, *The Life and Essays of Dr. Benjamin Franklin* (London: John M'Gowan, 1838), 327–328.

125. Federal Safety Net, "Welfare Opinion."

126. Peter Ferrara, "Liberating the Poor From Poverty," National Center for Policy Analysis, April 17, 2014 http://www.ncpa.org/pub/ib143 (accessed August 4, 2014).

127. Klein, "CRS Report: Number of Able-Bodied Adults on Food Stamps Doubled After Obama Suspended Work Requirement."

128. Daniel Halper, "Over $60,000 in Welfare Spent Per Household in Poverty."

129. Jenifer Zeigler, "War on Poverty Needs New Strategy," FoxNews.com, September 1, 2004, http://www.foxnews.com/story/2004/09/01/war-on-poverty-needs-new-strategy/ (accessed August 4, 2014).

130. Halper, "Over $60,000 in Welfare Spent Per Household in Poverty."

131. Carmen DeNavas-Walt, Bernadette D. Proctor, Jessica C. Smith, "Income, Poverty, and Health Insurance Coverage in the United States: 2011," United States Census Bureau, September 2012, http://www.census.gov/prod/2012pubs/p60-243.pdf (accessed August 4, 2014).

132. American Institute of Philanthropy, "Charity Watch: Criteria," http://www.charitywatch.org/criteria.html (accessed August 4, 2014).

133. See, for example, the testimony of Michael D. Tanner before the Finance Committee of the US Senate on welfare reform, March 9, 1995, transcript provided by the CATO Institute at http://www.cato.org/publications/congressional-testimony/welfare-reform (accessed August 4, 2014).

134. Robert Rector, "'Poverty' Like We've Never Seen It," The Heritage Foundation, November 27, 2012, http://www.heritage.org/research/commentary/2012/11/poverty-like-weve-never-seen-it (accessed August 4, 2014).

135. Ibid.

136. Robert Rector and Rachel Sheffield, "Understanding Poverty in the United States: Surprising Facts About America's Poor," The Heritage Foundation, September 13, 2011, http://www.heritage.org/research/reports/2011/09/understanding-poverty-in-the-united-states-surprising-facts-about-americas-poor (accessed August 4, 2014).

137. Ibid.; Rector, "'Poverty' Like We've Never Seen It."

138. Rector and Sheffield, "Understanding Poverty in the United States."

139. Susan Blumenthal, "Poverty and Obesity: Breaking the Link," Huffington Post, April 11, 2012, http://www.huffingtonpost.com/susan

-blumenthal/poverty-obesity_b_1417417.html (accessed August 4, 2012). See also Cynthia L. Ogden, et al., "Obesity and Socioeconomic Status in Children and Adolescents: United States, 2005–2008," National Center for Health Statistics Data Brief, no. 51, December 2010, http://www.cdc.gov/nchs/data/databriefs/db51.pdf (accessed August 4, 2014); Phil Izzo, "The Connection Between Obesity and Poverty," *Wall Street Journal*, July 7, 2011, http://blogs.wsj.com/economics/2011/07/07/the-connection-between-obesity-and-poverty/ (accessed August 4, 2014); and James A. Levine, "Poverty and Obesity in the U.S.," *Diabetes* 60, no. 11 (November 2011): 2667–2668, http://www.ncbi.nlm.nih.gov/pmc/articles/PMC3198075/ (accessed August 4, 2014).

140. Ronald Reagan, State of the Union Address, January 25, 1988, as quoted by the Miller Center at the University of Virginia, http://millercenter.org/president/speeches/detail/5684 (accessed August 4, 2014).

141. See, for example, Richard Peters, *A Sermon on Education, Wherein Some Account Is Given of the Academy, Established in the City of Philadelphia, Preached at the Opening Thereof on the Seventh Day of January 1750-1* (Philadelphia: B. Franklin and D. Hall, 1751); Cotton Mather, *Corderius Americanus*; Charles Nisbet, *The Usefulness and Importance of Human Learning: A Sermon Preached Before the Trustees of Dickinson College, Met at Carlisle, May 11, 1786, and Published at Their Desire* (Carlisle, PA: Kline and Reynolds, 1786); Tristram Gilman, *The Right Education of Children Recommended, in a Sermon Preached in a New Schoolhouse in North Yarmouth, September 23, 1788* (Boston: Samuel Hall, 1789); Levi Hart, *The Importance of Parental Fidelity in the Education of Children Illustrated, in a Discourse Addressed to the Congregation in the North Society of Preston, the Lord's Day Following the 28th of February 1792* (Norwich, CT: Bushnell and Hubbard, 1792); John Wesley, *On the Education of Children: A Sermon on Proverbs 22:6* (Newbern, NC: Hall and Bryan, 1811); Henry Ustick Onderdonk, *A Sermon on General Education Delivered Before the Female Charitable Society of Canandaigua, September 8, 1816* (Canandaigua, NY: J. D. Bemis, 1816).

142. National Center for Education Statistics, "Fast Facts: Expenditures," http://nces.ed.gov/fastfacts/display.asp?id=66 (accessed August 4, 2014).

143. WAMU885News, "Global Graduation Rates by Country," http://www.scribd.com/doc/82204617/Global-Graduation-Rates-By-Country-Source-OECD (accessed August 4, 2014); Kavitha Cardoza, "Graduation Rates Increases Around the Globe as US Plateaus," WAMU 88.5, February 21, 2012 http://wamu.org/news/morning_edition/12/02/21/

graduation_rates_increase_around_the_globe_as_us_plateaus
(accessed August 4, 2014).

144. Statistic Brain, "High School Dropout Statistics," January 1, 2014
http://statisticbrain.com/high-school-dropout-statistics/ (accessed
August 4, 2014).

145. Organization for Economic Cooperation and Development (OECD),
Program for International Student Assessment (PISA), 2000, 2003,
2006, 2009 and 2012, http://nces.ed.gov/surveys/pisa/idepisa/ (accessed
August 4, 2014).

146. Ibid.

147. Ibid.

148. Huff Post Books, "The US Literacy Rate Hasn't Changed in Ten Years,"
September 6, 2013, http://www.huffingtonpost.com/2013/09/06/
illiteracy-rate_n_3880355.html (accessed August 4, 2014).

149. NationMaster.com, "Education: Literacy (total population)," http://
www.nationmaster.com/graph-T/edu_lit_tot_pop&int=-1 (accessed January 27, 2004).

150. Huff Post Books, "The US Illiteracy Rate Hasn't Changed in Ten
Years."

151. Statistic Brain, "Illiteracy Statistics," April 28, 2013, http://
statisticbrain.com/number-of-american-adults-who-cant-read/
(accessed August 4, 2014).

152. Statistic Brain, "Private School Statistics," July 21, 2013, http://www
.statisticbrain.com/private-school-statistics/ (accessed August 4, 2014);
Statistic Brain, "Home School Statistics," April 28, 2013, http://www
.statisticbrain.com/home-school-statistics/ (accessed August 4, 2014);
Ian Slatter, "New Nationwide Study Confirms Homeschool Academic
Achievement," Home School Legal Defense Association, August 10,
2009 http://www.hslda.org/docs/news/200908100.asp (accessed August
4, 2014); and Florida Department of Education, "Student Achievement in Florida's Charter Schools: A Comparison of the Performance
of Charter School Students With Traditional Public School Students,"
https://www.floridaschoolchoice.org/pdf/Charter_Student_
Achievement_2012.pdf (accessed August 4, 2014).

153. National Center for Education Statistics, "Fast Facts: Expenditures."

154. Immigration Policy Center, "How the United States Immigration
System Works: A Fact Sheet," March 1, 2014, http://www
.immigrationpolicy.org/just-facts/how-united-states-immigration
-system-works-fact-sheet (accessed August 4, 2014).

155. Statistic Brain, "Illegal Immigrant Population Statistics," January 1, 2014 http://www.statisticbrain.com/u-s-unauthorized-immigrant -population/ (accessed August 4, 2014).

156. Steven A. Camarota and Jessica Vaughan, "Immigration and Crime: Assessing a Conflicted Issue," Center for Immigration Studies, November 2009, http://cis.org/ImmigrantCrime (accessed August 4, 2014).

157. Ibid.

158. Chuck Ross, "Murders, Rapists, Kidnappers: Over 36,000 Criminal Illegal Immigrants Released in 2013," The Daily Caller, May 12, 2014, http://dailycaller.com/2014/05/12/murderers-rapists-kidnappers-over -36000-criminal-illegal-immigrants-released-in-2013/ (accessed August 4, 2014).

159. Ibid.

160. Robert Rector and Jason Richwine, "The Fiscal Cost of Unlawful Immigrants and Amnesty to the US Taxpayer," The Heritage Foundation, May 6, 2013, http://www.heritage.org/research/reports/2013/05/ the
-fiscal-cost-of-unlawful-immigrants-and-amnesty-to-the-us-taxpayer (accessed August 4, 2014).

161. Dictionary.com, s.v. "Free Market," emphasis added, http://dictionary .reference.com/browse/free+market (accessed August 4, 2014).

162. *The Free Dictionary*, s.v. "Free Market," emphasis added, http://www .thefreedictionary.com/free+market (accessed August 4, 2014).

163. Thomas Jefferson, *The Writings of Thomas Jefferson*, vol. 14, ed. Andrew A. Lipscomb (Washington DC: Thomas Jefferson Memorial Association, 1903), 466.

164. Charles Thomson, letter to Benjamin Franklin dated September 24, 1765, as quoted in *The American Quarterly Review*, vol. 18 (Philadelphia: Lydia R. Bailey, 1835), 92.

165. Benjamin Franklin, *The Works of Benjamin Franklin*, vol. 1, ed. Jared Sparks (Boston: Charles Tappan, 1844), 251.

166. Kyle Pomerleau, "The High Burden of State and Federal Capital Gains Tax Rates," Tax Foundation, February 11, 2014, http://taxfoundation .org/article/high-burden-state-and-federal-capital-gains-tax-rates (accessed August 4, 2014).

167. Penny Starr, "Under Obama, 11,327 Pages of Federal Regulations Added," CNSNews.com, September 10, 2012, http://cnsnews.com/ news/article/under-obama-11327-pages-federal-regulations -added#sthash.TRHEldYE.dpuf (accesed August 28, 2014).

168. Santarelli, "Overreach?"

169. Michael Bastasch, "More Than 1,600 Pages of Regulations Added to Federal Register Last Week, Cost Now $1.8 Trillion per Year," The Daily Caller, September 11, 2012, http://dailycaller.com/2012/09/11/more-than-1600-pages-of-regulations-added-to-federal-register-last-week-cost-now-1-8-trillion-per-year/ (accessed August 4, 2014).

170. Karen Dennison, "Can Small Business Survive the High Costs of Regulations?" eZineArticles.com, August 19, 2008, http://ezinearticles.com/?Can-Small-Business-Survive-the-High-Costs-of-Regulations?&id=1424169 (accessed August 4, 2014).

171. Russell Huebsch, "The Disadvantages of a Small Business Complying With Government Regulations," *Houston Chronicle*, http://smallbusiness.chron.com/disadvantages-small-business-complying-government-regulations-2965.html (accessed August 4, 2014).

172. Antony Davies, "Regulation and Productivity," George Mason University Mercatus Center, 2014, http://mercatus.org/sites/default/files/Davies_Regulation&Productivity_v1.pdf (accessed August 4, 2014).

173. For explanations of the correlation between strong government regulations and increased rates of failure among those regulated businesses, see articles such as Peter J. Wallison, "Why Do We Regulate Banks," American Enterprise Institute, August 1, 2005, http://www.aei.org/article/economics/financial-services/why-do-we-regulate-banks-outlook/ (accessed August 14, 2014); and Andrew Beattie, "How Governments Influence Markets," Investopedia, http://www.investopedia.com/articles/economics/11/how-governments-influence-markets.asp (accessed August 14, 2014).

174. James L. Gattuso, Diane Katz, and Stephen Keen, "Red Tape Rising: Obama's Torrent of New Regulation," The Heritage Foundation, October 26, 2010 http://www.heritage.org/research/reports/2010/10/red-tape-rising-obamas-torrent-of-new-regulation (accessed August 4, 2014).

175. Brad Plumer, "America's Staggering Defense Budget, in Charts," *Washington Post*, January 7, 2013 http://www.washingtonpost.com/blogs/wonkblog/wp/2013/01/07/everything-chuck-hagel-needs-to-know-about-the-defense-budget-in-charts/ (accessed August 4, 2014).

176. USGovernmentSpending.com, "Government Spending Details": for 1795, http://www.usgovernmentspending.com/year_spending_1795USmf_15ms2n_3031F0F1_051#usgs302 (accessed August 4, 2014); for 1815, http://www.usgovernmentspending.com/year_spending_1815USmf_15ms2n_3031F0F1_051#usgs302 (accessed August 4, 2014); for 1825, http://www.usgovernmentspending.com/year_spending_1825USmf_15ms2n_3031F0F1_051#usgs302 (accessed August 4, 2014); for

1835, http://www.usgovernmentspending.com/year_spending_1835US mf_15ms2n_3031F0F1_051#usgs302 (accessed August 4, 2014).

177. George Washington, "First Annual Message to Congress on the State of the Union," January 8, 1790, as quoted in the American Presidency Project, http://www.presidency.ucsb.edu/ws/?pid=29431 (accessed August 4, 2014).

178. Ibid.

179. Jefferson, *Writings*, vol. 7, 624.

180. Plumer, "America's Staggering Defense Budget."

181. Ibid.

182. For nominal dollars, see "Federal Individual Income Tax Rates History: Nominal Dollars," http://taxfoundation.org/sites/taxfoundation .org/files/docs/fed_individual_rate_history_nominal.pdf (accessed August 4, 2014). For inflation-adjusted dollars, see "Federal Individual Income Tax Rates History: Inflation Adjusted," http://taxfoundation .org/sites/taxfoundation.org/files/docs/fed_individual_rate_history_ adjusted.pdf (accessed August 4, 2014).

183. National Taxpayers Union, "History of Federal Individual Income Bottom and Top Bracket Rates," http://www.ntu.org/tax-basics/history -of-federal-individual-1.html (accessed August 4, 2014).

184. Associated Press, "The Top 1 Percent of Americans Will Pay 30 Percent of the Nation's Federal Taxes in 2013: Report," March 3, 2013, http://www.huffingtonpost.com/2013/03/03/1-percent-taxes-2013_n _2802243.html (accessed August 4, 2014).

185. Tax Foundation, "Tax Freedom Day," http://taxfoundation.org/tax -topics/tax-freedom-day (accessed August 4, 2014).

186. Tax Foundation, "Tax Freedom Day 2014 Is April 21, Three Days Later Than Last Year," http://taxfoundation.org/article/tax-freedom-day -2014-april-21-three-days-later-last-year (accessed August 4, 2014).

187. Ibid.

188. Thomas Jefferson, *Writings of Thomas Jefferson*, vol. 15, ed. Andrew A. Lipscomb (Washington DC: The Thomas Jefferson Memorial Association, 1904), 39–40.

CHAPTER 8
THE CONDITION OF THE CHRISTIAN CHURCH

1. Barna Group, "OmniPoll 1-11 PH," national survey among 600 adults eighteen or over, January 2011.

2. Ibid.

3. Barna Group, "OmniPoll 1-14."

4. In the sections of this chapter regarding measures of health and born-again Christians, the comparison of data between 2004 and 2014 are drawn from the following national surveys of adults by the Barna Group: "OmniPoll 1-04" and "OmniPoll 1-14."

5. Barna Group, "OmniPoll 1-14" and "OmniPoll 1-04."

6. Ibid.

7. Ibid.; for a more extensive discussion about the unchurched and additional data regarding church attendance, see George Barna and David Kinnaman, gen. eds., *Churchless* (Carol Stream, IL: Tyndale, 2014).

8. Barna Group, "OmniPoll 1-14" and "OmniPoll 1-04."

9. Barna Group, "OmniPoll 1-03," national survey of 1,010 adults eighteen or older, conducted January 2003; and Barna Group, "OmniPoll 1-13 OL-PH," national survey of 2,083 adults eighteen or older, conducted January 2003.

10. Barna Group, "OmniPoll 1-14" and "OmniPoll 1-04."

11. See Table 8-1.

12. Barna Group, "OmniPoll 1-14" and "OmniPoll 1-04."

13. Ibid.

14. Ibid.

15. Ibid.

16. Ibid.

17. Ibid.

18. Ibid.

19. Ibid.

20. Ibid.

21. Ibid.

22. Ibid.

23. Ibid.

24. Ibid.

25. Ibid.

26. Barna Group, "OmniPoll 1-10," national survey of 1,005 adults eighteen or older, January 2010. The subsample of born-again Christians included 491 people who met the classification criteria.

27. Barna Group, "OmniPoll F-10," national survey of 1,022 adults eighteen or older, December 2010. The subsample of born-again Christians included 448 people who met the classification criteria.

28. Ibid.

29. Ibid.

30. Ibid.

31. Ibid.

32. For a more complete description about worldviews, their development, and how many Americans possess which worldviews, see George Barna, *Think Like Jesus: Make the Right Decision Every Time* (Nashville: Thomas Nelson, 2005). Other useful books on the topic include David Noebel, *Understanding the Times: The Religious Worldviews of Our Day and the Search for Truth* (Eugene, OR: Harvest House, 1994); Charles Colson and Nancy Pearcey, *How Now Shall We Live?* (Carol Stream, IL: Tyndale, 1999); James Sire, *The Universe Next Door*, 5th ed. (Downers Grove, IL: IVP Academic, 2009); Francis Schaeffer, *A Christian Manifesto* (Wheaton, IL: Crossway, 1981); and Nancy Pearcey, *Total Truth: Liberating Christianity From Its Cultural Captivity* (Wheaton, IL: Crossway, 2005).

33. Barna Group, "OmniPoll S-08," national survey of 1,003 adults eighteen or older, May 2008.

34. Barna Group, "PastorPoll W-03," national survey of 601 senior pastors of Protestant churches, November–December 2003.

35. Barna Group, "PastorPoll F-02," national survey of 601 senior pastors of Protestant churches, December 2002.

36. Ibid.

37. Statistics in this paragraph are drawn from Barna Group, "OmniPoll 1-14"; Barna Group, "OmniPoll 1-12," national survey of 1,005 adults eighteen or older, January 2012; and Barna Group, "OmniPoll F-12," national survey of 1,008 adults eighteen or older, November 2012.

38. Barna Group, "Frames Wave 1," national survey among 1,005 adults, June 2013.

39. Ibid.

40. Barna Group, "OmniPoll F-09," national survey among 1,002 adults eighteen or older, conducted September 2009.

41. Barna Group, "OmniPoll 2-10," national survey of 1,000 adults eighteen or older, August 2010.

42. American Culture & Faith Institute, "Conservative Clergy Canvass," a national survey among 412 theologically conservative senior pastors of Protestant churches, conducted October 2013.

43. Barna Group, "PastorPoll F-10," a national survey among 602 Protestant senior pastors, conducted November 2010; American Culture & Faith Institute, national surveys conducted among theologically conservative senior pastors: "C3-1," among 1,420 pastors in February 2014; "C3-3," among 1,036 pastors in April 2014; and "C3-4," among 1,679 pastors in June 2014.

CHAPTER 9
RESTORING THE GOVERNMENT

1. See Proverbs 15:14; 18:15;19:2; and Hosea 4:6.

2. See, for example, Marvin Olasky and Warren Cole Smith, *Prodigal Press: Confronting the Anti-Christian Bias of the American News Media,* rev. ed. (Phillipsburg, NJ: P and R Publishing, 2013); FoxNews.com, "Is There an Anti-Christian Bias in the Mainstream Media?," http://video.foxnews.com/v/2781548226001/is-there-anti-christian-bias-in-the-mainstream-media/#sp=show-clips (accessed August 5, 2014).

3. American Bible Society, *Bible Society Record,* vol. 46, no. 7 (New York: The American Bible Society, 1901), 99; Ferdinand Cowle Iglehart, *Theodore Roosevelt: The Man as I Knew Him,* (New York: The Christian Herald, 1919), 307–311.

4. Elias Boudinot, *The Age of Revelation: Or, The Age of Reason Shewn to Be an Age of Infidelity* (Philadelphia: Asbury Dickins, 1801), xv.

5. Wirt, *Sketches,* 402.

6. Webster, *History of the United States,* 310.

7. John Jay, *John Jay: The Winning of the Peace: Unpublished Papers 1780–1784,* vol. 2, ed. Richard B. Morris (New York: Harper and Row Publishers, 1980), 709.

8. Rush, *Essays,* 93.

9. Rush, *Letters,* vol. 1 936.

10. Adams, *Works,* vol. 10, 85.

11. Franklin D. Roosevelt, "Proclamation 2629: Thanksgiving Day, 1944," November 1, 1944, as quoted at the American Presidency Project, http://www.presidency.ucsb.edu/ws/?pid=72460 (accessed August 5, 2014).

12. Taylor, "The President and the Bible."

13. Abraham Lincoln, *Complete Works of Abraham Lincoln,* vol. 10, ed. John G. Nicolay and John Hay (Harrogate, TN: Lincoln Memorial University, 1894), 218.

14. Adams, *Letters to His Son,* 119.

15. B. B. Edwards and W. Cogswell, *The American Quarterly Register,* vol. 12 (Boston: Perkins and Marvin, 1840), 86.

16. Adams, *Letters to His Son,* 10–12.

17. Barna Group, "OmniPoll 1-13 OL." The survey revealed that 23 percent of the adults who describe themselves as Christian have read through the Bible, from start to finish, during the course of their life. The

statistic is somewhat higher among those who are classified as born-again Christians (36 percent). Just 10 percent of Catholics, who comprise more than one out of every five adults in the United States, have read through the entire Bible.

18. John Quincy Adams, *The Writings of John Quincy Adams*, vol. 6, ed. Worthington Chauncey Ford (New York: The Macmillan Company, 1916), 135.

19. Boudinot, *The Age of Revelation*, xv.

20. John Quincy Adams, *Letters to His Son*, 10–11.

21. Ronald Reagan, quoting Andrew Jackson in "Proclamation 5018—Year of the Bible, 1983," February 3, 1983, quoted at the American Presidency Project, http://www.presidency.ucsb.edu/ws/?pid=40728 (accessed August 5, 2014). See also George H. W. Bush, "Proclamation 6100—International Year of Bible Reading," February 22, 1990, quoted at the American Presidency Project, http://www.presidency.ucsb.edu/ws/?pid=1816 (accessed August 50, 2014); and *The American Missionary*, vol. 20, no. 8 (New York: American Missionary Association, 1876), 183.

22. Taylor, "The President and the Bible.

23. Franklin D. Roosevelt, "Statement on the Four Hundredth Anniversary of the Printing of the English Bible," October 6, 1935, quoted at the American Presidency Project, http://www.presidency.ucsb.edu/ws/?pid=14960 (accessed August 5, 2014).

24. Harry S. Truman, "Address Before the Attorney General's conference on Law Enforcement Problems," February 15, 1950, quoted at the American Presidency Project, http://www.presidency.ucsb.edu/ws/?pid=13707 (accessed August 5, 2014).

25. Ronald Reagan, "Proclamation 5018—Year of the Bible, 1983," February 3, 1983, quoted at the American Presidency Project, http://www.presidency.ucsb.edu/ws/?pid=40728 (accessed August 5, 2014).

26. Woodrow Wilson, as quoted in Jan Willem Schulte Nordholt, *Woodrow Wilson: A Life for World Peace*, trans. Herbert H. Rowen (Berkeley, CA: University of California Press, 1991), 47.

27. Lyndon B. Johnson, "Remarks at the Lighting of the Nation's Christmas Tree," December 22, 1963, quoted at the American Presidency Project, http://www.presidency.ucsb.edu/ws/?pid=26587 (accessed August 5, 2014).

28. Herbert Hoover, "Radio Address to the Nation on Unemployment Relief," October 18, 1931, quoted at the American Presidency Project, http://www.presidency.ucsb.edu/ws/?pid=22855 (accessed August 5, 2014).

29. Adams, *Works*, vol. 2, 6–7.

30. John Jay, *The Correspondence and Public Papers of John Jay*, vol. 1, ed. Henry P. Johnston (New York: G. P. Putnam's Sons, 1890), 163–164.

31. Adams, *Writings*, vol. 3, 349.

32. John Jay, *The Life of John Jay, With Selections From His Correspondence and Miscellaneous Papers*, vol. 2, ed. William Jay (New York: J and J Harper, 1833), 174.

33. Jay, *The Life of John Jay, With Selections From His Correspondence and Miscellaneous Papers*, vol. 1, ed. William Jay (New York: J and J Harper, 1833), 345.

34. John Hancock, as quoted in Louie R. Heller, *Early American Orations: 1760–1824* (New York: The MacMillan Company, 1912), 48–49.

35. John Witherspoon, *The Dominion of Providence Over the Passions of Men: A Sermon Preached at Princeton on the 17th of May 1776, Being the General Fast Appointed by the Congress Through the United Colonies* (Philadelphia: Bookfellers, 1777), 32.

36. John Quincy Adams, as quoted in Elbridge S. Brooks, *Historic Americans: Sketches of the Lives and Characters of Certain Famous Americans* (New York: Thomas Y. Crowell and Company, 1899), 209.

37. John Hancock, quoted in David Brewer, ed., *The World's Best Orations: From the Earliest Period to the Present Time*, vol. 6 (St. Louis: Ferd. P. Kaiser, 1900), 2399.

38. See Matthew 7:16–20; Luke 6:44–46; 1 Corinthians 6:2–3.

39. Adams, *Papers*, vol. 1, 81, emphasis in original.

40. Rush, *Essays*, 10–11.

41. Webster, *Letters to a Young Gentleman*, 18–19.

42. Webster, *Dictionary*, s.v. "evil."

43. *United States Oracle of the Day*, Portsmouth, NH (May 24, 1800); see also Maeva Marcus, *Documentary History of the Supreme Court*, vol. 3, 436.

44. Witherspoon, *Works*, vol. 3, 42.

45. John Jay, *The Correspondence and Public Papers of John Jay*, vol. 4 (New York: G. P. Putnam's Sons, 1893), 365.

46. Jay, *Life of John Jay*, vol. 2, 376.

47. Benjamin Franklin, *The Papers of Benjamin Franklin*, vol. 6, ed. Leonard W. Labaree (New Haven, CT: Yale University Press, 1963), 326.

48. Rush, *Essays*, 11.

49. Rush, *Letters*, vol. 1, 478.

50. Abigail Adams, in correspondence to her sister dated February 7, 1801, *New Letters of Abigail Adams, 1788-1801*, ed. Stewart Mitchell, (Boston, MA: Houghton Mifflin Company, 1947), 265–266.

51. Jonathan Elliott, ed., *The Debates in the Several State Conventions of the Adoption of the Federal Constitution*, vol. 2 (Washington DC: printed for the editor, 1836), 200.

CHAPTER 10
RESTORING THE CHURCH

1. Barna Group, "OmniPoll 1-10."

2. For more insights into understanding God's vision for your life, see George Barna, *The Power of Vision: Discover and Apply God's Vision for Your Life and Ministry*, rev. ed. (Ventura, CA: Regal, 2009); and George Barna, *Turning Vision Into Action* (Ventura, CA: Gospel Light, 1997).

3. Those findings are described in George Barna, *Maximum Faith: Live Like Jesus* (New York: SGG Publications, 2011), which describes the spiritual state of Americans, the stops on the transformational journey, and the barriers Americans face in seeking to become transformed individuals.

4. For the research and narrative describing the transformational journey, see George Barna, *Maximum Faith*. The text provides data and analysis from more than 17,000 interviews regarding how people grow spiritually and the nature of the journey to wholeness.

5. This is based on information that was tracked regularly by the Barna Group from October 1999 through May 2008. During that time the Barna Group conducted a series of ten national surveys tracking worldview status, each survey including a minimum of 1,000 adults. Those OmniPoll surveys were conducted in October 1999, January 2000, October 2001, August 2002, October 2002, September 2003, November 2003, July 2005, January 2006, and May 2008. The findings are described in *Think Like Jesus* by George Barna (Nashville, TN: Thomas Nelson, 2003).

6. Among the resources to consider would be George Barna, *Think Like Jesus*; David Noebel, *Understanding the Times*; Charles Colson and Nancy Pearcey, *How Now Shall We Live?*; and James Orr, *The Christian View of God and the World* (Grand Rapids, MI: Kregel Publications, 1989).

7. See Romans 14:19; 1 Corinthians 12:25; and Hebrews 3:13; 10:24–25; 12:15; and 13:17.

8. *Maximum Faith: Live Like Jesus* by George Barna (New York: SGG Publications, 2011) describes the spiritual state of Americans, the stops on the transformational journey, and the barriers Americans face in seeking to become transformed individuals.

9. See Deuteronomy 6:6–7; Psalm 78:4–7; Ecclesiastes 12:1; Isaiah 28:9–10; Ephesians 6:4.

10. Fisher Ames, *Notices of the Life and Character of Fisher Ames* (Boston: T. B. Wait and Co., 1809), 134.

11. Rush, *Essays*, 94.

12. See Varnum Lansing Collins, *President Witherspoon: A Biography*, vol. 1 (Princeton, NJ: Princeton University Press, 1925), 1. Other examples include John Trumbull; see Alexander Cowie, *John Trumbull: Connecticut Wit* (Chapel Hill, NC: University of North Carolina Press, 1936), 16–17.

13. The results of various national studies conducted by the Barna Group in relation to the importance of ministry to children are described in George Barna, *Transforming Children Into Spiritual Champions* (Ventura, CA: Regal, 2003).

14. Such insights are drawn from a variety of research studies comparing the views of young Christian adults and older Christian adults. Among the studies used were two conducted by the Barna Group: "OmniPoll 1-12" and "OmniPoll F-12"; and four studies conducted by the American Culture and Faith Institute: "RightView-3" (March 2014), "RightView-4" (April 2014), "RightView-5" (June 2014), and "RightView-6" (July 2014).

15. Barna Group, "OmniPoll 1-11 PH," a national survey among 600 adults eighteen or older, conducted January 2011.

16. Barna Group, "OmniPoll 2-09," a national survey among 1,005 adults eighteen or older, conducted August 2009; American Culture and Faith Institute, "RightView-6," a national survey among 1,612 adults eighteen or older, conducted July 2014; see also Pew Research Center, "U.S. Religious Knowledge Survey," September 28, 2010, http://www.pewforum.org/2010/09/28/u-s-religious-knowledge-survey (accessed August 14, 2014).

17. Barna Group, "OmniPoll 1-14."

18. A decade's worth of research by the Barna Group on this issue has concluded that very few clergy are called and gifted as both leaders and teachers. Less than one out of every four senior pastors of Protestant churches are called and gifted as leaders; roughly six out of ten

Protestant senior pastors are called and gifted as teachers. Substantially fewer than one out of every ten senior pastors possess the call and gift to carry out both the teaching and leading duties.

About George Barna

George Barna has filled executive roles in politics, marketing, advertising, media development, research, and ministry. He founded the Barna Research Group in 1984 (now the Barna Group) and helped it become a leading marketing research firm focused on the intersection of faith and culture before selling it in 2009. He currently serves as the executive director of the American Culture and Faith Institute and is president of Metaformation, a faith development organization.

Barna has written more than fifty books, addressing leadership, social trends, spiritual development, and church dynamics. They have included numerous best sellers and several award-winning volumes. He has sold more books based on survey research related to matters of faith than any author in American history.

He has served on the faculty at several universities and seminaries and also served as a pastor of a large, multiethnic church as well as a house church.

After graduating summa cum laude from Boston College, Barna earned two master's degrees from Rutgers University and has a doctorate from Dallas Baptist University.

George has been married to his wife, Nancy, since 1978. They have three daughters and one grandson. They all live in central California.

About David Barton

David Barton heads WallBuilders, a national pro-family organization that presents America's forgotten history and heroes with an emphasis on our moral, religious, and constitutional heritage.

David is the author of numerous best-selling books, with the subjects being drawn largely from his massive library museum of tens of thousands of original writings, documents, and artifacts from early America. A national news organization has described him as "America's historian," and *Time* magazine named him one of America's twenty-five most influential evangelicals.

He serves as a consultant to state and federal legislators, has participated in several cases at the Supreme Court, has been involved in the development of social studies standards for numerous states, and has helped produce some popular history textbooks now used in schools across the nation.

David and his wife, Cheryl, reside in Aledo, Texas, and have three grown children, Damaris, Timothy, and Stephen, and two grandchildren.

CREDIBLE, RELEVANT COVERAGE
of the issues that **matter most to you**

FrontLine brings you books, e-books, and other media covering current world affairs and social issues from a Christian perspective. View all of FrontLine's releases at the links below and discover how to bring your values, faith, and biblical principles into today's marketplace of ideas.